BUDDHISM HISTORY AND LITERATURE

Buddhism History And Literature

Dr. S.L. Misra

Mahaveer & Sons
(Publishers & Distributors)
New Delhi–110002

Edition 2015

ISBN-81-8377-302-7

Published by
MAHAVEER & SONS
3072/28, First Floor, Gola Market, Darya Ganj,
New Delhi–110002

Rs. 925/-

PRINTED IN INDIA

Published by Sh. Mukul Sharma for Mahaveer & Sons, 3072/28, First Floor, Gola Market, Darya Ganj, New Delhi–110002,
Printed at Nav Prabhat Printing Press, Delhi.

Preface

It has often been maintained that there is no nation or tribe without religion. But what is meant by religion ? The word, as is well known, is not found in languages not related to our own, and its derivation is uncertain.

Cicero, in one passage, derived it from re and lego and held that its real meaning was the repetition of prayers and incantations. Another interpretation derives the word from re and ligo, and makes its original sense that of attachment, of a continual binding (that is, no doubt, to the gods). A third derivation connects the word with lex, and explains it as a law-abiding, scrupulously conscientious, frame of mind.

This last seems to be most in accordance with the conceptions prevalent when the use of the phrase began, Buddhism and more in harmony with the similar expressions that arose under similar circumstances elsewhere in China, for instance, and in India.

In India, indeed, the same word is used by the followers of every school of thought for law and for religion the word Dharma, etymologically equivalent to the Latin forma^ and constantly reminding us in its implied connotation of the English phrase "good form."

Content

1

Religious Theories in India before Buddhism

IT has often been maintained that there is no nation or tribe without religion. But what is meant by religion ? The word, as is well known, is not found in languages not related to our own, and its derivation is uncertain. Cicero, in one passage, derived it from re and lego and held that its real meaning was the repetition of prayers and incantations. Another interpretation derives the word from re and ligo, and makes its original sense that of attachment, of a continual binding (that is, no doubt, to the gods). A third derivation connects the word with lex, and explains it as a law-abiding, scrupulously conscientious, frame of mind.

This last seems to be most in accordance with the conceptions prevalent when the use of the phrase began, Buddhism and more in harmony with the similar expressions that arose under similar circumstances elsewhere in China, for instance, and in India. In India, indeed the same word is used by the followers of every school of thought for law and for religion the word Dharma etymologically equivalent to the Latin forma^ and constantly reminding us in its implied connotation of the English phrase "good form."

Law did not, of course, in that early time, mean legislation. It was rather custom, established precedent ; and a sense of duty to the established order of things included and implied a reverential attitude toward the gods. This last side of the idea tended, even in Roman usage, to become predominant ; and when the early Christians began to write in Latin, they not only limited the sense of the word religion to this part of its original meaning, but so used it in this limited sense as to fit it in with their own theology, till it gradually becomes nearly a synonym first for Christianity, and then for Catholic Christianity. The completion of this revolution in meaning was, however, only opening the door to fresh modifications.

Thus we find St. Thomas Aquinas, in one place, defining religion as " goodness rendering to God the honour due to Him " ; and in another as " the mani festation of that faith, hope, and charity toward God to which man is, above all, ordained." But as the monastic system grew, a " religious house " came to mean a monastery, a " religious " that is a religious person a member of a monkish order, a " going into religion" the taking of the vows, and even a " religion " an order of monks.

Most curious is it to read the decree of the famous fourth Lateran council regretting the confusion brought about in the church of God by the diversity of " religions," and laying down that none should ferment a new "religion," but whoso desired to adopt "a religion," should select one of those already approved. Religion through-out this passage means simply an order of friars. An Irish Protestant, Archbishop Trench, finds in this use of the word a notable evidence of the moral contagion of papal domination, and asks " what an awful light does this one word, so used, throw on the entire state of mind and habit of thought in those ages!" Writers of all the numerous sects of Protestant belief have accordingly endeavoured to bring the meaning of the word religion back to those points which each of them regard as of vital importance.

But how can they hope to keep it there, and only there? For writers who discard the dogmas of Christianity endeavour to put a meaning into the word which will harmonise with their newer views of life. The author of Ecce Homo says that religion is "habitual and regulated admiration' or "worship of whatever in the known universe appears worthy of worship." Mr. Frederic Harrison defines it as "veneration for the power which exercises a dominant influence over our life." And Matthew Arnold found in it only "morality touched with emotion."

It is evident that man's definitions of religion will be precisely as numerous, as different, and as accurate as their own beliefs. There is only one definition which all must accept, the historical one, and the history of the word goes back a long way before Cicero, and is still, to-day, in the making. For the word is a convenient expression for a very complex set of mental conditions, including, firstly, beliefs as to internal and external mysteries (souls and gods) secondly, the mental attitude induced by those beliefs and thirdly, the actions and conduct dependent upon both. No one of these constituent elements of religion is stable. They are never exactly the same in any two individuals, even when these profess the same faith and live under the same conditions.

The beliefs especially (which are independent, except in a very indirect way, of the will of the individual) vary, and that in a definitely progressive way, from century to century. And in those countries where the expression " religion " has once obtained currency, it has been always and must still, in the future, be applied to each new variation.

The connotation of the word is determined by popular

usage, and popular convenience. It can never be limited by scholars or by the self-regarding definition of the apologists of any particular creed.

Of the paramount importance of religion, there can be no doubt. The life of every individual is profoundly affected by religious views and religious feelings, either his own or those of the people by whom he is surrounded, and there is nothing which so deeply affects the happiness of a nation as the predominant religion. It is not surprising, therefore, that the present revival of historical research should have been accompanied by a deep interest in the comparative study of the history of religious beliefs. And we may congratulate the Organising Committee of this scheme of lectures on their desire to bring before American students the latest results to which these enquiries have at present reached ; and on the wisely thought-out arrangements which ensure to their efforts so great a measure of success.

To me, I confess, the choice your Committee have made of the first subject for exposition seems particularly happy. For it is precisely in India that, for us Westerns, the evolution of religious belief is most instructive. It can be traced there with so much completeness, and so much clearness ; we can follow it there with so much independence of judgment, with so great an impartiality ; and it runs, in spite of the many differences, on general lines so similar to the history of religion in the West, that the lessons to be learnt from it are of the highest value. Nowhere else do we find the records of a movement stretching uninterruptedly over more than three thousand years. Nowhere else has greater earnestness or so much ability been devoted so continuously to religious questions. Nowhere else has there been so much freedom of thought. Nowhere else has the evolution of religion been so little influenced from outside. Yet nowhere else do we find a system at once so similar to our own in the stages and manner of its growth, and so interestingly and absolutely antagonistic to our own in the ultimate conclusions it has reached. And nowhere else do we find so complete a picture of the tendencies and influences which have brought about the marvellous change from the crude hypotheses of the earliest faith to the sublime conceptions of such original thinkers as those who put the finishing touches to the beautiful Indian picture of the Palace of Truth.

Our own religious beliefs grew up in the basin of the Mediterranean. Jews and Greeks, assisted and influenced in no small degree by Egyptians, laid the foundations. All the most earnest culture of the West has only availed, through so many centuries, to build the superstructure. Ideas similar to the two main and essential conceptions which underlie the whole the belief in " God " and the belief in the "soul" are no doubt to be found throughout the world. But in three places only do we find these two ideas developed into systems which can bear comparison with our own, either in the manner or in the length of the period of their growth, or in the complexity and richness of the final result. These three places are Persia, China, and India.

Now, as to Persia, the original beliefs of the Akkadians are only now just beginning to be known. Even as modified and recast by the Assyrians, the records are still for the most part unpublished and untranslated, and the few foremost scholars of Zoroastrianism are not in agreement either as to the date of its sacred books or as to the part it played up to the final struggle when all was submerged under the flood of a ruthless Muhammadanism. The labours of many generations of scholars will be required to unravel this strange story, and to tell, with any fulness and accuracy of detail, the tragic tale.

So in China history is almost a blank, a kind of battle-field for conjecture, before the time of Konfucius. Much has been done, no doubt, towards the elucidation of the religion founded by him on the more ancient faith. But Konfucius did not stand alone in China. We have only one work, of sufficient insight and authority, on the conceptions of Lao Tsu, which seem to the comparative student so much more original And of the curious history of Buddhism in that country, of the influence it exercised on other beliefs, of the modifications it had itself to submit to, we have no systematic account at all. It is only in India that we have a very complete and authentic record, from a period more than fifteen centuries before the birth of Christ down to the present time, of the evolution of religious belief among a people practically isolated from the rest of the world. There remains, it is true, here also a great deal of important work to be done.

But on the main lines at least the history is already remarkably clear. It is full of interest from the comparative point of view. And it reaches its culminating point in the Buddhist movement, the main subject of the present course of lectures, a movement which carried the evolution of religious belief one step farther than has been reached by any other of the numerous religions that history offers to our view.

That step and it is a step of the first importance is that Buddhism, alike in its ethics and in its views of the past and of the future, ignores the two theories of God and the soul. This came about in a very curious and instructive way. The oldest records in India (as is true also of the oldest recofds in every country that has records at all) show us a stage in culture in which the existence of gods and souls is taken for granted. The origin of these two theories is at present shrouded in mystery. Primitive man has left no records. We have only the evidence of those beliefs which are the later outcome of his crude hypotheses. And in attempting to read between the lines of these later records even in the light, itself very meagre and uncertain, of the existing beliefs of very savage peoples scholars are not altogether at one.

One or two principal points seem, amid difference of opinion as to details, to be generally admitted. Primitive man, whatever the race he belonged to, made no distinction at all between his experiences in every-day life and his experiences in dreams. And that was so, not because he looked upon life as a dream, but that he looked upon dreams as realities. When, in his dream, he saw a person he knew, on his awak-ening, to be dead, he at once concluded, on the mere evidence of his dream, that the person in question was still alive. And when he further recollected, as he sometimes must have done, that the body of the living man had been destroyed his very nightmare may have been the result of his having feasted on the body of his foe, then it was quite clear to him that there was a something (a breath, a life, he knew not what) which existed within the body, and was like the body, and which left it when the breath or life departed, to carry on a separate existence of its own. He did not reason much about it, or stay to consider whether its life was eternal or not. But he was too much frightened of it to forget it. And the dread reality afforded him a perfectly simple and a perfectly clear explanation of many otherwise mysterious things.

When he awoke in the morning after hunting all night in his dreams, and learnt from his companions that his body had been there all the time, it was of course his " soul " that had been away. The theory grew and flourished exceedingly. In all ancient books and in most modern ones too, and in travellers' tales about uncivilised and civilised men, refind it cropping up at every turn. Exactly how it grew, the order in which the applications of the theory took shape, is one of the battle grounds of the students of what is so oddly called Anthropology. To discuss the opinions on this point would take us too far from our subject. Suffice to say that the souls outside a man developed into gods. Souls were believed to wander from body to body. Animals had souls, and all things that men feared, and all that moved. The awe-inspiring phenomena of nature were instinctively regarded as the result of spirit action ; and rivers, plants, and stars, the earth and air and heavens, became full of ghosts.

One distinguished writer who has turned aside from the easy devious paths of philosophy to the straight and difficult one of history, thinks that all gods were, in origin, the ghosts of ancestors. So uniform an explanation is most improbable. A much more solid basis seems to support the argument that as the oldest recorded gods are goddesses, and as man makes God in his own image, the original deities must have arisen at a time when women were the leaders, as in other things, so also in theology. They were born of women, for it was woman who conceived them. And we must make room in our theory at least as much for the awe inspired by Mother Earth, and by the mysteries of the stars, as for the worship of ancestors. We have to explain how it was that the oldest divinities were almost, if not quite, exclusively feminine. We have to explain why the moon was worshipped before the sun, and certain stars before either, and the Mother Earth before them all It is precisely the succession of these curious beliefs that is the interesting point. It was only among the advancing peoples that the changes went very far at all. And these changes are full of information about tribal conflicts and social conditions. For the gods had no existence except in the brains of their worshippers. They were ideas, a rough kind of scientific hypotheses. The arrival of a new god meant the birth of a new idea ; and a book on The Birth Days of the Gods would be not only an epitome of human hopes and fears, but a history of men's views on social questions too.

For the gods, like the men who made them, grew old

and feeble and passed away, and their very ghosts were degraded in the minds of the descendants of their creators to the rank of devils. The change in the object of worship was not merely a change in name, with the same or a similar worship ; it was accompanied also by a change of view as to the relations of sex, as to mode of life, as to questions of organisation and government, and as to the forms of possession of goods and land. The worshippers of the new god thought themselves reformers, and often were so. The worshippers of the old gods looked upon the supporters of their rivals as atheists (just as the polytheists on the shores of the Mediterranean called the Christians atheists). But they were not in any case atheists, nor were they the founders of a new era, that was to last and to cure all woes. They only registered a new stage in the progress of thought, which (in this matter as in others) has, in the historic sense, an evolution of its own, independent of the men in whose brain the thought takes shape, and following (in all times and countries) precisely similar lines.

Many such changes had taken place in Indian spirit beliefs before the time of the oldest records that have come down to us. These show a very advanced stage in the ancient soul-theory. And there are no older records of its development along this particular line. The Akkadian records, it is true, go much farther back, and they have many points of analogy which seem to supply the actual historical origin of several later Hindu beliefs. But this is only because those beliefs have been incorporated into orthodox Hinduism from the descendants of those Dravidian peoples, related to the Akkadians, who preceded the Aryans in India. Nothing has yet been found in the Akkadian books showing any historical connection with Vedic beliefs.

On the other hand, we have in the ancient books of the Greeks and Persians, records of beliefs historically connected with the Indian. But these records are later in time than the oldest records in India, and preserve a later phase of the common beliefs.

When we find, for instance, in the Zoroastrian books, that the hypothetical beings called in the Vedas " gods " have there already become " devils," we know that we have a later phase of a common belief. For it is the new religion which looks upon the gods of its predecessor as devils, and it is unknown that, in the course of the development of the same system of faith, devils should ever become gods.

The oldest Indian books that is, the Vedas and Brahmanas therefore, though they themselves show us an advanced stage in ancient soul theory, are still the most ancient records of the particular line of development which we have to follow. And in them we find the germs of all the subsequent steps in philosophy and in religion that were taken in the valley of the Ganges.

The collection of Vedic hymns, as we now have it, bears of course no date. It resembles in this respect all other collections of similar antiquity, without exception, known to us. The date of the earliest books of each religion can be ascertained only by historical criticism, and so in India also.

We have to start with facts that are known. We can argue back from the well established date of the great Buddhist Emperor of India, the famous Asoka. For we find in the literature extant in his time a series of strata, so to speak, of literary and philosophic activity, each of them indisputable evidence of the previous existence of the one before it.

The last of these strata, the Buddhist Pitakas and the Sanskrit books of the same period, belong to his time. Estimates have been made of the previous interval that must be allowed successively for each of the other strata, between the time of Asoka and the close of the Vedic period, when the hymns were put into their present shape. And scholars are practically unanimous in the opinion that the Vedas must have been existing as we now have them at least 1000-1200 B.C., to allow time for the subsequent developments. Scholars also agree that they contain a good deal of material even much older than that, and the hymns stand in this last respect again on the same footing as the Buddhist Pitakas, or the Old Testament, or any other ancient canon. They reveal to us a most interesting and instructive picture of a number of clans, closely related to ourselves, engaged in forcing their way into a country already more or less occupied, and occasionally turning aside from their contests with the darker natives to fight among themselves.

Judging from the hymns, the invaders Aryans as we now call them were intensely religious ; but of morality, except as to customs within the clans, they seem to have had very primitive conceptions. To them the killing of opponents was no murder, and the " conveying*' of their neighbour's goods a matter of pride. They have left us no idea on the rights of man (or of woman either) ; and in foreign politics their guiding principle was conquest. Within the clan, too, life was simple for them. There were no poor, and none too rich. They were not troubled with either priests or landlords. And the desire of their hearts was for increase in children, and in cows. The picture afforded us in the hymns of their daily life, and of their habitual thoughts, has a peculiar charm. It was a childlike and clearly a still farther back, by arguments based on supposed astronomical allusions. But the basis for these arguments seems very unreliable happy race, full of activity, and but little troubled by contemplation or by doubt. Probably even their religion sat lightly upon them, but it would seem from the hymns that they had an unhesitating and childlike faith, which looked upon the great souls animating the nature round them as all-powerful in their worldly affairs.

As time went on it is evident that some of them had however commenced to speculate on the nature of the gods, and had dimly begun to think that there was a unity underlying the manifold forms of spirit life in which the people believed.

This is plain from those speculative hymns incorporated into the last and latest book of the great collection called the Rig Veda.

But it is also clear that the ancient Aryans were far too manly and free to be troubled much about their own souls, either before or after the death of the body. There are only a very few short and isolated passages bearing on this side of their spirit theory. They still held with a simple faith to the ancient hypothesis of their savage ancestors as to the existence of a " soul " inside their bodies. And it never occurred to them to doubt for a moment that these souls continued to exist in a sort of misty way after death, or to discuss the question of the duration or cessation of that future life. In all this by intercourse with other peoples, continually changed. The favour of the gods was to be won only by the spell, as it were, cast over them by the faithful repetition of the ancient words. The words themselves had now become but dimly understood.

Schools of priests had been formed to guard the words from destruction, not by writing which was unknown but by constant rehearsing. To aid them in their task, elaborate commentaries were composed and handed down, also by memory. Rules of grammar and of exegesis were devised and formulated into schemes of exposition. The whole intellectual power of the nation became for a time concentrated on these subsidiary studies. Works of original power, with the free and child-like spirit which animated the older hymns, became unknown.

The training in these schools was of a curious kind. History in our sense, and science too, were of course entirely unrepresented. The chief weight was placed on memory, and the ingenuity of commentators was much exercised in reconciling the diverse statements of the ancient texts which could not err and in finding mystic reasons to explain all the various details of the sacrifice.

Now one of the most striking things about the ancient hymns is the way in which each poet, partly no doubt through his want of expertness in we see the bright side of the ancient nature worship, of religion based on the soul theory as held in its early simplicity by a free and advancing and prosperous people. The darker side, which played in all probability a greater part in the daily thoughts and average life of the ordinary man and woman of those days, was that medley of strange beliefs and fears, revealed in the Atharva Veda, the reliance on omens, and spells, and magic rites, the vague terrors of a life surrounded by all sorts of malign influences, the poisonous fruit of the superstitions of demonology.

While all these ideas, good and bad, were fermenting together, the bolder spirits were ever pushing farther and farther on into the hot plains of India. The details of their gradual progress are indeed hidden in an obscurity which we can scarcely hope now ever to clear up. But the general results are already well ascertained. Before the rise of Buddhism the whole of the country as far East as Patna, had become more or less Aryanised, either by alliance or by conquest, and the Aryan gods (that is to say, the men who worshipped them) held sway from the Kabul hills down to the plains of Bengal.

The religion was, however, not altogether uniform. As the tribes pushed on, their language, partly by the ordinary and necessary growth or decay, partly the use of language, his inability to give due expression to shades of meaning; but partly also through the real fervour of his religious feeling, directed at the time on the one object of his praise is the way in which each poet so often refers to different gods (Indra, Agni, Prajapati, Varuna, etc.), as being, each one of them, the greatest and the best. There was not really any clear sense of comparison, though the words now seem to imply it. It was simply that the one God, that is to say, the one idea, loomed largest at the time before the mental eye of the poet. And in the explanation of such passages the Brahman Commentators carefully avoid all appearance of rivalry. A truer and what was probably of more importance from the theologian's point of view a more edifying explanation lay close to their hands. Already in the Vedas certain of the great souls, the gods, are identified with certain others, and there is even reference to a divinity which, as it were, lay behind them all, and was the basis of their godhead.

Thus there is a reference in the often quoted passage, Rig Veda, iii., 55, I, to that "great godhead of the gods which is one." And the Brahmans gradually elaborated out of such expressions a conception of a single being out of whom all gods, and all men, and all things had proceeded.

It may be noticed in passing that a precisely similar result was reached, though not exactly by the same process, and at a slightly different chronological stage, in both Greece and China. And though we have no evidence of a like logical process in Assyria, it would seem that Egyptian thinkers also had their speculations of a similar sort. There is nothing strange in this coincidence. It is the exception of Assyria that is really curious. And we need not think to explain the coincidence by any theory of borrowing by anyone of these peoples from the other. For the fact is, that, whenever there is sufficent intelligence and sufficient leisure in a country where the soul theory is held, there, by a logical process which is inevitable, men will come to believe in a number of gods ; and then, later on, to perceive a unity behind the many, and to postulate a single divinity as the supposed source of the many gods whom they themselves have really fashioned.

The characteristics of the new divinity, of the one god that is to say, the connotations of the new idea will differ according to the different conceptions out of which it has arisen. And in this respect the speculations of the Brahmans in India are especially worthy of consideration. With them the first conception was reached, not as among the Jews, by gradual additions to, and modifications of the character of one divinity, but by a purely philosophical reasoning as to the necessary nature of the first cause. The predicates they applied to him or, more accurately, to it were almost exclusively negative. It is the unknowable cause of the knowable, itself however without cause. It is the light in which all that is perceived is seen, but there is no light by means of which it can be seen. It is invisible, incomprehensible, without descent or colour, without eyes, or ears, or hands, or feet, the everlasting, all pervading, ever-present, extremely subtle, unchangeable source and support of all that is.

All the rest, including the great gods whom the ignorant worship and rightly worship as the highest that they know, is delusion. And the real insight, the only abiding salvation, consists in getting to know the impermanence of all else, and the identity of one's own soul with this Great Soul in which all else lives and moves and has its being.

There is great beauty and poetry in the passages in which this very ancient Pantheism is set out in the literature older than the rise of Buddhism, and though the exact formulation of this system of thought well known as Vedantism is due to later hands, it is evident that there was much earnest thinking and fearless philosophising in the time of the oldest Upanishads in which these ideas find their earliest and most poetical expression.

The Indian formulation of this monistic theory of the universe is indeed in all probability the most logical and most thorough-going of all similar at- tempts that have been preserved to us. The very striking analogies in Greek philosophy, more especially in Parmenides (though he was a century later), cannot even be properly worked out owing to the fragmentary condition in which alone the earlier Greek speculations have survived. And the corre sponding Chinese conceptions, either of the Konfucian or Taoist schools, seem to be altogether wanting in clearness and precision.

This very able and beautiful monistic philosophy was the dominant factor in Indian thought, when Gotama the Buddha appeared. Many centuries afterwards it was elaborated and systematiscd, more especially by Sankara, into that Vedantist philosophy now quite supreme in India. In those early days it had no doubt stronger rivals. When the Paftcaratra books have been made accessible to scholars it will be found, I think, that they contain a systematic philosophy built of the same cards, perhaps, as the Vedanta (god and soul) but independent of it, and at least equal to it in beauty if not in logical power. We hear also of Lokayatas, or Materialists, who must have preceded Buddhism, as they are mentioned in the oldest Buddhist books.

The Jaina faith, which arose at the same time as Buddhism, has also a voluminous literature. When that is published it cannot fail to throw much light upon the religious life of India at the time when the founders of the two new religions were rivals. But there was little original thought in Jainism. Its views are rather isolated propositions than a system of philosophy, and it would never have been a formidable rival to Vedantism.

It was quite otherwise with the Sankhya system. Centuries afterwards, when Buddhism had become corrupted, it would seem that the Sankhya was almost about to supplant the Vedanta ; and as it has often been held by European scholars that Buddhism is more or less based on the Sankhya, it will be necessary to consider the question of its priority.

Logically it stands half-way between the Vedanta and Buddhism, and was therefore a possible stepping-stone to the Buddhist position. And the Buddhists themselves acknowledge that Kapila, to whom the Sankhya books ascribe the foundation of their philosophy, lived several generations before the Buddha. It is therefore, to say the least, possible that the Sankhya system also preceded the Buddhist, or was the outcome of the same intellectual movement.

But what we know is, that in the centuries immediately before and after the birth of Christ (that is, some centuries after the rise of Buddhism) it was the Sankhya rather than the Vedanta, which was the predominant school; and that its adherents claimed a still more remote origin for their speculations. Professor Garbe, of Tubingen, who is the best authority on the subject, he has done for the Sankhya the same sort of service as has been so well rendered to the Vedanta by Professor Deussen, of Kiel, is of opinion that the Sankhya teachers are right, and that their teaching does indeed go back before the rise of Buddhism. The point seems to me, I confess, to be most doubtful. All the Sankhya books are much later in date.

The very oldest of them the Sankhya Karika of Isvara Krishna cannot be fixed at an earlier period than a full thousand years after the time of Gotama the Buddha. And though it is quite certain that the system, as a system already well worked out, was older than that, we find it referred to, and in great part adopted, along with Vedantism, in books, certainly two or three centuries older ; in Manu, for instance, and in the Bhagavad Glta, yet there is still a great gap to be bridged over. All the available evidence on the point is collected, with great care and completeness, by Professor Garbe, in his just published Sdnkhya Philosophie, a book which will, I hope, soon be translated into English. And on weighing all the evidence it seems to me that the only conclusion to be rightly drawn is that, though there is no evidence that Kapila was the real author of the whole Sankhya philosophy, there were; before the time of the Buddha, isolated thinkers, of whose words we have no trace, who elaborated views similar to those out of which the Sankhya was eventually developed.

For what do we find ? There is ample evidence even in the books of the orthodox body of Brahman teachers to show that when Buddhism arose there was not only much discussion of the ultimate problems of life, and a keen interest in the result, but also that there was a quite unusually open field for all sorts of speculations. In no other age and country do we find so universally diffused among all classes of the people so earnest a spirit of enquiry, so impartial and deep a respect for all who posed as teachers, however contradictory their doctrines might be.

It is true that the orthodox books are filled with the orthodox view. But this is only quite natural. How very little of precise and accurate information do we find even in Christian books of the early centuries concerning the views of opponents? Even the Buddhist writings do not tell us much. But we have a detailed list in the first Suttanta of the Digha Nikdya of sixty-two different theories of existence; and in the second Suttanta of the same collection, the views of six leading opponents are discussed at length. I shall return to these passages later on.

It is sufficient for the present argument to point out that they confirm in every particular the picture we find in the Brahmanas and in the old Upanishads, and that one at least of the sixty-two views thus condemned seems to be a forecast of the Sankhya.

The passage is as follows it is the Buddha himself who is represented as speaking :

"And in the fourth place, brethren, on what grounds and for what reason do the recluses and Brahmans who are believers in the eternity of existence declare that both the soul and the world are eternal ?

" In this case, brethren, some recluse or Brahman 5s addicted to logic and reasoning. He gives utterance to the following conclusion of his own reached by his argumentations, and based on his sophistry.

And though these living beings pass along, transmigrate, fall out of one state of existence and are born in another, yet they are for ever and ever.

Now this last is precisely the point in the soul theory on which the latter Sankhya teaching differs from the Vedanta. According to the latter it is only God who is everlasting, the world is a phantom as it were, a dream, a delusion, and has its only real existence in God. And the souls themselves have no independent existence. They are God itself. But the Sankhya on the other hand holds that there is no God, that the primordial Prakriti (or stuff out of which the world is formed) is eternal, and that the souls have a separate existence of their own, and continue to exist for ever in infinite numbers.

It will be noticed on the other hand that in the Buddhist description of this particular heresy the technical expression employed in the Sankhya books for the primordial stuff is not used. It is here " the world " which the heretics are said to consider eternal, and that is not the view entertained by the Sankhya. And if we should hold that the vague Nikaya edited by myself and Mr. J. Estlin Carpenter, for the Pali Text Society in 1890. Buddhaghosa's commentary on the passage has also been published by us in the Sumangala Vilasini, vol. i., pp. 105-107. (Pali Text Society, 1886.) expression " world " may be taken here in the special sense of the " original matter " of the Sankhya books, then we only come to another contradiction.

According to the Sankhya it is precisely out of the "original matter" and the individual souls that the visible world and living beings are produced.

The heretics described in our passage hold that the soul and the world are barren, give birth to nothing.

I am at a loss therefore to understand how this passage can be considered as good evidence that the Sankhya system existed as a whole, just as we find it in books many centuries later, at the time when the passage was composed, much less at the time of its legendary author, Kapila.

It is unfortunately impossible here to go into the details either of the Sankhya explanation of how the world and living beings arose out of the original Prakrit! (or matter) and the individual souls, or into the details of its psychological analysis. They also present very instructive analogies with the dualistic theories in Greece analogies which will be considered of greater importance as the Indian side of the picture becomes better known. It is sufficient to point out there is nothing at all in any of the details peculiar to the Sankhya which has been borrowed by Gotama, or is even to be found at all in any of the oldest Buddhist writings.

We have no body of writings other than those mentioned, to throw light on the religious speculations of India before Buddhism. But as regards the soul and salvation we have the very interesting list of the heresies on those points condemned by the early Buddhists, from which an extract has already been read. With your permission I will read this list. It does not follow, of course, that each one of the opinions quoted in it represents the teaching of a separate and distinct school. But the whole of it is full of suggestion as to the kind of discussions which were going on when Buddhism arose.

The extract occurs in a work of more importance than any other on Buddhism the collection of the dialogues, mostly of Gotama himself, brought together in the Dlgha and Majjhima Nikayas. This work contains the views of the Buddha set out, as they appeared to his earliest disciples, in a series of 186 conversational discourses which will some day come to hold a place, in the history of human thought, akin to that held by the Dialogues of Plato. The first of these 186 Dialogues is called the Brahma Jala, that is the Perfect Net the net whose meshes are so fine that no folly of superstition, however subtle, can slip through. In it are set out sixty-two varieties of existing hypotheses ; and after each of them has been rejected, the doctrine of Arahatship is put forward as the right solution.

These sixty-two heresies are as follows :

1-4 Sassata-Vadd. People who, either from meditation of three degrees, or fourthly through logic and reasoning, have come to believe that both the external world as a whole, and individual souls arc eternal.

5-8 Ekacca-Sassatika. People who, in four ways hold that some souls are eternal, and some are not.

a. Those who hold that God is eternal, but not the individual souls.

I. Those who hold that all the gods are eternal, but not the individual souls.

c. Those who hold that certain illustrious gods are eternal, but not the individual souls.

d Those who hold that, while the bodily forms are not eternal, there is a subtle something, called Heart or Mind, or Consciousness, which is.

9-12 Antanantika. People who chop logic about finity and infinity.

a. Those who hold the world to be finite.

b. Those who hold it to be infinite.

c. Those who hold it to be both.

d. Those who hold it to be neither.

13-16 Amara-Vikkhepika. People who equivocate about virtue and vice.

a. From fear lest, if they express a decided opinion, grief (at possible mis-take) will hurt them.

b. From fear lest they may form attachments which will injure them.

c. From fear lest they may be unable to answer skilful disputants.

d. From dulness or stupidity.

17-18 Adhicca-Samuppannika. People who think that the origin of things can be explained without a cause.

19-50 Uddhama-Aghatanikn. People who believe in the future existence of human souls.

a. Sixteen phases of the hypothesis of a conscious existence after death.

b. Eight phases of the hypothesis of an unconscious existence after death.

c. Eight phases of the hypothesis of an existence between consciousness and unconsciousness after death.

51-57 Uccheda-Vdda. People who teach the doctrine that there is a soul, but that it will cease to exist

a. On the death of the body here.

b. At the end of the next life.

c.-g-. At the end of subsequent lives.

58-62 Dittha-Dhamma-Nibbana-Vdda. People who hold that there is a soul, and that it can attain to perfect bliss in the present world, or wherever it happens to be

a. By a full, complete, and perfect enjoyment of the five senses.

I. By an enquiring mental abstraction (the first Jhana).

c. By undisturbed mental bliss, untarnished by enquiry (the second Jhana).

d. By mental calm, free alike from joy and pain and enquiry (the third Jhana), By that mental peace plus a sense of purity (the fourth Jhana).

The list is a formidable one, and it only trenches on certain selected points out of those that we know were the subjects of philosophical discussion in the India of that day. It must not be forgotten that we are dealing with an extent of country vastly greater than the region which was the seat, at a somewhat later period, of the beginning of Western philosophy. It is not only the numerous schools of the Brahmins in Middle India that we have to consider. We also must take into consideration the schools in the countries to the west of them (which the Aryans had left before the caste system had been established, and the Brahmin ritual had been developed), and the schools in the countries to the east of them where the Aryans, and no doubt Brahmins with them, had indeed penetrated, (which had been, so to speak, Aryanised,) but where the full power and influence of the Brahmins had not become so overwhelmingly predominant. It is precisely in these two regions, separated one from the other by a thousand miles of fertile and civilised plains, that we should expect to find the most unfettered thought, the widest dissension from the orthodox Vedantist view, the most original and daring speculation. And it is not without significance that it is precisely there that in after years the two great universities of India were established the one Takka Sila, in the extreme north-west, and the other, Nalanda, in Rajgir, in the extreme south-east.

I do not think, therefore, that the list I have read to you is at all exaggerated. The records of the thinkers referred to have all been lost. But this should raise no difficulty in our minds. Books were not written in India in those days. Even the wonderful powers of memory which those highly cultured people possessed, did not reach to learning by heart and handing down elaborate expositions of doctrines held to be insufficient or erroneous. To the life-long industry and marvellous memory of the scholars of that time, we owe the preservation of the extensive, and historically invaluable, literatures of the Vedic schools, and of the Buddhist Order; and instead of being astonished that the greater part of the rest has perished, we ought to be supremely grateful that so much has been preserved. After all, the old scholars of India, who were compelled to make a choice, were right in the choice they made.

These two systems are the highest expression, from the theological and the anti-theological points of view, respectively, of Indian thought. There is no one man to whom the original exposition of Vedantist philosophy can be ascribed, no one name pre-eminent in pre-Buddhistic Vedantism. But Sankar Acarya, centuries afterwards, systematised and formulated the Vedantist creed, and it is to Gotama the Buddha, that we owe what we call the Buddhist religion.

There can be no doubt that these two, Sankar Acarya and Gotama the Buddha, are the greatest names in the intellectual life of India, and that in preserving for us the records of the two systems of belief with which those names are associated, the repeaters of the Indian books have done for the world the greatest service they could do.

We have then in India in the valley of the Ganges, at the time when the Buddhist theory of life was first propounded, a maze of interacting ideas which may be divided for clearness sake, into the following heads. Firstly, the very wide and varied group of ideas about souls, whether in man or in the lesser powers of Nature and also in animals, and even in trees and plants. These may be summed up under the convenient modern term of Animism, and include all the conceptions preserved in the books of astrology, magic, and folk-lore, the ideas of a future life and of the transmigration of souls, the beliefs as to all sorts of minor demons, and fairies, and spirits, and ghosts, and gods.

Secondly, we have the later and more advanced ideas about the souls or spirits supposed to animate the greater forces and phenomena of Nature. These may be summed up under the convenient modern term of Polytheism, and include all the conceptions as to the great gods preserved in the Vedas, and elaborated and explained in the Brahmanas.

Thirdly, we have the still later and still more advanced idea of a unity lying behind the whole of these phenomena both of the first and of the second class, the hypothesis of a One First Cause on which the whole universe in its varied forms depends, in which it lives and moves, in which it has its whole and only being. This may be summed up in the convenient modern term of Pantheism. It is preserved in the Upanishads, and was subsequently elaborated and systematised by Sankar Acarya.

Then we have the still subsequent stage now preserved in the already quoted Sankhya books, and then probably already existing in earlier and less systematised forms, of a view of life in which the First Cause is expressly rejected, but in which with that exception the whole soul-theory is still retained side by side with the tenet of the eternity of matter.

This may be summed up under the convenient modern term of Dualism* And we have slight glimpses of very numerous other views (among others of philosophies allied to what we now understand in the West by Epicureanism and Materialism).

These modern Western terms, though most useful as suggestions, never, however, exactly fit the ancient Eastern modes of thought. And we must never forget that these really contradictory explanations of the problem of life, now so carefully differentiated and kept apart by modern scholars, were not then mutually exclusive. We have to deal with a state of society in which, not history, nor science, but precisely these ultimate questions engaged the ardent attention and passionate patience of a surprisingly large number of men, of whom only a very few had the logical clearness and moral fearlessness to take a deliberate and exclusive stand. Just as afterwards the Vedantist could accept parts of the Sankhya position really incompatible with the rest of his belief, and both of them could believe in the actual truth, if not in the supreme importance, of animistic delusions. You will follow this the more readily inasmuch as a similar state of mind is still the most prevalent one in the West when, for instance, a man may be a scientist and at the same time a spiritualist ; or may accept the

Darwinian hypothesis and the results of historical research, and also the substantial accuracy of the Hebrew cosmogony.

Such were the intellectual surroundings in which Buddhism arose. What I have had the honour of laying before you is of course the merest sketch. You will listen some day, I trust, to a whole course of lectures on Animism; to another on the Vedanta ; to another on the Sankhya; and to yet another on the remaining points of Indian belief in the sixth century B.C., to which allusion has been made. In the very narrow limits of time to which I am confined, it has only been possible to dwell on the more salient points, and I must apologise for having attempted to crowd so much into a single hour. But I have considered it my duty to bring out into as clear a relief as possible the points most essential to a right understnding of what we call Buddhism, and what the founder of that religion called the Dhamma, that is the Law, or the Norm.

Now the central position of the Buddhist alternative to those previous views of life was this that Gotama not only ignored the whole of the soul theory, but even held all discussion as to the ultimate soul problems with which the Vedanta and the other philosophies were chiefly concerned, as not only childish and useless, but as actually inimical to the only ideal worth striving after the ideal of a perfect life, here and now, in this present world, in Arahatship.

And I am only following the most ancient and the best of the Buddhist authorities in placing this most important point in the front of my exposition. The very first sermon which Gotama preached to his first converts is the Anatta Lakkhana Sutta, (the discourse on the absence of any sign of " soul " in any of all the constituent elements of individual life) preserved in the Vinaya and recapitulated in full in the Samyutta Niknya;^ and translated by Professor

Oldenbergand myself in our Vinaya Texts. The very first of the collection of the dialogues of Gotama, forming the principal book on the Dhamma in the Buddhist Scriptures, is the one already quoted in which the Buddha so completely, categorically, and systematically rejects all the possible current theories about " souls." And later books of the first importance follow the same order. The, Vatthu, a book of controversy composed in the third century B.C., against dissenters within the fold, is one of the latest included in the Buddhist Scriptures. But it also places this question of the " soul " at the head of all the points it discusses, and devotes to it an amount of space which makes it completely over-shadow all the rest.* So also with regard to the earliest Buddhist book after the canon was closed, the very interesting and instructive series of conver-sations between the Greek king, Menanda (Milinda), of Baktria, and N^gasena, the Buddhist teacher. It is precisely this question of the " soul " that the un-known author makes the subject of the very first dis-cussion in which Nagasena convinces the king that there is really no such thing as the " soul " in the ordinary sense. And he returns to the subject again and again. I have no time left in which to read you these clear and decisive passages of this most ancient Buddhist author outside the Scriptures known to us.

You can find them in full in my translation of the Milinda just published at Oxford, and in abstract in my little manual entitled Buddhism important from the historical point of view, is now being edited for the Pali Text Society, by Mr. Arnold C. Taylor.

We cannot be far wrong in attaching weight to a view considered in these ancient and authoritative Buddhist books to be of such transcendent importance. It is precisely the not having grasped this essential preliminary to a right understanding of Buddhism that has rendered so very large a portion of the voluminous Western writings on the subject of so little value. And the point is historically also of the very highest interest, for the Buddhist position is the inevitable logical outcome of all discussion of the soul theory; and the Buddhists of course hold that in the West also people must inevitably come to the same conclusion when they have leisure to turn from the at present all-engrossing questions of the accumulation and distribution of wealth.

You will, however, understand that this apparently at first sight purely negative position is not the Dharma proclaimed by the Buddha. It is merely his answer to the previous religious and philosophical systems. Without the " soul " they, one and all, fall at once to the ground. And the point is only made of so much importance in Buddhist writings, because the Buddhist teachers held, and rightly held, it impossible, before the rubbish had been cleared away from the site, to build the new Palace of Good Sense. They held it impossible, so long as men were harassed by doubts and fears about their " souls," to induce in them the emancipated state of mind essential to a calm pursuit of the higher life ; they held it impossible to stir men up to the ardent and earnest and hopeful struggle after a perfect life here and now, in this world, so long as they were still hampered, and all their virtue tarnished, by a foolish craving (that could never be satisfied, and would be a disaster if it could be) for an eternal future life in Heaven.

It must remain an open question how far this position is really negative. It is a matter to a great extent of degree. The rival theories are occupied, to the virtual exclusion of other matters, predominantly with questions of soul. Buddhism says that any real advance in ethical theory, and also in the practical conduct of life, really begins only when the delusions about the soul have been fully, and freely, and finally renounced. The rival theories purport to explain the origin and end of all things. Buddhism declares that everything has a cause ; and that it is not only a sufficient, it is the only true, method, to argue from one cause back to the next, and so on, without any hope or even desire to explain the ultimate cause of all things. The most famous Buddhist stanza found engraved on ten thousand votive gifts to Buddhist shrines in India, says, that, " Of all the things that proceed from a cause, The Buddha the cause hath told ; And he tells too how each shall come to its end, Such alone is the word of the Sage But the positive side of the Dharma must be reserved to a future lecture. The present one is only intended to show the surroundings among which this remarkably original and interesting view took shape, and its attitude towards the rival theories, not only of that day, but also of our own.

Months passed. Then, one day, the queen knew that the time was approaching for her son to be born. She went to King Suddhodana, and she said to him:

"My lord, I would wander through the happy gardens. Birds are singing in the trees, and the air is bright with flower-dust. I would wander through the happy gardens."

"But it will weary you, O queen," replied Suddhodana. "Are you not afraid?"

"The innocent being that I carry in my womb must be born amid the innocence of budding flowers. No, I will go, O master, I will go into the flower-gardens."

The king yielded to Maya's wish. He said to his servants:

"Go into the gardens and deck them out in silver and in gold. Drape the trees with precious hangings. Let everything be magnificent, for the queen will pass."

Then he addressed Maya:

"Array yourself, to-day, in great splendor, O Maya. Ride in a gorgeous palanquin; let your most beautiful maidens carry you. Order your servants to use rare perfumes; have them wear ropes of pearls and bracelets of precious stones; have them carry lutes and drums and flutes, and sing sweet songs that would delight the Gods themselves."

Suddhodana was obeyed, and when the queen reached the palace-gates the guards greeted her with joyous cries. Bells peeled gaily, peacocks spread their gorgeous tail-feathers, and the song of swans throbbed in the air.

They came to a wood where the trees were in bloom, and Maya ordered them to set down the palanquin. She stepped out and began wandering about, aimlessly. She was happy. And behold! she found a rare tree, the branches drooping under their burden of blossoms. She went up to it; gracefully extending her hand, she drew down a branch. Suddenly, she stood very still. She smiled, and the maidens who were near her received a lovely child into their arms.

At that same moment all that was alive in the world trembled with joy. The earth quivered. Songs and the patter of dancing feet echoed in the sky. Trees of all seasons burst into flower, and ripe fruit hung from the branches. A pure, serene light appeared in the sky. The sick were rid of their suffering. The hungry were satisfied. Those to whom wine had played false became sober. Madmen recovered their reason, the weak their strength, the poor their wealth. Prisons opened their gates. The wicked were cleansed of all evil.

One of Maya's maidens hastened to King Suddhodana and joyously exclaimed:

"My lord, my lord, a son is born to you, a son who will bring great glory to your house!"

He was speechless. But his face was radiant with joy, and he knew great happiness.

Presently he summoned all the Sakyas, and he

commanded them to accompany him into the garden where the child had been born. They obeyed, and, with a host of brahmans in attendance, they formed a noble retinue as they gravely followed the king.

When he came near the child, the king made a deep obeisance, and he said:

"Do you bow as I bow before the prince, to whom I give the name Siddhartha."

They all bowed, and the brahmans, inspired by the Gods, then sang:

"All creatures are happy, and they are no longer rough, those roads travelled by men, for he is born, he who gives happiness: he will bring happiness into the world. In the darkness a great light has dawned, the sun and the moon are like dying embers, for he is born, he who gives light: he will bring light into the world. The blind see, the deaf hear, the foolish have recovered their reason, for he is born, he who restores sight, and restores hearing, and restores the mind: he will bring sight, he will bring hearing, he will bring reason into the world. Perfumed zephyrs ease the suffering of mankind, for he is born, he who heals: he will bring health into the world. Flames are no longer pitiless, the flow of rivers has been stayed, the earth has trembled gently: he will be the one to see the truth."

Asita's Prediction

THE great hermit Asita, whose austerities were pleasing to the Gods, heard of the birth of him who was to save mankind from the torment of rebirth. In his thirst for the true law, he came to the palace of King Suddhodana and gravely approached the women's quarters. His years and his learning lent him great dignity.

The king showed him the courtesies that custom prescribed and addressed him in a seemly manner:

"Happy, indeed, am I! Truly, this child of mine will enjoy distinguished favor, for the venerable Asita has come purposely to see me. Command me. What must I do? I am your disciple, your servant."

The hermit, his eyes shining with the light of joy, gravely spoke these words:

"'This has happened to you, O noble, generous and hospitable king, because you love duty and because you are ever kind to those who are wise and to those who are full of years. This has happened to you because your ancestors, though rich in land and rich in gold, were above all rich in virtue. Know the reason for my coming, O king, and rejoice. In the air I heard a divine voice speaking and it said: 'A son has been born to the king of the Sakyas, a son who will have the true knowledge.' I heard these words, and I came, and my eyes shall now behold the glory of the Sakyas."

Overwhelmed with joy, the king went to fetch the child. Taking him from his nurse's breast, he showed him to the aged Asita.

The hermit noticed that the king's son bore the marks of omnipotence. His gaze hovered over the child, and presently his lashes were wet with tears. Then he sighed and turned his eyes to the sky.

The king saw that Asita was weeping, and he began to fear for his son. He questioned the old man:

"You say, O venerable roan, that my son's body differs little from that of a God. You say that his birth was a wondrous thing, that in the future his glory will be supreme, yet you look at him with eyes that are filled with tears. Is his life, then, to be a fragile thing? Was he born only to bring me sorrow? Must this new branch wither before it has burst into flower? Speak, O saintly man, speak quickly;

you know the great love a father bears his son."

"Be not distressed, O king," replied the hermit. "What I have told you is true: this child will know great glory. If I weep, it is for myself. My life draws to a close and he is born, he who will destroy the evil of rebirth. He will surrender sovereign power, he will master his passions, he will understand truth, and error will disappear in the world before the light of his knowledge, even as night flees before the spears of the sun. From the sea of evil, from the stinging spray of sickness, from the surge and swell of old age, from the angry waves of death, from these will he rescue the suffering world, and together they will sail away in the great ship of knowledge.

He will know where it takes its rise, that swift, wonderful, beneficent river, the river of duty; he will reveal its course, and those who are tortured by thirst will come and drink of its waters. To those tormented by sorrow, to those enslaved by the senses, to those wandering in the forest of existences like travellers who have lost their way, he will point out the road to salvation. To those burning with the fire of passion, he will be the cloud that brings refreshing rain; armed with the true law, he will go to the prison of desires where all creatures languish, and he will break down the evil gates. For he who will have perfect understanding will set the world free.

Therefore do not grieve, O king. He alone is to be pitied who will not hear the voice of your son, and that is why I weep, I who, in spite of my austerities, in spite of my meditations, will never know his message and his law. Yes, even he is to be pitied who ascends to the loftiest gardens of the sky."

Siddhartha at the Temple

THEY pleased Suddhodana at first, these words of

Asita's, and he pondered them. "So my son will live, and live gloriously," he thought, but then he became anxious. For it had been said that the prince would renounce royalty, that he would lead the life of a hermit, and did that not mean that at his death Suddhodana's family would cease?

But his anxiety was short-lived, for since the birth of Siddhartha the king could undertake nothing that did not prosper. Like a great river whose waters are swollen by many tributaries, each day new riches poured into his treasury; the stables were too small to hold the horses and elephants that were presented to him, and he was constantly surrounded by a host of loyal friends. The kingdom was rich in fertile lands, and sleek, fatted cattle grazed in the meadows. Women bore their children without suffering; men lived at peace with their neighbors, and happiness and tranquillity reigned in the land of Kapilavastu.

But the joy that had come to Maya proved too sweet. It soon became unbearable. The earth knew her as a mother but seven days; then she died and ascended to the sky, to be received among the Gods.

Maya had a sister, Mahaprajapati, who in beauty and virtue was almost her equal. The prince was given into Mahaprajapati's care, and she looked after his wants as tenderly as if he were her own child. And like fire fanned by an auspicious wind, like the moon, queen of the stars in the luminous skies, like the morning sun rising over the mountains in the East, Siddhartha grew in strength and stature.

Everyone now delighted in bringing him precious gifts. They gave him toys that would amuse a child of his age: tiny animals, deer and elephants, horses, cows, birds and fish, and little chariots; and they were toys made not of wood or of clay but of gold and of precious stones. And they brought him costly materials and rare gems, pearl necklaces and jewelled bracelets.

One day, while he was playing in a garden not far from the city, Mahaprajapati thought, "It is time I taught him to wear necklaces and bracelets," and she ordered the servants to bring the jewels that had been given to him. She clasped them around his arms and his neck, but it was as if he wore none at all. The gold and the precious stones seemed dull and lifeless, so brilliant was the light he diffused. And the Goddess who lived among the flowers of that garden came to Mahaprajapati and said:

"If the earth were made of gold, a single ray of light emanating from this child, the world's future guide, would be enough to dull its splendor. The light of the stars and the light of the moon, yes, even the light of the sun, are dimmed by his refulgence. And would you have him wear jewels, baubles crudely fashioned by jewellers and goldsmiths? Woman, remove those necklaces, take off those bracelets. They are only fit to be worn by slaves; give them to the slaves. This child will have his thoughts; they are gems of a purer water."

Mahaprajapati gave heed to the words of the Goddess. She unclasped the bracelets and the necklaces, and she never wearied of admiring the prince.

The time came to take Siddhartha to the temple of the Gods. By the king's command, the streets of the city and the public squares were superbly decorated; drums were sounded and bells joyously rung. While Mahaprajapati was dressing him in his richest apparel, the child asked:

"Mother, where are you taking me?"

"To the temple of the Gods, my son," she replied. The child smiled and quietly went with her to meet his father.

It was a magnificent sight. In the procession were brahmans from the city, warriors and all the chief merchants. A host of guards followed, and the Sakyas surrounded the chariot that bore the prince and the king. In the streets the air was heavy with incense, flowers were strewn in their path, and the people waved flags and streamers as they passed.

They arrived at the temple. The king took Siddhartha by the hand and led him to the hall where stood the statues of the Gods. As the child stepped across the threshold the statues came to life, and all the Gods, Siva, Skanda, Vishnu, Kuvera, Indra, Brahma, descended from their pedestals and fell at his feet. And they sang:

"Meru, king of the mountains, does not bow before a grain of wheat; the Ocean does not bow before a pool of rainwater; the Sun does not bow before a glowworm; he who will have the true knowledge does not bow before the Gods. Like the grain of wheat, like the pool of rainwater, like the glowworm is the man or the God with stubborn pride; like Meru mountain, like the Ocean, like the Sun is he who will have supreme knowledge. Let the world pay him homage, and the world will be set free!"

2

The Authorities on which our Knowledge of Buddhism is Based

HOW keen must have been the intellectual pleasure of that small band of scholars in the West of Europe, who, at the end of the fifteenth century, were able to appreciate the meaning and the value of Greek MSS. The taking of Constantinople by the Turks (1453) was the last ste Pina? reat catastrophe which threatened no less than destruction to the MS. treasures preserved in the Greek Empire, and death or poverty to their cultured if effeminate owners. The owners were scattered to the West, and their MSS. changed hands and found new homes. Whoever has had the good fortune to study the entrancing story of that time, more especially as it is focussed in the life of Scaliger, will be able to realise the vivid state of expectancy with which the advent of each new MS. was hailed.

The scholars had a very considerable knowledge of what had been written in Greece, and lost in the West ; and devoured each new MS. to see whether it would fill up any of the gaps. Too many of those gaps are, alas, still unfilled ; and hope has almost faded away now. But in those days almost anything could be hoped for, and the indescribable charm of reading something quite new, of editing a work never edited before, of translating a book never translated before, was within the reach of all.

Well we can now live a life of equal expectancy and hope, rewarded quite as often with an equal intellectual prize. The discoveries that have been made in the ancient libraries of Mesopotamia will no doubt have some day become of even greater importance to the historian of human ideas and institutions than the MSS. acquired by the scholars of the Renaissance.

For when completely understood and interpreted they will reveal a whole series of phenomena, independent of the Greek, and reaching farther back into the mists of antiquity. So also the discoveries in Egypt, made piecemeal from year to year, have the charm of constant expectancy in a very high degree. And now we have as a third factor of the same kind in the intellectual life of modern Europe, the gradual unveiling of that unique and original literature, which is our subject-matter to-day.

Compared with the Egyptian and the Assyrian, it has the disadvantage of youth. For the Pali books are no older than the Greek ones rediscovered in the fifteenth century. But they have the corresponding advantage of containing a rounded and complete picture of a new and strange religious movement, the outcome of many generations of intelligent and earnest thought, and of the very curious social conditions by which it was surrounded and furthered.

The story of the discovery of Pali is not without its interest. When in the thirties that most gifted and original of Indian archaeologists, James Prinsep clarum et venerabile nomen ,was wearing himself out in his enthusiastic efforts to decipher the coins and inscriptions of India, whilst the very alphabets and dialects were as yet uncertain, he received constant help from George Turnour, of the Ceylon Civil Service. For in Ceylon there was a history, indeed several books of history, whereas in Calcutta the native records were devoid of any reliable data to help in the identification of the new names Prinsep thought he could make out. It is not too much to say that without the help of the Ceylon books the striking indentification of the King Piyadassi of the inscriptions with the King Asoka of history would never have been made. Once made it rendered subsequent steps comparatively easy, and it gave to Prinsep and his co-adjutors just that encouragement, and that element of certainty, which were needed to keep their enthusiasm alive.

Tumour was of course much pleased. He was a very busy man, at the head of the Ceylon Civil Service. But he had most intelligent and learned native assistants at his command. And by their help he published in the Calcutta Asiatic Society's journal a short series of articles on the Pali books, and finally brought out in 1837 a complete edition of the text of the Mahd Vansa (or " Great Chronicle " of Ceylon) with a translation into English, and a most interesting introductory essay.

The value of this editio princeps was at once and widely acknowledged. But on the death of Tumour, no one was found to carry on his work. There was no dictionary of Pali, and no grammar worthy of the name. European scholars could not go out to Ceylon, and there enjoy the benefit of the help which had made Tumour's labours possible. His book remained, like a solitary landmark in an unexplored country, chiefly useful as a continual inducement to some scholar with ability and leisure to explore beyond. Only a few insignificant essays, nibbling inefficiently at the outskirts of the subject, appeared in Europe, till at last in 1855 Mr. Vincent Fausboll came forward with an editio princeps of an-other Pali text.

Mr. Fausboll, now Professor of Sanskrit at Copen hagen, was then engaged at the University Library there, and it was a very bold undertaking to attempt such a task with the limited aids at his disposal. He chose, not an historical work, but a religious one, the Dhammapada, a collection of 423 verses mostly culled from the Buddhist Scriptures (a sort of hymn-book); and he published, with the text, not only a translation into Latin, but also very copious extracts from the ancient Pali commentary upon it.

His work has been of the utmost service, and it is the second landmark in the story of our knowledge of Pali. It is pleasant to be able to remind the reader that the veteran scholar has steadily adhered to his first love. He subsequently brought out a number of specimens of that wonderful collection of ancient folk-lore included by a fortunate chance in the canon of the Buddhist Scriptures. And finding how great was the interest they excited, he has now, for many years, been printing an editio princeps of the whole collection. Five substantial volumes have already appeared, the sixth is well advanced in the press, and we may legitimately turn aside for a moment to send to Professor Fausboll our congratulations, and our thanks, and to express a hope, in the interests of historical study, that he will be spared not only to complete this magnum opus, but to add in other ways to the great services he has already rendered to historical research.

But to return to our story. After the publication of the Dhammapada by Professor Fausboll in 1855, the study of Pali again languished for a whole generation, and would in all probability have languished still had it not been for the third landmark in the history of our knowledge of Pali, the publication in two volumes in the years 1870 and 1873, f the Dictionary.

This great work was due to the self-sacrificing labour of Robert Caesar Childers of the Ceylon Civil Service. Soon after his retirement in 1866 he set to work to arrange alphabetically all the words found in the Abhidhana Padipika, a vocabulary of Pali in 1203 Pali verses, then already edited by Subhuti Unnanse, a well known Ceylon scholar. In making this re-arrangement Childers carefully added references to, and also other words taken from, the published texts, and from scholarly European books on the subject of Buddhism. His work rapidly improved as it went on, and there can be no doubt that its completion was almost a necessary preliminary to any further serious work in Pali scholarship.

The points to which I would most especially desire to invite your attention in this slight sketch are, that up to the year 1870 only two Pali texts of any size or importance had appeared in editions accessible to scholars in the West ; and that, of these two, only one was a book out of the Buddhist Scriptures, and that this one was a short collection of edifying stanzas, not composed as a book by themselves, but selected, without their original context, from other Buddhist books, then, in 1870, still buried in MS.

Nevertheless, the number of books, good, bad, and indifferent, published on the subject of Buddhism, was at that date very large. The reader will be able to judge how far they were likely to be of any permanent value when he calls to mind that no one of the authors of any one of these books had ever even read the Buddhist Bible in the original.

Now I would not for a moment quarrel with the enthusiasm for the study of Buddhism which leads people to write so much about it. But surely an enthusiasm according to knowledge would lead people to devote their leisure, their ability, and their means, rather to the publication and translation of the sacred books themselves, than to discussions about their contents carried on in much the same way as some chess-players play chess, sans voir, without seeing the pieces. What we want then is the texts themselves, and not extracts or abstracts, but the whole texts. And we want also the whole of such aids to the right understanding of the text, as are still extant in the shape of ancient Pali commentaries, and even of more modern Pali treatises, written by Buddhist authors. To this aim the publication and elucidation of the Buddhist texts I have devoted what remains of my life ; and I must trust myself entirely to your courtesy when I find myself here to-day in spite of what I have just said, and have so often said before turning away from that work to tell you how far it has got, what prospects it has of going on, and chiefly in some detail what is the nature and magnitude of the work that has to be accomplished.

A rough list of the Pitakas, with notes on the contents of each book, will be found in my little manual of Buddhism and another list in my Milinda gives the number of pages, printed and not yet printed, in each of the twenty-nine books.f A similar list brought up to date is appended to this lecture.

From this last list it appears that the whole of the Pitakas will occupy about 10,000 pages 8vo., of the size and type used by the Pali Text Society (about the same as these lectures). And from the calculations set out in the note to the list in Buddhism it follows that the number of Pali words in the whole is about twice the number of words in our English Bible. These figures are sufficient to show the extent of the Buddhist Scriptures.

To give an idea of their contents is not so easy, and it would be really impossible to frame any general description of the whole. The most accurate, and I believe also the most interesting method will be to run through the whole list (it is not a very long one), giving a paragraph or two to each. You will thus be able to realise what it is that the books do, and what is perhaps of more importance, what they do not, contain.

And firstly: The whole collection as we have it is divided into three parts, now called Pitakas or Baskets. In that technical sense the word Pitaka does not of course occur in the books themselves, just as the word Testament (in its technical sense of a division of the Bible) does not occur in the Bible itself. The meaning of the term Pitaka or Basket is not to be taken in the sense of a thing to put things away in, like a box or other receptacle, but in the sense of tradition. Excavations in early times, and not in the East only, used to be carried out by the aid of baskets handed on from workman to workman, posted in a long line from the point of removal to the point of deposit. So we are to understand a long line of teachers and pupils handing on, in these three sacred Pitakas or Baskets, from ancient times down to today, the treasures of the Dhamma (of the Norm),

The first of the three the Vinaya contains all that relates to the Order of Mendicant Recluses, how it came about that the Order was founded ; the rules which the Brethren and Sisters have to observe, and so on. The second the Suttas contains the truths of the religion itself presented from very varied points of view, and in very varied style; together with the discussion and elucidation of the psychological system on which those truths are based. The third the Abhidhamma contains a further supplementary and more detailed discussion of that psychological system, and of various points arising out of it.

So much for the leading division into Pitakas or Baskets. We will now consider the details of each. Vinaya the Canon Law (literally "guidance") is divided into three partitions, the Sutta Vibhanga, the Khandhakas, and the Parivara.

The word Sutta (sutra in Sanskrit) is a very ancient literary term in India. The literal meaning is "thread," and it is applied to a kind of book, the contents of which are, as it were, a thread, giving the gist or substance of more than is expressed in them in words. This sort of book was the latest development in Vedic literature just before and after the rise of Buddhism. The word was adopted by the Buddhists to mean a discourse, a chapter, a small portion of a sacred book in which for the most part some one point is raised, and more or less disposed of. But the Sutta par excellence, is that short statement of all the rules of the Order, which is also called the Patimokkha, and is recited on every Upo-satha day. On that day, the day of the full moon, the members of the Order resident in any one district are to meet together and hear this statement of the rules read.

The 227 rules are divided into eight sections, according to the gravity of the matter dealt with, and at the end of each section the reciter asks the assembly, whether it is blameless in respect thereof, and receives the assurance that it is. If any member has offended, he has then and there to confess, and receive absolution, or withdraw. The completion of the recitation is therefore evidence that all who have taken part in it are pure in respect of the specified offences. And this is the origin of that second name, the Patimokkha, which means the Acquittal, or Deliverance, or Discharge. A complete translation, with notes, of this statement of the Rules of the Order will be found in Vinaya Texts, the joint work of Professor Oldenberg and myself, contributed to the Oxford series of Sacred Books of the East.

This is the Sutta, of which the first book in the Vinaya, the Sutta Vibhanga, is the exposition in full for that is the meaning of Vibhanga. The book deals with each of the 227 rules in order and following throughout one set scheme or method. That is to say it tells us firstly how and when and why the particular rule in question came to be laid down.

This historical introduction always closes with the words of the rule in full. Then follows a very ancient word-for-word commentary on the rule a commentary so old that it was already about B.C. 400 (the probable approximate date of the Sutta Vibhanga) considered so sacred that it was included in the canon. And the Old Commentary is succeeded, where necessary, by further explanations and discussions of doubtful points. These are some-times of very great historical value. The discussions, for instance (in the rules as to murder and theft), of what constitutes murder, and what constitutes theft, anticipate m a very remarkable degree the kind of fine-drawn distinctions found in modern law books. These passages when made accessible, in translation, to Western scholars, must be of the greatest interest to students of the history of law, as they are quite the oldest documents of that particular kind in the world.

The second book in the Vinaya Pitaka is called simply the Khandhakas or Treatises. It deals one after another with all those matters relating to the Order which are not stated in so many words in the Rules of the Patimokkha. There are twenty of these treatises, and the points discussed in them are of the following kind :

1. Admission into the Order.
2. The Uposatha Ceremony and the Patimokkha.
3. On retreats, to be held during the rainy season
4. On a ceremony called Pavarana held at the end of the retreat.
5. On food, dwellings, etc.
6. On medicaments.
7. On clothes.
8. On the regulation by arbitration of differences of opinion.

9. On suspension and rehabilitation.

10. On the special rules for Sisters of the Order.

It would carry us too far to attempt a description in detail of these treatises. But I may describe one of them, as a specimen, and will choose that on medicaments, as it has an especial interest of its own.

The general rule as to the food of members of the Order is stated quite clearly in the Patimokkha.

There was a slight repast of fruit and cakes, with milk or water as the beverage, in the early morning, no doubt very early according to our ideas. Then between n and 12 was taken the principal meal of the day, usually consisting of curry and rice, and great importance was attached to the regulation that this meal was not to be prolonged beyond the time when the sun cast a shadow. In the latitude of the valley of the Ganges that means midday. After sunturn no more solid substantial food was to be taken that day. But slight repasts in the after-noon, and at what we should call supper-time, were allowed and practised. Now it became a pretty point of casuistry to determine what was solid food and what was not, and a longish list of things held permissible might be compiled from the earlier portions of the Khandhakas. Among the rest there was a considerable number of things allowed as medicine in the case of sufferers from certain specified diseases. And so in the Khandhaka or Treatise on this matter we obtain quite incidentally a very fair insight into a good deal of the medical lore current at that early period, that is about 400 B.C., in the valley of the Ganges, It is a pity that the current authorities on the history of law and medicine have entirely ignored the details obtainable from these ancient books of Buddhist Canon Law. The whole of these Khandhakas have been translated by myself and Professor Oldenberg in the Vinaya Texts already referred to.

There is only one other book included in the canon under the head of Vinaya. This is the book called the Parivara (or Appendix). It is very short, and is little more than a kind of student's manual, containing lists to assist the memory, and various sets of puzzles which are not unlike some modern examination papers. It is of course later than the other books on which it is founded, and is a very-interesting bit of evidence on early methods of education.

SUDDHODANA kept thinking of what Asita had told him. He did not want his family to die out, and he said to himself: "I will arouse in my son a desire for pleasure; then, perhaps, I shall have grandchildren, and they shall prosper."

So he sent for the prince, and he spoke to him in these words:

"My child, you are at an age when it would be well to think of marriage. If there is some maid that pleases you, tell me."

Siddhartha replied:

"Give me seven days to consider, father. In seven days you shall have my answer."

And he mused:

"Endless evil, I know, comes of desire. The trees that grow in the forest of desire have their roots n suffering and strife, and their leaves are poisonous. Desire burns like fire and wounds like a sword. I am not one of those who seek the company of women; it is my lot to live in the silence of the woods. There, through meditation, my mind will find peace, and I shall know happiness. But does not the lotus grow and flourish even amid the tangle of swamp-flowers? Have there not been men with wives and sons who found wisdom? Those who, before me, have sought supreme knowledge spent many years in the company of women.

And when the time came to leave them for the delights of meditation, theirs was but a greater joy. I shall follow their example."

He thought of the qualities he would value most highly in a woman. Then, on the seventh day, he returned to his father.

"Father," said he, "she whom I shall marry must be a woman of rare merit. If you find one endowed with the natural gifts I shall enumerate, you may give her to me in marriage."

And he said:

"She whom I shall marry will be in the bloom of youth; she whom I shall marry will have the flower of beauty; yet her youth will not make her vain, nor will her beauty make her proud. She whom I shall marry will have a sister's affection, a mother's tenderness, for all living creatures. She will be sweet and truthful, and she will not know envy. Never, not even in her dreams, will she think of any other man but her husband.

She will never use haughty language; her manner will be unassuming; she will be as meek as a slave. She will not covet that which belongs to others; she will make no inconsiderate demands, and she will be satisfied with her lot. She will care nothing for wines, and sweets will not tempt her. She will be insensible to music and perfume; she will be indifferent to plays and festivals. She will be kind to my attendants and to her maidens.

She will be the first to awaken and the last to fall asleep. She whom I shall marry will be pure in body, in speech and in thought."

And he added:

"Father, if you know a maid who possesses these

qualities, you may give her to me in marriage."

The king summoned the household priest. He enumerated the qualities the prince sought in the woman he would marry, then:

"Go," said he, "go, brahman. Visit all the homes of Kapilavastu; observe the young girls and question them. And if you find one to possess the necessary qualities, bring her to the prince, even though she be of the lowest caste. For it is not rank nor riches my son seeks, but virtue."

The priest scoured the city of Kapilavastu. He entered the houses, he saw the young girls, he cleverly questioned them; but not one could he find worthy of Prince Siddhartha. Finally, he came to the home of Dandapani who was of the Sakya family. Dandapani had a daughter named Gopa. At the very sight of her, the priest's heart rejoiced, for she was beautiful and full of grace. He spoke a few words to her, and he doubted no longer.

The priest returned to King Suddhodana. "My lord," he exclaimed, "I have found a maid worthy of your son."

"Where did you find her?" asked the king. "She is the daughter of the Sakya, Dandapani," the brahman replied.

Though he had great confidence in his household priest, Suddhodana hesitated to summon Gopa and Dandapani. "Even the wisest men can make mistakes," he thought. "The brahman may be exaggerating her perfections. I must put the daughter of Dandapani to a further test, and my son himself shall judge her."

He had many jewels made out of gold and silver, and by royal command a herald was sent through the streets of Kapilavastu, crying:

"On the seventh day from this day, Prince Siddhartha, son of King Suddhodana, will present gifts to the young girls of the city. So may all the young girls appear at the palace on the seventh day!"

On the day announced, the prince sat on a throne in the great hall of the palace. All the young girls of the city were present, and they filed before him. To each one he presented a jewel, but, as they approached the throne, his striking beauty so intimidated them that they lowered their gaze or turned their heads away. They hardly took the time to receive their presents; some were even in such haste to leave that they merely touched the gift with the tips of their fingers, and it fell to the floor.

Gopa was the last one to appear. She advanced fearlessly, without even blinking her eyes. But the prince had not a single jewel left. Gopa smiled and said to him:

"Prince, in what way have I offended you?"

"You have not offended me," replied Siddhartha.

"Then why do you treat me with disdain?"

"I do not treat you with disdain," he replied. "You are the last one, and I have no jewel to give you."

But suddenly he remembered that on his finger he was wearing a ring of great value. He took it off and handed it to the young girl.

She would not take the ring.

She said, "Prince, must I accept this ring from you?"

"It was mine," replied the prince, "and you must accept it."

"No," said she, "I would not deprive you of your jewels. It is for me, rather, to give you a jewel." And she left.

When the king heard of this incident he was elated.

"Gopa, alone, could face my son," he thought;

"she alone is worthy of him. Gopa, who would not accept the ring that you took from your finger, Gopa, O my son, will be your fairest jewel."

And he summoned Gopa's father to the palace.

"Friend," said he, "the time has come for my son Siddhartha to marry. I believe your daughter Gopa has found favor in his eyes. Will you marry her to my son?"

Dandapani did not answer at once. He hesitated, and again the king asked him:

"Will you marry your daughter to my son?" Then Dandapani said:

"My lord, your son has been brought up in luxury; he has never been outside the palace-gates; his physical and intellectual abilities have never been proven. You know that the Sakyas only marry their daughters to men who are skillful and strong, brave and wise. How can I give my daughter to your son who, so far, has shown a taste only for indolence?"

These words disturbed King Suddhodana. He asked to see the prince. Siddhartha came immediately.

"Father," said he, "you look very sad. What has happened?"

The king did not know how to tell him what Dandapani had so bluntly expressed. He remained silent.

The prince repeated:

"Father, you look very sad. What has happened?"

"Do not ask me," replied Suddhodana.

"Father, you are sad, what has happened?"

"It is a painful subject; I would rather not speak of it."

"Explain yourself, father. It is always well to be explicit."

The king finally decided to relate the interview he had had with Dandapani. When he had finished, the prince began to laugh.

"My lord," said he, "you are needlessly disturbed. Do you believe there is anyone in Kapilavastu who is my superior in strength or in intellect? Summon all who are famous for their attainments in any field whatsoever; command them to measure their skill with mine, and I shall show you what I can do."

The king recovered his serenity. He had it proclaimed throughout the city:

"That on the seventh day from this day, Prince Siddhartha will compete with all who excel in any field whatsoever."

On the day designated, all those who claimed to be skillful in the arts or in the sciences appeared at the palate. Dandapani was present, and he promised his daughter to the one, whether of noble or of humble birth, who would be victorious in the contests which were to take place.

First, a young man, who knew the rules of writing, sought to challenge the prince, but the learned Visvamitra stepped before the assembly and said:

"Young man, such a contest would be futile. You are already defeated. The prince was still a child when he was placed in my care; I was to teach him the art of writing. But he already knew sixty-four varieties of script! He knew certain varieties that were unknown to me even by name!"

Visvamitra's testimony was enough to give the prince a victory in the art of writing.

Then they sought to test his knowledge of numbers. It was decided that a certain Sakya named Arjuna, who had time and again solved intricate problems, would act as judge in the contest.

One young man claimed to be an excellent mathematician, and to him Siddhartha addressed a question, but the young man was unable to reply.

"And yet it was an easy question," said the prince. "But here is one that is still easier; who will answer it?"

No one answered this second question.

"It is now your turn to examine me," said the prince.

They asked him questions that were considered difficult, but he gave the answers even before they had finished stating the problem.

"Let Arjuna himself examine the prince!" came the cry from all sides.

Arjuna gave him the most intricate problems, and never once was Siddhartha at a loss for the correct solution.

They all marvelled at his knowledge of mathematics and were convinced that his intelligence had probed to the bottom of all the sciences.

They then decided to challenge his athletic skill, but at jumping and at running he won with little effort, and at wrestling he had only to lay a finger upon his adversary, and he would fall to the ground.

Then they brought out the bows, and skillful archers placed their arrows in targets that were barely visible. But when it came the prince's turn to shoot, so great was his natural strength that he broke each bow as he drew it. Finally, the king sent guards to fetch a very ancient, very precious bow that was kept in the temple. No one within the memory of man had ever been able to draw or lift it. Siddhartha took the bow in his left hand, and with one finger of his right hand he drew it to him. Then he took as target a tree so distant that he alone could see it. The arrow pierced the tree, and, burying itself in the ground, disappeared. And there, where the arrow had entered the ground, a well formed, which was called the Well of the Arrow.

Everything seemed to be over, and they led toward the victor a huge white elephant on which, in triumph, he was to ride through Kapilavastu. But a young Sakya, Devadatta, who was very proud of his strength, seized the animal by the trunk and, in fun, struck it with his fist. The elephant fell to the ground.

The prince looked reprovingly at the young man and said:

"You have done an evil thing, Devadatta."

He touched the elephant with his foot, and it stood up and paid him homage.

Then they all acclaimed his glory, and the air rang with their cheers. Suddhodana was happy, and Dandapani, weeping with joy, exclaimed:

"Gopa, my daughter Gopa, be proud to be the wife of such a man."

The next great division is the Sutta Pitaka, or the Basket of Discourses, and here we come to the sources of our knowledge of the most ancient Buddhism. The whole Basket consists of four great Nikayas (or collections), and of these the first two form what we should now call a single book. It is in two volumes, so to speak, called respectively Dlgha is to say, long and of medium length (or to translate more idiomatically, longer and shorter). It contains 186 dialogues of Gotama arranged according to their length. They are discussions on all the religious and philosophical points of the Buddhist view of life. The Buddha himself is the principal interlocutor, but several of his principal disciples play a distinguished part in the book. In depth of philosophic insight, in the method of Socratic questioning often adopted, in the earnest and elevated tone of the whole, in the evidence they afford of the most cultured thought of the day, these discourses constantly remind the reader of the Dialogues of Plato. It would be worse than foolish to attempt any description of their contents. Each of the 183 dialogues would demand at least a single lecture to make its meaning clear. They have a style of their own, always dignified and occasionally rising into eloquence. It is a style intended, however, not to be read, but to be learnt by heart. You will easily understand therefore that it is a style intensely abhorrent to the modern devourer of newspapers and reviews and the last new novel Scholars however will revere this book as one of the most priceless of the treasures of antiquity still preserved to us. And it is quite inevitable that, as soon as it is properly translated and understood, this collection of the Dialogues of Gotama will come to be placed, in our schools of philosophy and history, on a level with the Dialogues of Plato.

Ninety-one out of the 186 have now been edited in the original Pali for the Pali Text Society, and about a dozen have been translated into English, seven of them by myself in the volume entitled " Buddhist Suttas " in the Sacred Books of the East.

A disadvantage of the arrangement in dialogues, more especially as they follow one another according to length and not according to subject, is that it is not easy to find the statement of doctrine on any particular point which is interesting one at the moment. It was very likely just this consideration which led to the compilation of the other two collections included in this Pitaka. In the first, called the Anguttara Nikaya, all those points of Buddhist doctrine capable of expressipn in classes are set out in order. This practically includes most of the psychology and ethics of Buddhism. For it is a distinguishing mark of the Dialogues them-selves to arrange the results arrived at in carefully systematised groups. You are familiar enough in the West with similar classifications, summed up in such expressions as the Seven Deadly Sins, the Ten Commandments, the Thirty-nine Articles, the Four Cardinal Virtues, the Seven Sacraments, and a host of others. These numbered lists (it is true) are going out of fashion. The aid which they afford to memory is no longer required in an age in which books of reference abound. It was precisely as a help to memory that they were found so useful in the early Buddhist times, when the books were all learnt by heart, and had never as yet been written.

And in the Anguttara we find set out in order first of all the ones, then all the pairs, then all the trios, and so on up to the thirty-four constituent parts of the human organism, or the thirty-seven constituent elements of Arahatship. It is the longest book in the Buddhist Bible and will fill 1800 pages 8vo. About two-fifths of the Pali text has been published by the Pali Text Society, and none of it has yet been translated into English.

The next and lastof these great collections contains again the whole of the Buddhist doctrine, but arranged this time in the order of subjects. It consists of fifty-five so-called Samyuttas, or Groups, and in each of these a number of short chapters (Suttas), either on the same subject or addressed to the same sort of people, are grouped together. The Samyutta is divided into five volumes, four of which have been already published by the Pali Text Society, the fifth and last being in preparation. None of it has been translated into English.

It would be useless to speculate whether these two re-arrangements of the Buddhist doctrine are entirely dependent upon the Dialogues for their matter, or vice versa, or whether they are drawn also from other sources. We know that large portions of them recur bodily in the Dialogues, and that those portions not yet traced in the Dialogues contain nothing inconsistent with them. And it will not be very long before the publication of the whole of the three books, Dialogues, Anguttara, and Samyuttas, will enable us to state with accuracy the relation between them. This concludes the second Basket, The third and last of the Pitakas or Baskets, is the Abhidhamma Pitaka, containing seven books of which at present only three have been published by the Pali Text Society. Abhidhamma has hitherto been rendered Metaphysics. But this is an entirely misleading translation. You will have realised from the previous lecture that the whole Buddhist view of life is constructed without the time-honoured conception of a soul within the body. We know nothing, according to Buddhism, except that which is derived from experience, the apprehension of phenomena.

In such a system there is no room for Metaphysics at all. The noumenon is not discussed. What the Buddhists themselves understand by Abhidhamma is clear from the explanation given of the word by the great Buddhist scholar and commentator, Buddhaghosa. The passage, discovered by Mr. Arnold C. Taylor, has been edited and translated by him in a recent issue of the Journal of the Royal Asiatic Society. According to that greatest of Buddhist scholars, Abhidhamma means merely the expansion, enlarged treatment, exposition in detail, of the Dhamma. And the Dhamma, as you know, is the Religion, the Truth, the Norm. The three books already published entirely, and the complete abstract of a fourth printed by me two years ago,f entirely confirm this view.

One, the Puggala Pannatti, or " Identification of Individuals," is a small tract of less than eighty pages, in which men and women are considered and classified from the ethical point of view. Another, the Dhatu Kathd, is on the bases of character, and discusses the mental characteristics most likely to be found in conjunction in converted and earnest folk.

The third already printed is the Dhamma Sangani, or " Enumeration of States and it analyses the states of mind reached by religious people, Buddhists and others.:]: The fourth book above referred to is the Katha Vatthu, or " Account of Opinions," and is the only book in the Buddhist Scriptures of which we know the author and date. It was written (or rather put together, for books were not then written) by Tissa, the son of Moggali, about the year 250 B.C., at the Court of Asoka, the famous Buddhist Emperor of India. At that late period in the history of early Buddhism, the church or community was much torn by dissension and heresies. Asoka took great pains to restore the purity of the original faith. And Tissa, in furtherance of that object, re-futed in this most curious ancient book two hundred and fifty-two of the most dangerous and important heresies put forward by the leading opponents of the orthodox school There is nothing metaphysical in it. But it is most interesting from the comparative point of view that the most far-reaching cause of the decay of the primitive faith is here shown to have been the growth of what we should call superstitious views about the person of the Buddha. You will recollect how, in the history of the Christian Church, a very similar state of things existed, how the early Church was rent by dissensions arising out of the differing views as to the person of Christ, and as to his relation to the First Person in the Trinity.

But in the Christian Church it was the new views, not found in the New Testament, that prevailed. In the Buddhist community, the new views were held at bay, and only succeeded, after a long interval, and in distant lands, in obtaining wide recognition. We shall have to deal with this subject further in our last lecture, so it need not detain us longer here. Mr. Arnold C. Taylor has nearly completed his edition of the Kathd Vatthu for the Pali Text Society, and has undertaken to translate it also.

We have now gone through the principal books in the Three Pitakas, but there is a miscellaneous collection, mostly of shorter works, which has come to be included in the Canon. I have left this to the last, because Buddhists . themselves from the very earliest times have been divided in opinion about it ; some of them considering this Nikaya as an appendix to the Sutta Pitaka, some of them considering it as an appendix to the Abhidhamma Pitaka. The reason of this difference of opinion was probably something of the following kind. The most important things for the members of the Buddhist Order to preserve most carefully in their memory were essentially the Rules of the Community or Association they had joined, and the tenets of the Faith they professed. These were contained in the Canon Law, and in the Dialogues of Gotama, and in the various other books already referred to in which the doctrine set out in the Dialogues was re-arranged, elucidated, and expounded. During the time when the Canon was still unsettled, there was great activity in learning, rehearsing, repeating, and discussing these sacred books. But there was also considerable activity in what we should now call a more literary direction.

PRINCE Siddhartha lived happily with his wife, the princess. And the king, whose love for his son now verged on adoration, took infinite care to spare him the sight of anything that might distress him. He built three magnificent palaces for him: one for the winter, one for the summer, and the third for the rainy season; and these he was forbidden ever to leave, to wander over the broad face of the earth.

In his palaces, white as autumn clouds and bright as the celestial chariots of the Gods and Goddesses, the prince drained the cup of pleasure. He led a life of voluptuous ease; he spent languid hours listening to music played by the princess and her maidens, and when beautiful, smiling dancers appeared before him and performed to the sound of golden kettle-drums, with delight he watched them as they swayed with a grace and loveliness rare even among the happy Apsarases.

Women cast furtive glances at him: their eyes boldly offered or archly pleaded, and their drooping lashes were a promise of ineffable delight. Their games amused him, their charms held him in thrall, and he was content to remain in these palaces so full of their laughter and song. For he knew nothing of old age and sickness; he knew nothing of death.

Suddhodana rejoiced at the life his son was leading, though his own conduct he judged with the utmost severity. He strove to keep his soul serene and pure; he refrained from doing evil, and he lavished gifts on those who were virtuous. He never yielded to indolence or pleasure; he was never burned by the poison of avarice. As wild horses are made to bear the yoke, even so did he subdue his passions, and in virtue he surpassed his kinsmen and his friends. The knowledge he acquired he placed at the service of his fellow-men, and he only studied those subjects that were useful to all. He not only sought the welfare of his own people but he also wanted the whole world to be happy. He purified his body with the water from the sacred ponds, and he purified his soul with the holy water of virtue. He never uttered a word that was pleasant and yet a lie; the truths he spoke never gave offense or pain. He tried to be just, and it was by honesty, not by force, that he defeated the pride of his enemies. He did not strike, he did not even look with anger upon those who deserved the penalty of death; instead, he gave them useful advice, and then their freedom.

The king was an example to all his subjects, and Kapilavastu was the happiest and most virtuous of kingdoms.

Then beautiful Gopa bore the prince a son, and he was given the name of Rahula. King Suddhodana was happy to see his family prosper, and he was as proud of the birth of his grandson as he had been of the birth of his son.

He continued in the path of virtue, he lived almost like a hermit, and his actions were saintly; yet he kept urging on his beloved son to new pleasures, so great was his fear to see him leave the palace and the city and seek the austere refuge of the holy forests.

The Three Encounters

ONE day, some one spoke in the presence of the prince and told how the grass in the woods had become a tender green and the birds in the trees were singing of the spring, and how, in the ponds, the great lotuses were unfolding. Nature had broken the chains that winter had forged, and, around the city, those gardens so dear to young maidens were now gaily carpeted with flowers. Then, like an elephant too long confined in his stable, the prince had an irresistible desire to leave the palace.

The king learned of his son's desire, and he knew no way to oppose it.

"But," he thought, "Siddhartha must see nothing that will trouble the serenity of his soul; he must never suspect the evil there is in the world. I shall order the road cleared of beggars, of those who are sick and infirm and of all who suffer."

The city was decorated with garlands and streamers; a magnificent chariot was prepared, and the cripples, the aged and the beggars were ordered off the streets where the prince would pass.

When the time came, the king sent for his son, and there were tears in his eyes as he kissed him on the brow. His gaze lingered over him, then he said to him, "Go!" And with that word he gave him permission to leave the palace, though his heart spoke differently.

The prince's chariot was made of gold. It was drawn by four horses caparisoned in gold, and the charioteer held gold reins in his hands. Only the rich, the young and the beautiful were allowed on the streets he drove through, and they stopped to watch him as he went by. Some praised him for the kindness of his glance; others extolled his dignified bearing; still others exalted the beauty of his features; while many glorified his exuberant strength. And they all bowed before him, like banners dipped before the statue of some God.

The women in the houses heard the cries in the street. They awoke or left their household tasks and ran to the windows or quickly ascended to the terraces. And gazing at him in admiration, they murmured, "Happy the wife of such a man!"

And he, at the sight of the city's splendor, at the sight of the wealth of the men and the beauty of the women, felt a new joy pour into his soul.

But the Gods were jealous of the celestial felicity enjoyed by this city of the earth. They made an old man, and, in order to trouble Siddhartha's mind, they set him down on the road the prince was travelling.

The man was leaning on a staff; he was worn out and decrepit. His veins stood out on his body, his teeth chattered, and his skin was a maze of black wrinkles. A few dirty grey hairs hung from his scalp; his eyelids had no lashes and were red-rimmed; his head and limbs were palsied.

The prince saw this being, so different from the men around him. He gazed at him with sorrowful eyes, and he asked the charioteer:

"What is this man with grey hair and body so bent? He clings to his staff with scrawny hands, his eyes are dull and his limbs falter. Is he a monster? Has nature made him thus, or is it chance?"

The charioteer should not have answered, but the Gods confused his mind, and without understanding his mistake he said:

"That which mars beauty, which ruins vigor, which causes sorrow and kills pleasure, that which weakens the memory and destroys the senses is old age. It has seized this man and broken him. He, too, was once a child, nursing at his mother's breast; he, too, once crawled upon the floor; he grew, he was young, he had strength and beauty; then he reached the twilight of his years, and now you see him, the ruin that is old age."

The prince was deeply moved. He asked:

"Will that be my fate, also?"

The charioteer replied:

"My lord, youth will also leave you some day; to you, too, will come troublesome old age. Time saps our strength and steals our beauty."

The prince shuddered like a bull at the sound of thunder. He uttered a deep sigh and shook his head. His eyes wandered from the wretched man to the happy crowds, and he spoke these solemn words:

"So old age destroys memory and beauty and strength in man, and yet the world is not frantic with terror! Turn your horses around, O charioteer; let us return to our homes. How can I delight in gardens and flowers when my eyes can only see old age, when my mind can only think of old age?"

The prince returned to his palace, but nowhere could he find peace. He wandered through the halls, murmuring, "Old age, oh, old age!" and in his heart there was no longer any joy.

He decided, nevertheless, to ride once more through the city.

But the Gods made a man afflicted with a loathsome disease, and they set him down on the road Siddhartha had taken.

Siddhartha saw the sick man; he stared at him, and he asked the charioteer:

"What is this man with a swollen paunch? His emaciated arms hang limp, he is deathly pale and pitiful cries escape from his lips. He gasps for breath; see, he staggers and jostles the bystanders; he is falling. . . . Charioteer, charioteer, what is this man?"

The charioteer answered:

"My lord, this man knows the torment of sickness, for he has the king's evil. He is weakness itself; yet he, too, was once healthy and strong!"

The prince looked at the man with pity, and he asked again:

"Is this affliction peculiar to this man, or are all creatures threatened with sickness?"

The charioteer answered:

"We, too, may be visited with a similar affliction, O prince. Sickness weighs heavily upon the world."

When he heard this painful truth, the prince began to tremble like a moonbeam reflected in the waves of the sea, and he uttered these words of bitterness and pity:

"Men see suffering and sickness, yet they never lose their self-confidence! Oh, how great must be their knowledge! They are constantly threatened with sickness, and they can still laugh and be merry! Turn your horses around, charioteer; our pleasure trip is ended; let us return to the palace. I have learned to fear sickness. My soul shuns pleasure and seems to close up like a flower deprived of light."

Wrapped in his painful thoughts, he returned to the palace.

King Suddhodana noticed his son's sombre mood. He asked why the prince no longer went out driving, and the charioteer told him what had happened. The king grieved; he already saw himself forsaken by the child he adored. He lost his usual composure and flew into a rage at the man whose duty it was to see that the streets were clear; he punished him, but so strong was his habit of being indulgent that the punishment was light. And the man was astonished at being thus upbraided, for he had seen neither the old man nor the sick man.

The king was more anxious now than ever before to keep his son from leaving the palace. He provided him with rare pleasures, but nothing, it seemed, could arouse Siddhartha. And the king thought, "I shall let him go out once more! Perhaps he will recover the joy he has lost."

He gave strict orders to have all cripples and all who were ill or aged driven out of the city. He even changed the prince's charioteer, and he felt certain that this time there would be nothing to trouble Siddhartha's soul.

But the jealous Gods made a corpse. Four men carried it, and others followed behind, weeping.

And the corpse, as well as the men who carried it and the men who were weeping, was visible only to the prince and to the charioteer.

And the king's son asked:

"What is he that is being carried by four men, followed by those others, wearing dark clothes and weeping?"

The charioteer should have held his peace, but it was the will of the Gods that he reply:

"My lord, he has neither intelligence nor feeling nor breath; he sleeps, without consciousness, like grass or a piece of wood; pleasure and suffering are meaningless to him now, and friend and enemy alike have deserted him."

The prince was troubled. He said, "Is this a condition peculiar to this man, or does this same end await all creatures?"

And the charioteer answered: "This same end awaits all creatures. Whether of humble or of noble birth, to every being who lives in this world, death comes inevitably."

Then Prince Siddhartha knew what death was.

In spite of his fortitude, he shuddered. He had to lean against the chariot, and his words were full of distress:

"So to this does destiny lead all creatures! And yet, without fear in his heart, man amuses himself in a thousand different ways! Death is about, and he takes to the world's highroads with a song on his lips! Oh, I begin to think that man's soul has become hardened! Turn your horses around, charioteer; this is no time to wander through the flower-gardens. How can a sensible man, a man who knows what death is, seek pleasure in the hour of anguish?"

But the charioteer kept on driving toward the garden where the king had ordered him to take his son.

There, at Suddhodana's command, Udayin, who was a son of the household priest and Siddhartha's friend since childhood, had assembled many beautiful maidens, skilled in the art of dancing and of song, and skillful also in the game of love.

Gopa's Dream

THE chariot entered the wood. The young trees were in bloom, birds fluttered about joyously as though intoxicated by the light and atmosphere, and on the surface of the pools the lotuses had cupped their petals to drink in the cool air.

Siddhartha went unwillingly, like a young hermit, still new to his vows, who fears temptation and is taken to some celestial palace where lovely Apsarases are wont to dance. Filled with curiosity, the maidens rose and came forward as though to greet a betrothed. Their eyes were bright with admiration, and the hands they extended were like flowers. They all thought, "This is Kama himself come back to earth." But they did not speak nor even smile, so timid were they in his presence.

Udayin called to the boldest and the most beautiful, and he said to them:

"Why do you fail me to-day, you whom I have chosen from among many to captivate the prince, my friend? What makes you behave like shy, silent children? Your charm, your beauty, your boldness would win even a woman's heart, and you tremble before a man! You mortify me. Come, wake up! Use your charms! Make him yield to love!" One of the maidens spoke up:

"He frightens us, O master; his majestic splendor frightens us."

"Great as it is," replied Udayin, "it should not frighten you. For strange is the power of women. Let him remind you of all those who, in the past, have been at the mercy of a tender glance. Once upon a time the great hermit Vyasa, whom even the Gods were afraid to offend, was kicked by a courtesan called the Belle of Benares, and he was not displeased. The monk Manthalagotama, who was famous for his long penances, became an undertaker's assistant, in order to win the favor of the wanton Jangha, a woman of the very lowest caste. Santa artfully managed to seduce Rishyasringa, a learned man who had never known woman; and that most pious of all men, glorious Visvamitra, one day, in the forest, yielded to the importunities of the Apsaras Ghritaki. And I could name many more who succumbed to women like you, O lovely maidens! Come, do not be afraid of the king's son. Smile at him, and he will fall in love with you."

Udayin's words encouraged the maidens. Smiling, and with exquisite grace, they gradually formed a ring around the prince.

They used the most engaging wiles in order to approach Siddhartha, in order to brush past him or hold him and steal a caress. One pretended to stumble and clung to his girdle. Another drew near and mysteriously whispered in his ear, "Deign to hear my secret, O prince." Another feigned intoxication; she slowly unwound the blue veil that bound her breasts, then came and leaned against his shoulder. Another jumped down from the branch of a mango-tree and laughingly tried to stop him as he passed. Still another offered him a lotus-flower. And one sang: "Look, dear love, this tree is covered with blossoms, with blossoms whose perfume cloys the air; in the branches, rare birds trill their happy songs, as though in a golden cage. Listen to the bees, hovering over the flowers; they are roused and consumed by a burning ardor. Look at those creepers, warmly embracing the tree; the breeze ruffles them with a jealous hand. Over there, in that lovely glade, do you see the silver pool asleep? It is smiling, drowsily, like a maiden caressed by a bold moonbeam."

But the prince was not smiling; he was unhappy, for he was thinking on death.

He thought, "They do not know these maidens, that youth is fleeting, and that old age will come and strip them of their beauty! They are blind to the menace that is sickness, though it is already master of the world! They know nothing of death, of imperious death, of death that destroys everything! And that is why they can laugh, that is why they can play!"

Udayin tried to interrupt Siddhartha's thoughts.

He said, "Why are you so discourteous to these maidens? Perhaps they do not interest you? What matter! Be kind to them, even at the cost of a few lies. Spare them the shame of being spurned. How can your beauty profit you if you are ungracious? You will be like a forest without flowers."

"What good are lies, what good is flattery?" replied the prince. "I would not deceive these women. Old age and death lie in wait for me. Do not try to tempt me, Udayin; do not ask me to join in any vulgar amusement. I have seen old age, I have seen sickness, I am certain of death; nothing now can give me peace of mind. And you would have me yield to love? Of what metal is that man made who knows of death and still seeks love? A cruel, implacable guard stands at his door, and he does not even weep!"

The sun was setting. The maidens had ceased their laughter; the prince had no eyes for their garlands and their jewels. They felt their charms were of no avail, and slowly they took the road back to the city.

The prince returned to the palace. King Suddhodana heard from Udayin that his son was shunning all pleasure, and that night he found no sleep.

Gopa was waiting for the prince. He avoided her. It made her anxious, and when she finally fell asleep, she had a dream:

The whole earth shook; the tallest mountains swayed; a savage wind blew, shattering and uprooting the trees. The sun, the moon and the stars had fallen from the sky to the earth. She, Gopa, was stripped of her clothes and of her ornaments; she it had lost her crown; she was naked. Her hair was cut. The bridal bed was broken; the prince's robes and the precious stones with which they were embroidered were scattered about. Meteors sped across the sky over a darkened city, and Meru, king of the mountains, trembled.

There was a great love of poetry in the communities among which Buddhism arose. The adherents of the new faith found pleasure in putting into appropriate verse the feelings of enthusiasm and of ecstasy which their faith inspired. When peculiarly happy in their literary finish, or peculiarly rich in religious feeling, such poems would not be lost. They would be handed on from mouth to mouth in the small companies of the Brethren or Sisters, and some of them, either the oldest or the most popular, would gradually come to inspire so much veneration, so much love, that when the Canon was finally fixed, they could scarcely be left out. The question where to put them was however difficult. They could not, except in a very few instances, be inserted either in the books on the Rules of the Order, nor in the collection of the Dialogues of the Master. They must be added therefore either to the other parts of the Sutta Pitaka in which the doctrine is set out, or to the Abhidhamma where the psychological side of it is enlarged upon in detail. It was not a point of vital importance, and we need not be too much surprised that some put these books as an appendix in one place, and some in another.

It was not only poems that found their way into this appendix. It contains at least one very ancient commentary ascribed to a famous leader and teacher in the Order. There is also a book on the Lives of the Saints, and another of ancient folk-lore. But the same sort of reason that led to the inclusion of the poetry, covered also these other works. And the whole collection is so very interesting as evidence of the literary life in the valley of the Ganges in those early times, that I hope you will allow me to devote a short time to each of these curious books.

The first, the Khuddaka Patha, or " Short Recitations," is a little tract of only a few pages, starting with the so-called Buddhist creed :

" I take my refuge in the Buddha, I take my refuge in the Religion, I take my refuge in the Order."

Then follows a paragraph setting out the thirty-four constituents of the human body bones, blood, nerves, and so on, strangely incongruous with what follows. For that is simply a selection of a few of the most beautiful poems to be found in the Buddhist Scriptures. There is no apparent reason, except their exquisite versification, why these particular pieces should have been here brought together. I cannot help thinking that this tiny volume was simply a sort of first lesson book for young neophytes when they joined the Order. In any case that is one of the uses to which it is put at present.

The Dhammapada, already mentioned to you (as having been edited by Professor Fausboll in 1855), is another of such selections, but this time not of entire poems. Here are brought together from ten to twenty stanzas on each of twenty-six selected points of Buddhist self-training or ethics. In almost all cases these verses, gathered from various sources, are here strung together without any other internal connection than that they relate more or less to the same subject, and the collector has not thought it at all necessary to choose stanzas written in the same metre or in the same number of lines. We know that the early Christians were accustomed to sing hymns both in their homes and on the occasions of their meeting together.

These hymns are now irretrievably lost. Had some one made a collection of about twenty isolated stanzas, chosen from those hymns, on each of about twenty subjects such as Faith, Hope, Love, The Converted Man, Times of Trouble, Quiet Days, The Saviour, The Tree of Life, The Sweet Name, The Dove, The King, The Angels, The Land of Peace, The Joy Unspeakable, and so on we should have a Christian Dhammapada; and very precious such a collection would be. The Buddhist Dhammapada has been frequently translated. Where the verses deal with those ideas that are common ground to Christians and Buddhists, the versions are easily intelligible and some of the verses appeal very strongly to the Western sense of religious beauty. Where the stanzas are full of the technical terms of the Buddhist system of self-culture and self-control, it is often impossible, without expansions that spoil the set of the thought, or learned notes that ruin the poetry, to convey the full sense of the original. In all these distinctively Buddhist verses the existing translations are inadequate, and sometimes quite erroneous. The ancient commentary on these 423 verses tells a story about each of them, setting forth how, and when, and by whom, and on what occasion each of these stanzas was originally pronounced.

These stories are written in very easy Pali and many of them are full of human interest. The late Dr. Wenzel and myself were preparing in collaboration a complete editio princeps of these stories the copy is finished and nearly ready for the press, and will be issued as soon as I can find the time and the money.

Cannnot some one undertake a translation for us into English of these strange and interesting old-world stories about a collection of verses so widely popular among Buddhists, and now attracting so much attention in the West?

As a general rule such stories explanatory of ancient verses and without which very often the verses themselves would be quite unintelligible were handed down in India by way of traditional comment. In two cases the Buddhists have included the stories themselves as well as the verses in the miscellaneous appendix to their Canon. One instance is the Uddna^ or " Ecstatic Utterances." The Buddha is represented on various occasions during his long career to have been so much moved by some event, or speech, or action, that he gave vent, as it were, to his pent up feelings in a short ecstatic utterance, couched for the most part in one or two lines of poetry. These outbursts, very terse and enigmatic, are charged with religious emotion, and turn often on some subtle point of Arahatship, that is of the Buddhist ideal of life. The original text has been published by the Pali Text Society. But the little book a garland of fifty of these gems has not yet been translated.

The other instance (also edited but not translated) is the Iti Vuttakam. This contains 120 short passages, each of them leading up to a terse, deep saying of the Buddha's, and introduced in each case with the words Iti Vuttam Bhagavata, " Thus was it said by the Blessed One." It is always invidious to look a gift horse in the mouth, and even did we wish to do so, the time has not yet come to discuss with profit whether these sayings were actually said as here represented. What we know, is, that these (often delicately beautiful) puzzles of thought on some of the deepest questions of human life were actually extant and so widely known and appreciated that they were included in the Canon, when the Canon was finally fixed. I think it would be impossible to assign them to a later date than 400 B.C., and I have no hesitation in saying that, at that time, there had been produced nowhere in the world any works approaching to these four booklets in delicacy of construction, in exquisite beauty of terse enigmatic expression, in depth of earnestness, and in real grasp of the most difficult problems that mankind has had to face.

These ecstatic utterances and deep sayings are attributed to the Buddha himself. There is also in-cluded in the Canon a collection (called, the Thera-theri-gdthd, or "Songs of the Elders," men and women) of stanzas attributed to 107 of the leading .

The stories explanatory of the verses, giving a short account of the life history of each of the authors and authoresses, are handed down in the commentary. The commentary on the men's verses has not yet been published; but that on the women's verses has just been edited by Professor Eduard Miiller, of Bern, for the Pali Text Society. With the help of this commentary my wife wrote an account of these Buddhist lady scholars for the Oriental Congress, held in London in 1892. It is published in the Proceedings of the Congress, and affords a very instructive picture of the life they led in the valley of the Ganges in the time of Gotama the Buddha. It was a bold step on the part of the leaders of the Buddhist reformation to allow so much freedom, and to concede so high a position to women. But it is quite clear that the step was a great success, and that many of these ladies were as distinguished for high intellectual attainments as they were for religious earnestness and insight. A good many of the verses ascribed to them are beautiful in form, and not a few give evidence of a veiy high degree of that mental self-culture which played so great a part in the Buddhist ideal of the perfect life.

Women of acknowledged culture are represented as being the teachers of men, and as expounding, to less advanced Brethren or Sisters in the Order, the deeper and more subtle points in the Buddhist philosophy of life.

As I have not so far troubled you with quotations, I venture to give the substance of two of these legends. The first is about Soma. She was born, says the Commentator, Dhammapala, as the daughter of the Court Chaplain of King Bimbisara at Rajagaha. Then, after taking the -vows, she, with insight and good works, became an Arahat (that is, attained to Nirvana, the Buddhist ideal of the perfect life). Dwelling thus in the happiness of freedom at Savatthi, she entered one day the Andha Grove to pass the heat of the day, and sat there at the foot of a tree. Then Mara, the Evil One, wishing to frighten her from her meditations, stood there in invisible form and uttered the words, " The vantage ground the sages may attain, is hard to reach.

With her two-finger test, woman cannot achieve those distant heights." The Commentator pauses here to explain that what the Evil One refers to, is that women, though from their seventh year upwards they are always cooking rice, yet they cannot tell whether it has been boiled or not. They have to take some out in a spoon and squeeze it between their two fingers ; then they know.

Now when she heard this the Then rebuked the Evil One, and said : " How should our woman's nature hinder us, Whose hearts are firmly set, whose feet mount up Unfaltering to those cool heights of Truth, In growing knowledge of the Arahat way ?

On every hand the love of pleasure yields, Borne down by knowledge and the sense of Law, And the thick gloom of ignorance is rent In twain. Know this, Evil One ! and know Thyself, death ! found out and worsted ! "

Then the Evil One, thus rebuked, vanished away ; and the Then, strong in the sense of base suggestions overcome, continued in meditation till the cool of the evening.

The other poem is Sukka's. Born of a wealthy family in Rajagaha, she became an adherent of the Buddha's, already in the first year of his public appearance as a teacher, and afterwards studying under another famous lady teacher (the Dhamma Dinna, whose story Mrs. Bode has told us in the J. R. A. S. for 1893), she was converted, and became an Arahat. She then attained to such mastery in exegesis and extemporary exposition that, in her hermitage near Rajagaha, she gave lectures open to the public, and gained great influence for good among the residents in her native city. Such was her eloquence as she taught, walking to and fro in her shady terrace, all who came from the city to see her, that the Dryad in the tree at the end of the terrace was filled with impetuous enthusiasm at her wisdom, and quitting its cool shrine, went off to Rajagaha and called aloud :

" What would ye men of Rajagaha have ?

What have ye done ? that mute and idle here Ye lie about, like men bemused with wine, Nor upon Sukka wait, while she reveals The precious truths of the Ambrosial way.

The wise in heart, methinks, were fain to quaff That

life's Elixir (once gained, never lost, That welleth ever up in her sweet words) E 'en as the wayfarer * welcomes the rain."

And when the people heard, they forthwith with eagerness went forth to Sukka, and would not make an end of listening to her.

And when the Then had reached her appointed span of life, and was about to pass away, she bore witness to the victory she had gained, and to her- self, as to another person, uttered these words:

" child of light, Sukka, f by Truth set free From cravings dire ; firm, self-possessed, serene, Bear to the end thy last incarnate frame ; For thou hast conquered Mara and his hosts ! "

There is one instance, and one only, of a commentary, detached from its subject-matter, having been allotted a place among the Sacred Books. There must be some special reason for this. But it would be premature to discuss the matter till we have the text before us, and I am very happy to say that a distinguished American scholar, Professor Lanman of Harvard College, has undertaken an edition of this unique text for the Pali Text Society. It is called the Niddesa ; and it is a commentary ascribed to Sariputta, one of the most distinguished of the personal disciples of the Buddha, on the first part of the Sutta Nipata. This last book, also included in our appendix to the canon, has been edited and translated! by Professor Fausboll of Copenhagen.

It consists of poems arranged in five books, the first four of which contain fifty-four separate poems, each of them only a page or two in length. But the fifth book is one poem almost certainly forming an independent whole. It is very unlikely that the other poems are all the work of the same hand. In all probability we have here another collection, this time not of verses, but of complete hymns, popular among the early Buddhists, but due to separate minds.

I hope to read to you in a future lecture translations of two of these lyrics.

There are two other short poems included in our appendix, each of them the work of one unknown author, and probably later than the other books in the appendix. One of these is the Buddha Vansa poetical memoranda on the legends of the Buddhas supposed to have preceded the historical Buddha, the founder of Buddhism. The other is the Cariya Pitaka a fragment never completed giving a few short verses (scarcely more than an aid to the memory) on thirty-four of the supposed previous births of the historical Buddha himself. Both of these short, and from a literary point of view uninteresting, texts have been published for the Pali Text Society.

There are two other short poems in which legends regarding the future life are put into verse. They are called respectively the Peta- and Vimftna-Vatthu, and have been edited for the Pali Text Society, but not yet translated. Some of the longer legends are interesting as poems, and the whole set of beliefs exemplified in these books is historically interesting as being in all probability the source of a good deal of mediaeval Christian belief in Heaven and Hell.

But the greater part of these books, composed according to a set pattern, is devoid of style ; and the collection is altogether of an evidently later date than the bulk of the books included in this appendix.

We now come to the Jdtakas. These are stories nominally of the 550 previous births of the Buddha, but really a collection of the most popular folk-lore tales of all kinds fables, fairy tales, riddles, puzzles, old-world legends, clever and witty judgments, instances of current superstitions good-humouredly laughed at, tales of magic cups and vanishing caps and wishing trees, stories of old mythology, and so on. At some period not quite ascertained, but certainly before 300 B.C., it had become the custom to identify the principal hero of each of these popular tales with the Buddha himself in a previous birth.

It would be ungenerous to lay stress on the fact that this identification is entirely without foundation. For it is solely due to the fortunate chance of the growth of this idea that we have thus preserved to us the most complete, the most authentic, and the most ancient collection of folk-lore in the world a collection entirely unadulterated, as modern folk-lore stories so often are, by the inevitable process of passing through a Western mind. Each story contains a stanza or stanzas attributed to the Buddha himself, either in his present or in his previous births. And it is only the verses that are included in the canon.

They are usually unintelligible by themselves ; but the comment, which gives the whole story in prose, gives also a further explanation of them ; and Prof essor Fausboll edits the whole, text and commentary, together. I had at one time contemplated a translation into English of this most interesting, but also most voluminous work. The first volume of this translation appeared in 1881, under the title of Buddhist Birth Stories. But I have long been obliged to give up the hope of carrying on this work, and am now delighted to be able to say that a complete translation is being brought out by a syndicate of English scholars, under the editorship of Professor Cowell of Cambridge, and that the first two volumes, by Mr. Robert Chalmers and Mr. W. H. D. Rouse, members of the Pali Text Society, have just been issued by the Cambridge University Press.

There are one or two other books included in this appendix to the Three Pitakas, but as they are not yet published, it would be premature to discuss their contents. You will have sufficiently understood the nature of the authorities on which our knowledge of early Buddhism must principally rest. You will have noticed that the rules of the Order the books of Canon Law, if I may be allowed so to describe them and the books of the Abhidhamma, the expansion of the psychological doctrines laid down in the Dialogues, are of historical rather than of literary value.

But in the Dialogues themselves, and in some of the more ancient poems, we have documents of the first literary importance. You will have observed also that the contents of the books are not mythological, nor theological, nor metaphysical, but above all ethical, and in the second place psychological. You will have observed also that there is very little of what is popularly supposed to be the essential characteristic of religion nothing about God and the soul, and the nature of them both, and the relation between the two. But Buddhism is none the less a religion ; and it is the religion which comes nearest of all the other religions in the world to Christianity, and the religion which has influenced more lives than any other religion, not excepting even Christianity. It would not be the place here to discuss the doctrines of Buddhism, or to attempt to give the reasons of its great successes, and of its equally great failures. I shall have time in the sub-sequent lectures to lay before you the essence at least of its positive philosophy of life. Here I would only invite your attention to the fact that a small band of scholars are endeavouring, without pecuniary reward of any kind, to make accessible to the West the earliest documents of one of the most important and most interesting intellectual movements the world has ever seen. And I do not hesitate to appeal to you for your cordial sympathy with their self-denying labours.

When I returned from Ceylon, I made up my mind that, if my life was spared, I would try to get the whole of this literature edited and translated.

When I began to speak of the advisability of starting a Pali Text Society with this object, I was told that the project was doomed to failure. No one cared enough for Pali to contribute the necessary funds ; and even if they did, there were no competent scholars, not already otherwise engaged, to carry out the work. Well ! the King of Siam, one of the most cultured and enlightened of sovereigns, sent me enough money to bring out the first volume ; and private friends of my own showed their interest in historical enquiry by subscribing enough to bring out a second ; and I soon had a small list of supporters, mostly poor men and scholars, willing to subscribe a guinea a year. This was enough for me to venture on a beginning. It was no easy task to find MSS. and competent scholars willing to spend years of labour without fee or reward of any kind. But both difficulties have been surmounted.

The work has now gone on for twelve years. We have published thirty-four volumes, amounting in the whole to 7200 pages. Out of the twenty-seven books in the Buddhist Pitakas, thirteen are now published in full, five others in part, one more is in the press, and nearly all the remainder are in preparation.

About one half of the work has been done, and the interest of scholars throughout the world has been so thoroughly aroused, that it is now only a question of money whether the work shall go on, and how soon it shall be completed. There are already three or four public libraries in Europe which have a fair collection of Buddhist MSS. ; and I have a good many in my private collection, and correspondents both in Burma and Ceylon, who are helping to procure others as they are wanted. The number of scholars able and willing to co-operate in the undertaking is slowly but steadily increasing. But the printers will not work for nothing, and the only difficulty is the want of money to pay the printer's bills.

Will not America come forward to assist in the important work of disentombing this ancient literature, now buried in MSS.?

I shall be happy to receive the subscriptions or donations of any one intelligent enough to see the importance of the work, and generous enough to give.

3

The Life of the Buddha

IT is a strange thing, and very characteristic of the real meaning of the true Buddhism, that there is no life of Gotama the Buddha in the Buddhist Scriptures. Indeed the only work, so far known to us, that can be called a biography in our Western sense is a quite modern book called the Mdldlankdra Wattku, of unknown date, but almost certainly quite two thousand years later than the Buddha himself.* There is a much older sketch of the first part of the Buddha's life, down to his thirty-sixth year, in the Introduction to the collection of Buddhist Folk-Lore called the Jataka Book, and written about the fifth century of our era.f Both of these prose works rest on the same tradition, and are written in Pali, one in Burma and the other in Ceylon.

Then there is a Pali poem called the Jina Carita, " The Conqueror's Career' written in Ceylon by Buddhadatta in the twelfth century of our era, and dealing at length with the traditional episodes down to the thirty-sixth year, and also with the events of the last few months of the Teacher's life.* There are also two well known Sanskrit poems, the Buddha Carita and the Lalita Vistara, both of which have been translated, the first into English by Professor Cowellf and the second into French by Professor Foucaux.J The former, of which a portion is lost, can be dated with considerable certainty at the end of the first century of our era, and the second (though its date is unknown) is probably even later still.

These poems are not historical biographies. Milton's Paradise Regained is of value not for what it tells us about the life of its hero, but for the literary ability with which it has recast a story derived entirely from older documents. The historical value of those documents must be determined by a criticism which will, of course, take no notice of the later poetical version. A corresponding argument ought to hold good with respect to these Pali and Sanskrit poems, and a fortiori with respect to the Chinese and Tibetan reproductions of the San Edited in the native character both in Burma and in Ceylon, but not yet translated. Sacred Books of the East, Oxford, 1894. Muste Guimet, Paris, 1888. They are literary not historical documents, and such historical value as they have is the very instructive way in which they show how far the older beliefs about the life of the Buddha had been, at the time when these books were composed, developed (or rather corrupted) by the inevitable hero-worship of the followers of his religion.

It is unfortunately precisely these later Sanskrit poetical accounts which have been the source of modern popular notions about the life of the Buddha, and the beautiful poem of Sir Edwin Arnold entitled the Light of Asia, no doubt well known to many of you, is an eloquent expression in English verse of the Buddhist beliefs at the stage when those later poems were composed. Clearly the only proper course to pursue is to go back, behind these later poetical documents, to the -actual text of the Three Pitakas themselves, to collect there whatever is said incidentally about the life, family, and personal surroundings of the Buddha, and to piece them together into a connected whole. This has not yet been done, and cannot of course be done in a satisfactory way until the whole of the text of the Sacred Canon shall have been published by the Pali Text Society or elsewhere. But certain progress has been made. There are accounts more or less circumstantial, in the introductory parts of many of the Dialogues, of various episodes in Gotama's career. Occasionally in an argument in support of one or another ethical pro-position, autobiographical reminiscences are placed in the mouth of the Buddha himself as the principal interlocutor in the dialogue. Some of the ancient poems also relate to similar episodes, and in the introductory stories to certain of the rules of the Order, specifying the occasion on which the rule in question was originally established by the Founder, other autobiographical incidents are incidentally alluded to.

It will be impossible for me, within the limits of time at my disposal, to do more than summarise the results which can be reached from a comparison of such passages as these.

As you are all aware, the actual date of the birth of the Buddha is still a matter of controversy, but may be fixed approximately at about B.C. 600. He was born in the city of Kapila-vastu, about one hundred miles north-east of the city of Benares.

This was one of those portions of the valley of the Ganges which had been the last to be brought under the influence of the Brahmins. It was far to the east of the Holy Land of Brahmin tradition, and there can be but little doubt that, at the time of which we speak, the inhabitants of that district were in many respects more independent of the Brahmins than the countries farther west. We have no evidence that there was any large number of Brahmins settled in the country, which was inhabited by a high-caste tribe, forming the Sakya clan. Mr. Beal, the late translator of so many Chinese Buddhist books, was of opinion that this very word " Sakya " was sufficient evidence to show that the clan was of Skythian, and therefore of Mongolian, origin. This seems to me a very wide conclusion to draw from a chance similarity of name, and also a very rash con-clusion when so many details confirm the native tradition that the clan, or at least its principal members, was of Aryan descent. Its government was certainly aristocratic. We find indeed, in the sixth century before Christ, in the valley of the Ganges, a stage of social evolution very similar to that reached in Greece at the time of Plato. With one or two exceptions, kingdoms had not yet arisen. The country was politically split up into small communities, governed under republican institutions, some aristocratic, and some more democratic in character.

These were just beginning to lose their independence by being merged into kingdoms formed by some successful despot. The later legends represent the Buddha as having been the son of such a king. But this is distinctly contradicted by the earliest documerits. The texts are most particularly, almost ludicrously, careful to speak of everyone with the exact degree of reverence or respect due to their worldly position. Now Gotama's father is not spoken of as a king until we come to later documents, whereas his first cousin, Bhaddiya, is addressed by the title of Raja. Even Raja, however, is not necessarily the same as " king" in English. It means "ruler," and may well have no stronger signification than that of "archon" or "consul."

The probability therefore is that Gotama was born in a family belonging to the highest ruling caste of the small Aryan community centred at Kapila-vastu in Kosala. The later accounts would lead one to infer that the Sakya domain was a rich and extensive country. There is nothing in the older books to confirm this opinion. Indeed, from the references to the adjoining states, it would seem to have been a small territory ; not much more than 150 square miles in extent.

His people were agriculturists and, no doubt, the

economic position even of the principal families among them was of a very simple kind. All the marvellous details of the wealth and glory of the royal palace, in which he lived in Oriental luxury, are due to the natural desire to magnify the splendour of the position he renounced, when, for the sake of others, he "came out" as a mendicant teacher. The name of his mother has not yet been found in the oldest texts, but it is given in the Buddhavansa as Maya, and we are told that she died when he was seven days old, and that he was brought up by his aunt, Maha Pajapati of the Gotamids. We also know that he was married (though the name of his wife is not given), that he had a son named Rahula, and that this son afterwards became an insignificant member of the Order founded by his father. Of Gotama's childhood and early youth we know next to nothing from the earlier texts. But there are not wanting even there descriptions of the wonders which attended his birth, and of the marvellous precocity of the boy. " He was not born as ordinaiy men are ; he had no earthly father; he descended of his own accord into his mother's womb from his throne in heaven ; and he gave unmistakable signs, immediately after his birth, of his high character and of his future greatness.

Earth and heaven at his birth united to pay him homage, the very trees bent of their own accord over his mother, and the angels and archangels were present with their help. His mother was the best and the purest of the daughters of men, and his father was of royal lineage, a king of wealth and power. It was a pious task to make his abnegation and his condescension greater by the comparison between the splendour of the position he was to abandon, and the poverty in which he afterwards lived. And in countries distant from Kapila-vastu the inconsistencies between such glowing accounts, and the very names they contain, passed unnoticed by credulous hearers." Such legends are indeed of the greatest possible historical value from the comparative point of view.

Similar legends are related of all the founders of great religions, and even of the more famous kings and conquerors in the ancient world. In a certain stage of intellectual progress it is a necessity of the human mind that such legends should grow up.

They are due, in every case, to similar causes, and most instructive is it to watch those causes at work. I have dealt with this most interesting subject at considerable length both in my manual Buddhism and in my Hibbert Lectures. I have there pointed out the sources of the Buddhist Legend, and have shown how the two ideas of the King of the Golden Age and of the Prophet-Sage have influenced Buddhists in precisely the same way as the two ideas of the Messiah and the Logos have influenced Christians, and how strikingly similar are the results attained by each. I will therefore content myself with referring on this occasion to those expositions, and will only remind you of the extreme importance of noting, not only the source of each particular incident in the legend, but also the date, as nearly as possible, when each episode became actually incorporated into the ever-growing tale. How long does it take people, perfectly sincerely and honestly, to believe in the Divine fatherhood of their hero, in his immaculate conception, in the extraordinary and even supernatural instances of the precocity of the child, and so on through all the list ?

In this respect it is desirable to call attention to the publication by Mr. Robert Chalmers in the last volume of the Journal of the Royal Asiatic Society of the important text entitled the Acchariya Abbhuta Sutta, or "The Discourse on Wonders and Marvels." This is one of the dialogues referred to in the last chapter, No. 123 in the shorter collection.

In it is laid down as true of each Buddha (and therefore also of the historical Buddha) that the universe is illumined with brilliant light at the moment of his conception ; that the womb is transparent so that his mother can see the babe before it is born ; that the pregnancy lasts exactly 280 days; that the mother stands during parturition ; that on the birth of the babe it is received first into the hands of heavenly beings, and that supernatural showers provide first hot and then cold water in which the child is bathed ; that the future Buddha walks and speaks at once, and that the whole universe is again illumined with a brilliant light. There are other details, but this is enough to show as the collection of dialogues is certainly one of the very oldest texts we have how very short is the time (less than a century) required for such belief in the marvellous to spring up.

We know that in his twenty-ninth year Gotama abandoned his home, his young wife, and his infant son, and went forth into the world to become a homeless wanderer, and to spend his life, first in thinking out for himself the deepest problems of experience, and then in spreading abroad to others the good tidings of the salvation which he deemed himself to have discovered. It may seem strange to western people, even of the most earnest and cultured sort, that any man, aiming at such results, should have thought it necessary to take this step.

But the conditions of life at that time in the valley of the Ganges were very different from those obtaining at present. To work in one's study for the regeneration of mankind was almost impossible. There were no written books through which to communicate with the outside world. On the other hand the necessities were much fewer and much simpler.

In that gorgeous climate and in that half occupied

country, to retire into the woods and devote one's self to the higher life was not only practicable, but was even not uncommon. We hear of many instances of a similar kind. In the law-books, by which the lives of the Brahmins were regulated, it is considered so much a matter of course that a man should retire from the world, that the life of the good Brahmin is divided into three stages, during the first of which he is to be a student during the second of which he is to marry, rear a family, and perform all the religious rites and sacrifices, and the household duties of a good Brahmin and during the third of which he is to leave his home and retire, with or without his wife, into the forest, and live, as a recluse, a life of meditation. We are not unfamiliar, even among Christians, with the idea of a Retreat, into which a man may retire and, getting rid of the world, devote himself to the education of his heart. And at that time in India the doctrine of the Retreat was a favourite one, not only among Brahmins, but among the numerous sects which professed, each in a different way, to propound a solution, independent of the Brahmin theories, of the problems of life. We have constant reference in the Buddhist books to wandering ascetics of every race and caste and sect, men and women alike, who wandered from village to village, and were ready to hold discussions with all the world.

Thus we are told, in the just published Paramat-tha Dipani, of a lady who was in the habit of wandering from village to village, and setting up at the entrance to the village a broomstick with the announcement, that she was willing to discuss with anyone who should overturn the broomstick.

At one village which she reached a follower of the Buddha accepted her challenge. On the following day a public discussion was held between the two in the presence of all the village. The Buddhist answered all her puzzles, but she could not answer his, and full of confusion at a defeat (which for so many years she had never suffered) she threw her-self at the feet of her opponent, and acknowledged herself a disciple from that day forth of the Blessed One. Again, in the Ratthapala Suttanta, one of the dialogues of Gotama, translated by Mr. Lupton, of the Indian Civil Service, in the Journal of the Royal Asiatic Society for 1894, there is a full discussion of the motives which led at that time in India to the adoption of such a life. Ratthapala, I may add, who is the recluse of this dialogue, is represented as young and rich, and in every sense of the word happy, when he retired from the world. And he explains to the king why persons should adopt this course from other motives than those of disappointment, poverty, or old age.

Having " gone forth," as the technical expression runs, Gotama went first to Rajagaha, the capital city of the neighbouring kingdom of Magadha.

His visit is described in one of the ancient poems I have referred to as being included in the canon, and I will quote it as a specimen of the kind of bio-graphical material we find in these records. It is called the Pabbajjd Sutta, and is contained in the Sutta Nipata. Of course all the beauty of the rhythm in the Pali text of the simple ballad is lost in my prose version.

1. I will praise the homeless life, such as the Far-Seeing One led, such as when he had thought the matter o'er he deliberately chose as the homeless life.

2. " Full of hindrances is this household life, the haunt of passion ; free as -the air is the homeless state." Thus he considered, and went forth.

3. And when he had gone forth he gave up wrong-doing, both in action and in words, and he made his mode of livelihood quite pure.

4. To the King's town the Buddha went, to Giribioo Buddhism baja in Magadha; full of outward signs of worth, he collected alms for food.

5. Him saw Bimbisara, standing on the upper terrace of his palace. On seeing him with such signs, he spake as follows :

6. " Be careful, Sirs, of this man, handsome is he, great and pure ; guarded in conduct, he looks not more than a fathom's length before him.

7. " With downcast eye, and self-possessed is he. Such an one is of no low caste. Let the king's messengers run forth and ask: Where is the mendicant going?"

8. Thus sent, the messengers hurried after him.

   They asked : " Where is the Bhikkhu going ? Where does he mean to stay ? "

9. Wandering straight on from house to house, guarded as to the door (of his senses), well restrained, mindful and self-possessed, he quickly filled his bowl.

10. When he had finished his round for alms the Sage went forth from the city, and gained the mountain Pandava. "There shall my dwelling be."

11 On seeing where he stopped, there the messengers stayed ; and one messenger went back, and told this to the king :

12. "The mendicant, King, is now seated on Pandava hill, like to a mighty tiger, Kke a lion in a mountain cave."

13. On hearing the messenger's words the prince in a state chariot hurriedly went forth towards the Pandava rock.

14. And where the carriage road ended there alighting from his car, on foot the prince went on till he came near ; and then sat down.

15. On sitting down, the King, with courtesy, exchanged with him the greetings of a friend. Then he spake thus :

16. "Young art thou and delicate, a lad in his first youth ; fine is thy colour, like a high-born noble's,

17. "The glory of the vanguard of the army, at the head of a band of heroes. I will give thee wealth. Do thou accept it, and tell us thy lineage, when asked."

18. " Hard by Himalaya's slopes, King, there is a country strong in wealth, the dwellers therein are of the Kosalas,

19. " Descendants of the Sun by race, Sakyas they are by birth. T is from that stock I have gone forth, longing no more for sensual delights.

20. " Seeing the danger therein, looking on going forth as bliss, I shall go on in the struggle, for in that my mind delights."

Here ends the Pabbajja Sutta.

Having thus rejected the royal offer the recluse placed himself as a pupil under one of the recluses who had established themselves in the mountains near Rajagaha. We have an account in the Ariya Pariyesana Sutta, given by Gotama himself, of the essence of the teaching of this sage, whose name was Alara Kalama, and of the reasons which led Gotama to be dissatisfied with the result.

He then went to another of these recluses, to Uddaka, the son of Rama, but was again dissatisfied with the teaching that he heard.

We have other accounts of these two sages, propos of certain propositions which they put for. ward, in passages of the Samyntta, in which similar propositions are discussed. From these passages it appears that the teaching of these masters was of no simple kind. It was an elaborately thought-out solution of the problems discussed (as already pointed out in our first lecture) by such later schools as the Sankhya and Vedanta. And it is certainly evident that Gotama, either during or before this period, must have gone through a very systematic and continued course of study in all the deepest philosophy of the time. All the oldest accounts agree in stating that after working as a pupil under Alara and Uddaka, Gotama devoted himself, during a period the length of which is not known, to a regular system of what we should now call penance.

It was a matter of common belief at that time, that by the practice of austere self-mortification a man could compel the gods to manifest themselves to him and reveal the truth ; and also that the sup-pression of bodily feeling would in itself open out the way to a greater vigour of the mind, and to extraordinary insight. From one or other of these motives Gotama accustomed himself gradually to live on smaller and smaller quantities of food, and, by checking and repressing his breath, sought to plunge himself into that state of trance in which he might experience the illumination that he sought for.

In carrying out these self-mortifications he was watched by five ascetics, who wondered at his self-resolution and waited to see him made partaker of the long-expected enlightenment. We need not, therefore, be surprised to learn that his fame is said to have spread round about like the sound of a great gong hung in the canopy of the skies.

But he found himself no nearer the goal ; and one day,

after he had suddenly staggered and fallen in a faint to the ground, he determined to give up this method also, and again gradually to return to the ordinary life of a recluse. Then, when he was apparently most in need of sympathy, when his sense of failure might have been assuaged by the tender trust and respect of faithful followers, his companions forsook him, and went away to Benares.

To them it was an axiom that mental conquest lay through bodily suppression. In giving up his penance he had to give up their esteem ; and, in what might have been his sore distress, they left him to bear, alone, the bitterness of doubt.

There then ensued that mental struggle which culminated on the day when, under the Bo Tree, Gotama the recluse attained to Buddhahood and to Nirvana, deemed himself to have discovered at last the right solution of the mysteries of life, and became henceforth Gotama the Buddha. The later legends have described this, the most important event in Gotama's career, in poetical language not found in the earliest texts. Even the well-known scene of the temptation by Mara, the Evil One (which fills so many pages in the later records, and in Sir Edwin Arnold's beautiful poem), is in those accounts entirely wanting. And when it is first incidentally referred to f we find only the bare men-Sutta Nipata (FausbSll's translation, pp. 69-72) where the suggestion is quite different. The origin of this whole legend of Mara, to which we have two of these early references, inconsistent with one another, is perhaps to be found in the simple words at the end of the Ariya having solved the mystery, his work is done, and that the time had arrived for him to pass away without attempting to proclaim to others the glad tidings of the Noble Way.

But he rejected the thought (veiled under this figure of a suggestion from without), and resolved to preach his gospel to the world. First he sought out and proclaimed it to the five recluses who had been till lately his companions. In the oldest account of this episode * it is stated that when they saw him coming, they concerted with each other, saying:

" Friends, there comes the Samana Gotama, who lives in abundance, who has given up his exertions, and has turned back to a life of ease. Let us not salute him, nor rise from our seats when he approaches, nor take his bowl and his robe from his hands. But let us just put there a seat. If he likes, let him sit down."

But when the Blessed One gradually approached nigh unto those five recluses, the five could not keep their agreement. They went forth to meet the Blessed One. One took his bowl and his robe, another prepared a seat; a third brought water wherewith to wash his feet, and a footstool thereto and a towel. Then the Blessed One sat down on the seat they had prepared.

Now they addressed the Blessed One by his name, and with the appellation " Friend.** But he said to them : " Do not address the Tathagata by his name, or by the appellation ' Friend.* The Tathagata has become an Arahat, the supreme Buddha. Give ear, recluses. The ambrosia has been won by me. I will teach you. To you I preach the Dharma (the Law, the Norm). If you walk in the way that I will show, you will ere long, having yourselves known it and seen it face to face, live in the possession of that highest goal of the holy life, for the sake of which noble youths give up the world and go forth into the homeless state.

They then object that, having given up his austerities, how can he claim to have gained the insight he had been seeking. But he repeats to them his assurance of knowledge; and when they again object, he says : " Do you admit that I have never unburdened myself to you in this way before this day?

" You have never spoken so, lord," is the reply. He then sets out to them his view of life in a discourse called the DJiamina-cakka-ppavattana-sutta, or the " Foundation of the Kingdom of Righteousness

In my next lecture I shall give you the actual words which he is related to have used on this important occasion, which the later accounts have surrounded once again with poetical legends which are sometimes of surprising beauty, and are remarkable as anticipating some of the very expressions used in the Christian legend of the day of Pentecost"

The five recluses were converted to the new doctrine, and Gotama stayed with them in the hermitage near Benares. There he preached his doctrines and made other conversions until, after three months, the number of his disciples amounted already to sixty persons. Then he sends out his disciples to wander through the villages, and preach the glorious gospel to the world ; and himself goes on to Uruvela with a similar purpose in view.

From this time his career as a teacher may be fairly said to have commenced. Henceforth till his death his mode of life was very simple. Like other recluses of the time he was in the habit of spending three months of each year the three months of the rainy season in residence at some particular spot.

The other nine months of the year he wandered from village to village, through the valley of the Ganges, preaching and teaching his new gospel. I have not time, and it would be tedious, to attempt to follow him through all these wanderings. It is true that, in each dialogue and poem, we have the account of the place at which it was spoken, and of the occasion which gave rise to it But it is difficult to trace any chronological sequence, as the principal thing in the minds of the narrators has always been, not the time at which any word was spoken, but the portion of truth which it revealed.

We know that he returned eventually to his home, and very affecting is the account of his interview with his father, his wife, and his only son. And there are a number of other episodes which are both interesting in themselves as stories, and as throwing light upon the character of the Buddha. I have given in my Manual a statement of the most important of these episodes for the first twenty years of his career as a teacher. But I can here only deal with the more general features.

Now there is a very interesting picture in Buddhaghosa's commentary on the first of the Dialogues of Gotama, of the manner in which Gotama was wont, under ordinary circumstances, to spend each day.

As this has never been translated, it may interest you to hear it. It runs as follows :

" For the Blessed One used to rise up early (i. e. about 5 A.M.), and, out of consideration for his personal attendant, was wont to wash and dress himself, without calling for any assistance.

Then, till it was time to go on his round for alms, he would retire to a solitary place and meditate. When that time arrived he would dress himself completely in the three robes (which every member of the Order wore in public), take his bowl in his hand and, some-times alone, sometimes attended by his followers, would enter the neighbouring village or town for alms, sometimes in an ordinary way, sometimes won- ders happening such as these.

As he went towards the village soft breezes would waft before him cleansing the way, drops of rain would fall from the sky to lay the dust, and clouds would hover over him, spreading as it were a canopy protecting him from the sun. Other breezes would waft flowers from the sky to adorn the path ; the rough places. would be made plain and the crooked straight, so that before his feet the path would become smooth and the tender flowers would receive his footsteps.

And betimes a halo of six hues would radiate from his form (as he stood at the threshold of the houses) illuminating with their glory, like trails of yellow gold or streamers of gay cloth, the gables and veran-dahs round about. The birds and beasts around would, each in his own place, give forth a sweet and gentle sound in welcome to him, and heavenly music was wafted through the air, and the jewellery men wore jingled sweetly of itself.

At signs like these the sons of men could know' To day it is the Blessed One has come for alms/ Then clad in their best and brightest, and bringing garlands and nosegays with them, they would come forth into the street and, offering their flowers to the Blessed One, would vie with one another, saying, ' To-day, Sir, take your meal with us ; we will make provision for ten, and we for twenty, and we for a hundred of your followers.' So saying they would take his bowl, and, spreading mats for him and his attendant followers, would await the moment when the meal was over.

Then would the Blessed One, when the meal was done, discourse to them, with due regard to their capacity for spiritual things, in such a way that some would take the layman's vow, and some would enter on the paths, and some would reach the highest fruit thereof.

And when he had thus had mercy on the multitude, he would arise from his seat and depart to the place where he had lodged.

And when he had come there he would sit in the open

verandah, awaiting the time when the rest of his followers should also have finished their meal. And when his attendant announced they had done so, he would enter his private apartment. Thus was he occupied up to the mid-day meal.

"Then afterwards, standing at the door of his chamber, he would give exhortation to the brethren such as this: 'Be earnest, my brethren, strenuous in effort. Hard is it to meet with a Buddha in the world. Hard is it to attain to the state of (that is to be born as) a human being. Hard is it to find a fit opportunity. Hard is it to abandon the world.

Difficult to attain is the opportunity of hearing the word

" Then would some of them ask him to suggest a subject for meditation suitable to the spiritual capacity of each, and when he had done so they would retire each to the solitary place he was wont to frequent, and meditate on the subject set.

Then would the Blessed One retire within the private chamber, perfumed with flowers, and calm and self-possessed would rest awhile during the heat of the day. Then when his body was rested he would arise from the couch and for a space consider the circumstances of the people near that he might do them good.

And at the fall of the day the folk from the neighbouring villages or town would gather together at the place where he was lodging, bringing with them offerings of flowers. And to them, seated in the lecture hall, would he, in a manner suitable to the occasion, and suitable to their beliefs, discourse of the Truth. Then, seeing that the proper time had come he would dismiss the folk, who, saluting him, would go away. Thus was he occupied in the afternoon.

" Then at close of the day should he feel to need the refreshment of a bath he would bathe, the while some brother of the Order attendant on him would prepare the divan in the chamber, perfumed with flowers.

And in the evening he would sit awhile alone, still in all his robes, till the brethren returned from their meditations began to assemble.

Then some would ask him questions on things that puzzled them, some would speak of their meditations, some would ask for an exposition of the Truth.

Thus would the first watch of the night pass, as the Blessed One satisfied the desire of each, and then they would take their leave.

And part of the rest of the night would he spend in meditation, walking up and down outside his chamber ; and part he would rest lying down, calm and self-possessed, within.

And as the day began to dawn, rising from his couch he would seat himself, and calling up before his mind the folk in the world he would consider the aspirations which they, in previous births, had formed, and think over the means by which he could help them to attain thereto'

It is true that this picture is charged with super-natural details such as we must expect to find in the wording of a tradition which had been handed down for about a thousand years, but the expressions used are not without a certain poetical beauty of their own ; and in the incidents which are here said to have filled up the time of the teacher, we have a picture substantially confirmed, as to its main features, by the incidental references in the earlier books.

I have no doubt that this was actually the way in which the Buddha used to spend the working days of his useful and peaceful career ; and that the tone of the narrative, the life of intellectual activity, the peace and harmony and gentleness pervading the picture, may be actually regarded as true.

Of course we have here the description of a day spent altogether at one place, and it should not be for- gotten that the Buddha was constantly moving about, and that then the hours of the early morning as well as of the close of the day would have been occupied, not in meditation, but in actual walking from one place to another.

There is one book or chapter, included in the Dialogues, and the longest of them all, which approaches in character to a gospel, and gives a detailed description of all the events of , the last three months of his career.

This Suttaf I have translated in full in my volume entitled Buddhist Suftas, and have analysed in my Manual. It is plain from this document, as well as from other passages in the earlier books, that, in his wanderings during the nine months of good weather, the Buddha was accustomed, as a regular practice, to walk from fifteen to twenty miles a day ; and this may account, in great measure, for the vigorous health which he enjoyed, and for the ripe old age to which he at- tained.

He retired from the world at twenty-nine ; he spent six years in study and meditation prior to his appearance as a teacher, and for forty-five years after that he lived this life of constant travelling, teaching, thinking.

He had time, therefore, during this long period, to think out very thoroughly the views of life which are set out in the Dialogues and which will form the subject of our next two lectures.

And by his constant intercourse with all the most cultured and earnest thinkers of the day through a large extent of territory, stretching from Patna in the south-east to Savatthi in the north-west, about three hundred miles long by one hundred miles in breadth, he had frequent opportunities of comparing his views with those of such men.

Moreover, by mixing daily with all sorts and conditions of men, from kings and wealthy merchants down to the peasants in the villages, as well as with Brahmins and leaders of sects, he was able, in an extraordinary degree, to enter into the needs and aspirations, the hopes and fears, of our common humanity.

It is very interesting, as evidence of the wonderful toleration which prevailed at that time, through the valley of the Ganges, that a teacher, whose whole system was so diametrically opposed to the dominant creed, and logically so certain to undermine the influence of the Brahmins, the parsons of that day, should, nevertheless, have been allowed to carry on his propaganda so ceaselessly and so peacefully through a considerable period of time.

It is even more than that. Wherever he went, it was precisely the Brahmins themselves who often took the most earnest interest in his speculations, though his rejection of the soul theory, and of all that it involved, was really incompatible with the whole theology of the Vedas, and therefore, with the supremacy of the Brahmins. Many of his chief disciples, many of the most distinguished members of his Order, were Brahmins.

He admitted equally, it is true, men from all the other castes, and there were certain individuals, among the dominant school, who foresaw that this course of action would, in the long run, be fatal to the maintenance of the distinguished social position arid pecuniary advantages of the Brahmins.

But on the whole he was regarded by the Hindus of that time as a Hindu.

We hear of no persecution during his life, and of no persecution of his followers till many centuries afterwards.

And it is a striking result of the permanent effect which this spirit of toleration had, that we find the great Buddhist Emperor Asoka, in his famous edicts, inculcating reverence to the Brahmins and to the teachers of rival sects, as much as to the leaders of his own persuasion.

Throughout the long history of Buddhism, which is the history of more than half the people in the world for more than two thousand years, the Buddhists have been uniformly tolerant ; and have appealed, not to the sword, but to intellectual and moral suasion.

We have not a single instance, throughout the whole period, of even one of those religious persecutions which loom so largely in the history of the Christian church. Peacefully the Reformation began; and in peace, so far as its own action is concerned, the Buddhist church has continued till to-day.

But this is only one proof out of many of the fact we should never forget, that Gotama was born and brought up and lived and died a Hindu.

His teaching, far-reaching and original as it was, and really subversive of the religion of the day, was Indian throughout. Without the intellectual work of his predecessors his own work, however original, would have been impossible.

He was no doubt the greatest of them all ; and most probably the world will come to acknowledge him as, in many respects, the most intellectual of the religious teachers of mankind. But Buddhism is essentially an Indian system. The Buddha himself was, throughout his career, a characteristic Indian.

And, whatever his position as compared with other

teachers in the West, we need here only claim for him, that he was the greatest and wisest and best of the Hindus.

[Note on page 104. Since the above was in type Professor Windisch, of Leipzig, has published his very able and interesting monograph Mara and Buddha in which all the documentary evidence as to the growth of the legends about the relation of the Buddha to Mara is critically set forth.]

4

The Secret of Buddhism

Part I. The Signs, the Path, and the Fetters.

YOU have all heard of the wonderful remains of Buddhist art which are the wonder and admiration of all travellers in India. Amongst the most striking of these ancient relics of a faith now forgotten in India are the Buddhist caves, the most famous of which have been discovered in the Centre and the West. There are the wonderful caves of Elephanta on an island in what was once a lonely bay, and has now become the busy centre of English trade in the Eastthe harbour of Bombay, There, remote from all the thronged haunts of men, the Indians of old hollowed out of the solid rock a number of apartments, some of them small, some of them so large as to be spacious halls, in which the recluses of that age might dwell far from the madding crowd, living a life of meditation and of peace.

There are the still more impressive caves of Ajanta in Central India, where in a woody and hilly region now called the district of Nagpur, equally remote from busy life, the Buddhists of that time hollowed out the perpendicular face of a granite bluff, carving the entrance like some cathedral doorway and fagade, and the interior into a series of lecture-halls and dwelling-places, supported by pillars left untouched in the solid rock, and ornamented with elaborate carvings and paintings, which make these caves one of the wonders of the world. Abandoned for centuries, the frescoes have yielded to the ravages of time, until in many instances, it is difficult to recognise what the artists intended to depict. I am glad to say that the School of Art at Bombay has made careful copies of what remains of these precious records of the past, and it is a great pity that these copies have not been reproduced in lithograph so as to make them accessible to scholars throughout the world.

One of the pictures so copied was long supposed to be an ancient representation of the signs of the Zodiac, and it is so called in the Bombay copy. It gives the figure, unfortunately in a very incomplete state, of a wheel divided Into six compartments separated by spokes, and containing figures both in these compartments and around the rim. Mr. Waddell, of the Indian Medical Service, has shown in an article read this year before the Royal Asiatic Society of England, that the subject of this curious fresco is not anything so material as the signs of the Zodiac at all, but is an attempt to represent the so-called "Wheel of Life" or "Chain of Causation."

Gotama in one of the most ancient of the Buddhist texts,* is said to have thought out this wheel in that supreme moment of his life when, sitting under the Bo Tree, he attained to that high degree of insight which gave him his name of "The Buddha," " The Enlightened One." There is no doubt about this result, Dr. Waddell having discovered in Thibet an almost exact reproduction of this ancient picture, which reproduction being both complete and intact is readily intelligible.

I will read you from the Maha Vagga the words in which this " Wheel of Life " or " Chain of Causation " was first formulated, and I venture to predict that though it is written in English, you will not understand a word of it.

" From Ignorance spring the Sankharas.

" From the Sankharas springs Consciousness.

" From Consciousness spring Name and Form.

" From Name and Form spring the Six Provinces (of the six senses).

" From the Six Provinces springs Contact.

" From Contact springs Sensation.

* Vinaya,) i., I.

" From Sensation springs Thirst (or Desire), " From Thirst springs Attachment.

" From Attachment springs Existence.

" From Existence springs Birth.

" From Birth spring Old Age and Death, grief, lamentation, suffering, dejection, and despair."

Now what does all this mean ?

It would be impossible to explain it without first setting forth certain fundamental principles of the Buddhist doctrine which are here taken for granted and not expressed.

In the first place, it is an essential doctrine, constantly insisted upon in the original Buddhist texts, and still held, so far as I have been able to ascertain, by all Buddhists, that there is nothing, either divine or human, either animal, vegetable, or material, which is permanent. There is no being, there is only a becoming. And this is true of the mightiest god of gods, as much as of the tiniest material atom. The state of an individual, of a thing or person, distinct from its surroundings, bounded off from them, is unstable, temporary, sure to pass away. It may last, as for instance in the case of the gods, for hundreds of thousands of years

; or, as in the case of some in-sects, for some hours only ; or, as in the case of some material things (as we should say, some chemical compounds), for a few seconds only. But, in every case, as soon as there is a beginning, there begins also, that moment, to be an ending.

In the lowest class of being, we have form of one sort or another, and various material qualities ; in the higher classes, we find also mental qualities. The union of these constitutes the individual. Every person, or thing, or god is, therefore, a putting together, a component individuality, a compound, a confection (to coin an equivalent for the Buddhist technical term).* As the relation of its component parts one to another is ever changing, so it is never the same for two consecutive moments; and no sooner has separateness, individuality begun, than dissolution, disintegration, also begins. There can be no individuality without a putting together.

There can be no putting together, no Confection, without a becoming different. And there can be no becoming different without, sooner or later, a passing away.

Such thoughts are really quite familiar to us. We acknowledge them as true of all inorganic substances, and of living organisms, including our own. " eternal hills," and the deepest ocean depths grow into being and pass gradually away, as surely, and, compared with eternity, as quickly, as the gorgeous butterfly. Astronomy has taught us how the broad earth itself had once no individuality, and how, as soon as it began to be, it entered also on a progress of becoming, of continual change, which will never end till it has ceased to be. But the peoples of the West have inherited a belief in spirits inside their bodies, and in other spirits, good and evil, outside them-selves, and to these spirits they attribute an individuality without change, a being without becoming, a beginning without an end. The

Buddhists, like them, inherited from the Animism (the spirit theories) of their remote ancestors the belief in the existence of these external spirits. But the belief (which is not necessarily false because it is derived from the Animism of the savage) has not constituted in their minds any exception to the great Law of Impermanence, the most important of the conceptions which underlie the Buddhist religion.

Buddhism goes even further, and says that all those subtle and excellent qualities, emotions, sentiments, and desires which make up the noblest life of man (and are now often referred to as " soul ") are really discouraged and hindered by this belief in the permanence and eternity of a semi-material soul.

No training in ethics will be of any real advantage to the man who still nourishes this worst of all superstitions.

Secondly, it is a belief common to all schools of the Buddhists that the origin of sorrow is precisely identical with the origin of individuality. Sorrow is in fact the result of the effort which an individual has to make to keep separate from the rest of existence.

To the universal law of composition and dissolution men and gods form no exception. The unity of forces which constitutes essential Being must sooner or later be dissolved ; and it is to the effort to delay that dissolution that all sorrow and all pain are due.

Wherever an individual has become separate from the rest of existence, then immediately disease, decay, and death begin to act upon it. Wherever there is individuality there must be limitation; wherever there is limitation there must be ignorance ; wherever there is ignorance there must be error; wherever there is error there must sorrow come. As soon as an individual begins to be, the outside world plays upon that individual through the open doors of its six senses, sensations are stirred up within it, giving rise to ideas of attachment or of repugnance, and hence to a desire to satisfy the feelings so excited. Sometimes, more often indeed than not, it is

The Signs, the Path, and the Fetters 125 impossible for the being thus affected to satisfy these cravings; it cannot gain what it wants, it cannot avoid what it dislikes. This inability involves pain or sorrow. Birth (the springing of the being into temporary individuality) is fraught with pain. It brings in its wake the liability to disease and to de-cay. And no separate entity can escape from change, disintegration, and at last from death. All these result inseparably from the struggle necessary to maintain and to carry on its separateness, its in-dividuality. This is indeed, as I have elsewhere pointed out, a larger generalisation than that which says " A man is born to trouble as the sparks fly upward." It is an attempt to give a scientific ex-planation of the great fact of the existence of evil, and certainly the most consistent, if not the most successful, of all the efforts that have been made in that direction.

The third doctrine only applies and carries on these teachings of Buddhism with regard to indi-viduality. It will be seen that individuality is not denied. The quarrel of the Buddhist teacher is against those delusions with respect to individuality by which all persons still in the animistic stage of thought are necessarily deceived. People naturally think that they are quite separate both from the world on which they tread, and from the people and other beings who inhabit it. They naturally think that they are separate both from all things and beings who have existed in the past, and all things and beings who will have their existence in the future.

They even think that their own self is so important that it cannot possibly ever cease to be, and they are constantly concerning themselves with the ways and means of making that little self of their own happy and comfortable for ever. The Buddhist theory is, that these ideas are for the most part delusions ; that men are blinded by delusion as to their separateness from the external world, that they are blinded by delusion as to their separateness from other beings in the past and in the future. Men overlook the fact that they are really no more separate than a bubble in the foam of an ocean wave is separate from the sea, or than a cell in a living organism is separate from the organism of which it forms a part.

It is ignorance that thus leads them to think " This is I," or " This is mine/' just as a bubble or a cell might think itself an independent being.

A watchman in a lofty tower sees a charioteer driving his horse along the plain. The driver thinks he is moving rapidly, and the horse in the pride of life seems to scorn the earth from which it thinks itself so separate ; but to the watchman above, horse and chariot and driver seem to crawl along the ground, and to be as much a part of the earth as the horse's mane, waving in the wind, is a part of the horse itself. As a child grows up, its mind reflects as in a mirror the image of the surrounding world, and practically though unconsciously it regards itself as the centre round which the whole universe turns.

Gradually its circle widens somewhat. But the grown man never escapes from the delusions of self, and spends his life in a constant round of desires and cares, longing for objects which, when attained, produce not happiness, but fresh desires and cares.

With the majority of men these cares are mean, petty, and contemptible ; but even those whose am-bition urges them to higher aims are equally seeking after vanity, and only laying themselves open to greater sorrows and more bitter disappointments.

So also it is with regard to the past and to the future. Men, dazed by the soul theory, and wrapped up in the present, are full of delusions about that.

But they fail also to see that they are the mere ternporary and passing result of causes that have been at work during immeasurable ages in the past, and that will continue to act for ages yet to come. It has been the great service which Comtism has ren-dered to humanity, that it has taught people to try to realise the solidarity of the human race. The Buddhist doctrine of Karma is an attempt made five hundred years before the birth of Christ to formulate a similar but wider idea. Men are merely the present and temporary links in a long chain of cause and effect, a chain in which no link is independent of the rest, can get away from the rest, or can really, as men think they can, start off, and continue to be by itself without the rest. Each link is the result of all that have gone before, and is part and parcel of all that will follow. And just as truly as no man can ever escape from his present surroundings, so can he never really dissociate himself, though he always takes it for granted that he can, either from the past which has produced him, or from the future he is helping to make. There is a real identity between a man in his present life and in the future. But the identity is not in a conscious soul which shall fly out away from his body after he is dead. The real identity is that of cause and effect. A man thinks he began to be a few years twenty, forty, sixty years ago. There is some truth in that ; but in a much larger, deeper, truer sense he has been (in the causes of which he is the result) for countless ages in the past ; and those same causes (of which he is the temporary effect) will continue in other like temporary forms through countless ages yet to come. In that sense alone, according to Buddhism, each of us has after death a continuing life.

It is worse than no use, it is full of hindrance to a man to " Inflate himself with sweet delusive hope " in the impossible. And not only is there no such thing as an individuality which is permanent ; even were a permanent individuality to be possible, it would not be desirable, for it is not desirable to be separate. The effort to keep oneself separate may succeed indeed for a time ; but so long as it is suc-cessful it involves limitation, and therefore ignorance, and therefore pain. "No! It is not separateness you should hope and long for," says the Buddhist, " it is union the sense of oneness with all that now is, that has ever been, that can ever be the sense that shall enlarge the horizon of your being to the limits of the universe, to the boundaries of time and space, that shall lift you up into a new plane far beyond, outside, all mean and miserable care for self.

Why stand shrinking there? Give up the fool's paradise of This is I,' and ' This is mine.' It is a real fact the greatest of realities that you are asked to grasp. Leap forward without fear ! You shall find yourself in the ambrosial waters of Nir-vana, and sport with the Arahats who have conquered birth and death ! "

This theory of Karma is the doctrine which takes the place in the Buddhist teaching of the very ancient theory of " souls/' which the Christians have inherited from the savage beliefs of the earliest periods of history. It is, at the same time, the Buddhist explanation of the mystery of Fate, of the weight of the universe pressing against each individual, which the Christians would explain by the doctrine of predestination. As I have said elsewhere : " The fact underlying all these theories is acknowledged to be a very real one. The history of an individual does not begin with his birth, but has been endless ages in the making; and he cannot sever himself from his surroundings, no, not for an hour. The tiniest snowdrop droops its fairy head just so much and no more, because it is balanced by the universe.

It is a snowdrop, not an oak, and just that kind of snowdrop, because it is the outcome of the Karma of an endless -series of past existences, and because it did not begin to be when the flower opened, or when the mother plant first peeped above the ground, or first met the embraces of the sun, or when the bulb began to shoot above the soil, or at any time which you and I can fix," A great American writer says : " It was a poetic attempt to lift this mountain of Fate, to reconcile this despotism of race with liberty, which led the Hindoos to say, Fate is nothing but the deeds committed in a prior state of existence. I find the coincidence of the extremes of Eastern and Western speculation in the daring statement of the German philosopher, Schelling.

1 There is in every man a certain feeling that he has been what he is from all eternity.' We may put a new and deeper meaning into the words of the poet:

It follows from the above that the good Buddhist cannot seek for any salvation which he is himself to enjoy in any future world. The result of his good actions, the fruit of his Karma, as the Buddhists would call it, will survive when he is dead, and advance the happiness of some other being, or of some other beings, who will have no conscious identity with himself. But, so far as he can reach salvation, he must reach it in this present world, he must enjoy it in this present life. The Buddhist books are constantly insisting upon the foolishness of wasting time (when there is so much to do, both for one's self and for others) in any hankering after a supposed happiness of heaven. And salvation here is precisely the being delivered from delusions with regard to individuality, in which the ordinary unconverted man is still entangled. When the mind has become clear from these delusions, a new and wider, brighter world reveals itself to the mind of him who has " entered upon the Path/' And the Buddhist books are full of descriptions of the means which must be adopted first to get rid of the delusions, and secondly to gain the full heights of the peaceful city of Nirvana, in which he who is free from these delusions lives and moves and has his being.

It was necessary to explain these three fundamental ideas, or what follows would not have been understood; for, though much in them is undeniably true, and quite familiar to Western thought, yet the union of the three implies a view of life quite contradictory to the animistic notions accepted in the West. For, if the very conditions of individuality prevent its being permanent, and render inevitable its subjection to sorrow, then most of the Western ideas on the subject would require modification. And though the Buddhists do believe, in a sense of their own, in a future life, in the hereafter, yet that sense is so different from the one in which Christians use the terms, that Christian theologians would rightly class the Buddhists among those who do not believe in it at all.

For two essential conditions of a future life, as held in the West, and indeed wherever the " soul " theory is in vogue, are the continuation of memory and the consciousness of identity. The " soul/' in flying away from the body, is supposed, by those hypotheses, to carry with it the memory of these things at least which it recollected when in the body (and even, in some writers, of things which it had then forgotten), and to retain quite distinctly the sense of personal identity. The " soul " then enters upon a new life, either of weal, or of woe ; and though there has of late years been much discussion whether the life of woe is permanent or not, there is no question either as to the permanence or the happiness of the life of those who are supposed to have entered the state of bliss. All this would be denied by the Buddhists. There is no passage of a " soul " or of an " I " in any sense, from the one life to the other, Their whole view of the matter is independent of the time-honored soul theories, held in common by the followers of every other creed. The only link they acknowledge between the two beings (in the one existence and in the next) who belong to the same series of Karma, is the Karma itself.

The new existence is never either absolutely permanent or absolutely free from sorrow. And it is not a future life of the same being, but a new life of (what we should call) another being. For there is neither memory nor conscious identity to make the two lives one.

It would be a pretty piece of casuistry to say the Buddhist believes in a future life in our sense. But they are none the less earnest in their belief in it in their own. In that, it has been a deep reality to them, all through the long history of their faith, and in whatever age or clime their religion has been adopted. This is at least suggestive, in showing that one may pour a very different meaning into the terms " future " and " life,*' and yet they may still retain their influence over the hearts of men.

We have had thus far an explanation of three fundamental doctrines which are to be understood as underlying all Buddhist statements. These are the three doctrines of Aniccam, Dukkham, and Anattam, that is to say, The Impermanence of every Individual, The Sorrow inherent in Individuality, The Non-reality of any abiding Principle, of any Soul in the Christian sense. How then did Gotama, having accepted propositions so fundamentally opposed to all that we are accustomed to find in our own religion, propose to solve the problem of salvation, to untie the knot of existence, to find a way of escape.

The solution was summed up in that memorable discourse to his first converts, the circumstances of which were described to you at some length in the last lecture. I told you then how, in the discourse entitled the " Foundation of the Kingdom of Right-eousness " the Buddha had laid down the essence of his system. This sermon has a merit very great in sermons, that of exceeding brevity, and with your permission I will read it you, omitting repetitions, and adding a few notes of my own.

" There are two extremes, recluses, which he who has gone forth ought not to follow : The habitual practice, on the one hand, of those things whose attraction depends upon the pleasures of sense, and especially of sensuality (a practice low and pagan, fit only for the worldly-minded, unworthy, of no abiding profit) ; and the habitual practice, on the other hand, of self-mortification (a practice painful, unworthy, and equally of no abiding profit).

"There is a Middle Way, recluses, avoiding these two extremes, discovered by the Tathagata a path which opens the eyes and bestows under-standing, which leads to peace of mind, to the higher wisdom, to full enlightenment, to Nirvana.

" And which is that Middle Way ? Verily it is the Noble Eightfold Path. That is to say: "Right Views (free from superstition or delusion)

" Right Aspirations (high, and worthy of the intelligent, worthy man)

" Right Speech (kindly, open, truthful)

" Right Conduct (peaceful, honest, pure)

" Right Livelihood (bringing hurt or danger to no living thing)

"Right Effort (in self-training and in self-control)

"Right Mindfulness (the active, watchful mind)

" Right Rapture (in deep meditation on the realities of life).

"Now this, recluses, is the noble truth concerning suffering.

" Birth is painful, and so is old age ; disease is painful, and so is death. Union with the unpleasant is painful, painful is separation from the pleasant ; and any craving that is unsatisfied, that too is painful. In brief, the five aggregates which spring from attachment (the conditions of individuality and its cause), they are painful.

" Now this, recluses, is the noble truth concerning the origin of suffering. Verily it originates in that craving thirst which causes the renewal of becomings, is accompanied by sensual delight, and seeks satisfaction now here, now therethat is to say, the craving for the gratification of the passions, or the craving for a future life, or the craving for success in this present life (the lust of the flesh, the lust of life, or the pride of life).

" Now this, recluses, is the noble truth concern- ing the destruction of suffering.

" Verily, it is the destruction, in which no craving remains over, of this very thirst ; the laying aside of, the getting rid of, the being free from, the harbouring no longer of, this thirst.

" And this, recluses, is the noble truth concerning the way which leads to the destruction of suffering.

"Verily, it is this Noble Eightfold Path; that is to say :

" Right Views (free from superstition and delusion)

" Right Aspirations (high, and worthy of the intelligent, earnest man)

" Right Speech (kindly, open, truthful)

" Right Conduct (peaceful, honest, pure)

" Right Livelihood (bringing hurt or danger to no living thing)

"Right Effort (in self-training and in self-control)-

" Right Mindfulness (the active, watchful mind)

" Right Rapture (in deep meditation on the realities of life)."

Then with regard to each of the Four Truths, the Teacher declared that it was not among the doctrines handed down ; but that there arose within him the eye firstly to see it, then to know that he would understand it, and thirdly, to know that he had grasped it; there arose within him the knowledge (of its nature), the understanding (of its cause), the wisdom (to guide in the path of tranquillity), and the light (to dispel darkness from it). And he said :

" So long, recluses, as my knowledge and in-sight were not quite clear regarding each of these four noble truths in this triple order, in this twelve-fold manner so long I knew that I had not at-tained to the full insight of that wisdom which is unsurpassed in the heavens or on earth, among the whole race of recluses and Brahmins, gods or men.

But now I have attained it. This knowledge and insight have arisen within me. Immovable is the emancipation of my heart. This is my last existence. There will be no rebirth for me.

" Thus spake the Blessed One. The five ascetics, glad at heart, exalted the words of the Blessed One,"

The passages in brackets have been added chiefly from the commentary, for the reasons stated in my Buddhist Suttas. There is no doubt, I think, that we have here not only the actual basis of the Buddha's teaching, but also the very words in which he was pleased to state it. The early disciples who have preserved this record are not likely to have been mistaken on the first point, and the essential words of the discourse, however shortened, are not likely to have been much altered. The views here set forth are so remarkable as the basis of a religion promulgated in the sixth, century B. C., that to suppose the disciples to have invented them is to credit them with a power of intelligence and imagination no less than that of their revered master. But to the historian it would be much the same thing whether the Foundation of the Kingdom of Right-eousness were really due to the master or his followers. The remarkable fact is, that we have here set forth a view of religion entirely independent of the soul theories, on which all the various philosophies and religions then current in India were based ; entirely free from the idolatries and superstitions of the day. And if this Buddhist ideal of the perfect life is remarkable when compared with the thought of India at that time, it is equally instructive when looked at from the comparative point of view.

We are struck at once with the analogy between it and the ideals of the last pagan thinkers in Europe before the rise of Christianity, and of some of the most advanced thinkers of to-day. And the similarity is no mere chance. It is due to the influence of similar causes. When, after many centuries of thought, a pantheistic or monotheistic unity has been evolved out of the chaos of polytheism which is itself only a modified form of animistic polydae-monism, there is a natural tendency towards the formation of a school in which theological discussions have lost their interest ; and men have sought for a new solution of the deeper questions of life in a new system in which man was to work out, here on earth, his own salvation. It is their place in the progress of thought that explains why there is so much in common between the greatest philosopher of India, the Konfucian School in China, the Stoics of Greece and Rome, and some of the newest schools in France, in Germany, and among ourselves.

But we must not push the analogy too far. Each of these schools, though dispensing with the theologies, has peculiarities of its own, the result of the circumstances of its birth. None of the others are quite so frankly and entirely independent as Buddhism of the two theories of God and the soul.

None of them have laid quite the same stress on the necessity of a co-ordinated activity of moral earnestness, emotional culture, and intellectual strength.

There is a sentence, often repeated in the oldest Suttas, which runs as follows :

"Great is the fruit, great the advantage of the rapture of contemplation (Samadhi) when set round with upright conduct. Great is the fruit, great the advantage of intellect when set round with the rapture of contemplation. The mind set round with intelligence is set free from the great evils that is to say, from sensuality, from future life, from de-lusion, and from ignorance."

Now we have here set forth in this Eightfold Noble Path the positive side of Gautama's ideal.

In discussing the path in other Dialogues or Suttas, there is constant reference to the Ten "Samyo-janas" or Fetters, which those who have entered upon the Path have gradually to break. It would complete the picture if I give you a short sketch of these ten points, though of course to make them fully clear one ought to have a lecture for each.

The first is the " SAKKAYA-DITTHI," or Delusion of Self. After what has been said, you will easily understand what is implied by this term. And it is most significant that this delusion of self should be the very first fetter that the good Buddhist has to break, should be placed at the very entrance, as it were, of the path to perfection. So long as a man harbours any of those delusions of self which are the heritage of the thoughtless, so long is it impossible for him even to enter upon the path.

So long as a man does not realise the identity of himself with those incalculable causes in the past, which have produced his present temporary fleeting individuality, so long as he considers himself to be a permanent being, and is accustomed to use the ex- pression " This is I " and " This is mine without a full knowledge of the limitations which the actual facts of existence impose upon their meaning, so long is it impossible for him to make any progress along the line of Buddhist self-culture and self-control.

Until he has become fully conscious of the sorrow that is inherent in individuality, it will be impossible for him to begin to walk along the path which is the destruction of sorrow, and the end whereof is peace.

The next Fetter that he has to break is the fetter of VICIKICCHA, or Doubt. This is already defined in the Dhamma sangani (1004), one of the books of the Abhidhamma, as being divided into eight divisions. It is doubt in the Teacher, in the Dhamma, in the Order ; in the System of Training, and in the past, future, and present action of Karma, and in the qualities which arise from Karma.

Having realised the impermanence of self and the sorrow wrapped up in individuality, he must be harassed by no doubts as to the insight of the Blessed One, or as to the efficacy of the means set forth in the Dhamma by which a man (working himself for himself, and being a lamp and a guide to himself) can, without relying on any external assistance, realise his aspirations after the higher life. In this connection I would like to read you a few words from the Maha Parinibbdna Sutta (or Book of the Great Decease), addressed by Gotama, just before his death, to his favourite disciple Ananda.

" Now very soon afterwards the Blessed One began to recover. When he had quite got rid of the sickness he went out and sat down behind his chamber, on a seat spread out there. And the venerable Ananda went to the place where the Blessed One was, and saluted him, and took a seat respectfully on one side, and addressed the Blessed One and said:

" I have beheld, Lord, how the Blessed One was in health, and have beheld how the Blessed One had to suffer, and though at the sight of the illness of the Blessed One my body became weak as a creeper, and the horizon became dim to me, and my faculties were no longer clear, yet notwithstanding I took some little comfort at the thought that the Blessed One would not pass away until at least he had left instructions as touching the Order."

" What then, Ananda ? Does the Order expect that of me ? I have preached the Truth without making any distinction between exoteric and esoteric doctrine.

For in respect of the truth, Ananda, the Tathagata has no such thing as the closed fist of a teacher who keeps some things back. Surely, Ananda, should there be anyone who harbours the thought, ' It is I who should lead the brotherhood or ' The Order is dependent upon me/ it is he who should lay down instructions in any matter concerning the Order.

Now the Tathagata, Ananda, thinks not that it is he who should lead the brotherhood, or that the Order is dependent upon him. Why then should he leave instructions in any matter concerning the Order? I too, Ananda, am now grown old and full of years, my journey is drawing to a close, I have reached my sum of days, I am turning eighty years of age. And just as a worn out cart, Ananda, can only by careful tying up be made to move along, so, methink, the body of the Tathagata can only by much patching up be still kept going. It is only, Ananda, Wffen the Tathagata, ceasing to attend to any outward thing, or to experience any sensation, becomes plunged in the rapture of contemplation that is concerned with nc material object it is only then that the body of the Tathagata is at ease.

"Therefore, Ananda, be ye lamps unto your- selves. Be ye a refuge to yourselves. Betake your- selves to no external refuge. Hold fast to the truth (the Dhamma) as your lamp. Hold fast as a refuge to the truth. Look not for refuge to any one except yourselves . . . and whosoever, Ananda, either now or after I am dead, shall act thus, it is only they among my recluses who shall reach the very Top-most Height, (that is, the Nirvana of Arahatship) and even they must be willing to learn."

It is perfectly clear from this striking passage that doubt in the Buddha cannot mean doubt in his ability to save. No man can save another. No one can save a man, save only himself. But the Master has discovered and shewn the way by which a man can save himself. It is that which constitutes his Buddha-hood, and the doubt referred to is doubt in that.

And there is a good reason for the place this link, the link of doubt, occupies in the chain. To enter on the path one has to get rid, not of individuality, but of the delusions that cluster round the idea.

When a man has seen through the mist, and realised that there is no permanent ego within him to gain an eternal paradise beyond the grave, then the temptation lies near, having found the old theologies wanting, to give up everything in despair, and betake himself to the lower life of ease and pleasure. Then is felt the necessity of confidence in the insight of the Buddha who has pointed the way along which a man may work out his own salvation, confidence in the adequacy of the Dhamma he has proclaimed, confidence in the reliability of the Order who hand it on, confidence in the unchangeable reality of the law by which the past and the future are bound in one.

The third Fetter is the Fetter of SILABBATAPARA-MASA, or of the efficacy of good works and cere-monies. It is essential that the man, who enters on the system of ethical training which we now call Buddhism, should begin by clearing away the rubbish of false beliefs, of sham supports which really afford no aid. Years ago, in Ceylon, when my old teacher Yatramulle Unnanse was explainingthis term to me, he let drop the admission that in his eyes Christianity came under this category. But of course in the early days of Buddhism the protest was against the existing rites and ceremonies then practised by the Brahmins in India ; and it also included a protest (precisely similar to one that has often been urged by Christian theologians of the reformed schools) against the notion, that mere morality in the ordinary sense, the mere performance, however exact, of outward duties, can alone suffice.

To have broken these three Fetters constitutes what the Buddhists call conversion, a state of mind similar in its results, and in much of its connotation, to conversion as understood by Christians. A con-verted man, free from the delusions of self, from doubt, and from dependence upon works and ceremonies, is called technically the sotapanno he who has entered upon the stream. And having once entered upon the stream he can never be turned back. For the doctrine of the Final Assurance of the saints is part of the Buddhist system.

The fourth Fetter that he has to break is the Fet- ter of KAMA (not Karma), or sensuality, bodily passions. This protest is common to all the ethical systems of the world ; and the centre of interest from the comparative point of view is the degree in which the suppression of the bodily passions is inculcated in any one of them. In the Buddhist system

we find that asceticism is as strongly objected to on the one hand as lust is on the other. You will have noticed that point in the first sermon, and also in the description of the Buddha's daily life. The Buddha himself is always represented as having been well clothed, well fed. And there are elaborate regulations in the rules of the order for the constant use of the bath, with which most of the hermitages were provided. Lay Buddhists were mostly monogamists, but the practice of celibacy and abstinence from intoxicating drinks was enjoined upon the members of the Order, and was a necessary condition of Arahatship. The point evidently is, that the mind should not be occupied either with the satisfaction or with the suppression of the ordinary passions of mankind, and, with the two exceptions above mentioned (of celibacy and abstinence in the Order), the doctrine was one of moderation and temperance.

The next Fetter, the fifth, which the converted man has to break is PATIGHA, or ill-will. The state of mind here denoted is that which is produced by a consciousness of difference, and is best illustrated by the meditation called the Brahma Vihara, or "the Highest Condition practised by the early Buddhists to get rid of this sense of difference. It is the Buddha who is represented as speaking :

" And he lets his mind pervade one quarter of the world with thoughts of love, and so the second, and so the third, and so the fourth. And thus the whole wide world, above, below, around and everywhere, does he continue to pervade with heart of Love, far reaching, grown great, and beyond measure.

"Just, Vasettha, as a mighty trumpeter makes himself heard, and that without difficulty, towards all the four directions ; even so of all things that have shape or form, there is not one that he passes by or leaves aside, but regards them all with mind set free and deep-felt love."*

The exercise is then repeated, substituting each time for Love, first Pity, then Sympathy, and then Equanimity. By this means the strength of the fifth fetter is gradually weakened, and at last destroyed.

To have conquered these two enemies of the higher life lands the " sotapanno " at the end of the Third Stage, the whole of the Second and Third Stages being occupied with the struggle against them. The path leading immediately to Arahatship is occupied with sundering the last five of these fetters, which one may take together. They are : (6) RUPARAGA, the love of life on earth, literally, in the worlds of Form ; (7) ARtPARAGA, desire for a future life in heaven, literally, in the Formless worlds ; (8) MANO, which is Pride; (9) UDDHACCA, or Self- righteousness, and (10) AVIJJA, or Ignorance. We find here again that the Bud.dhist ethics harps once more upon the old quèstion, which crops up so often, of the folly of a craving after a future life. And we ought not to be surprised to find that it is not ex- pected that this inherited desire, which really owes its strength to the great length of time during which it has grown up, should be quite extinguished until nearly the end of the struggle, until victory is nearly won. It is quite characteristic also of the Buddhist faith to find self-righteousness and ignorance placed at the very end of the list, as the last and most diffi-cult enemies which the good Buddhist, in his struggle for self-mastery, has to overcome.

To have acquired, as an habitual frame of mind, the eight positive characteristics laid down in the Noble Path, to have got rid of the ten failings speci-fied in the list of the

Fetters, constitutes Arahatship, the Buddhist ideal of life. Directly or indirectly this is the one subject of the earliest Buddhist books.

The most eloquent passages lead up to it ; the longest (and to us, sometimes I am afraid, the most tedious) deal with the details of it. One might fill pages with the awe-struck and ecstatic praise lavished in the writings of the early Buddhists, men or women, who had reached this state, upon the glorious bliss and peace of the mental condition it in- volved. They had endless love names for it, each based on one of the phases of the many-sided whole.

It is Emancipation, the Island of refuge, the End of craving, the State of purity, the Supreme, the Transcendent, the Uncreate, the Tranquil, the Un-changing, the Going-out, the Unshaken, the Imperish-able, the Ambrosia, and so on, in almost endless variety. One of the epithets is very familiar to us in the West ; being indeed much more exclusively used by European, than by Buddhist writers, as a name for the Buddhist ideal. This epithet is Nirvana, " the going out " ; that is to say, the going out, in the heart, of the three fires of lust, ill-will, and dulness. It is very characteristic that the going out of dulness should be part of the Buddhist salvation.

But our hour has come to its close. We have no time left in which to discuss the exact force of each of these epithets, or to attempt, further than has already been possible, to describe the Arahat. We shall have to return to the subject in the next lecture. It must suffice to remind you here that so predominant is this subject in the Buddhist Pitakas that it is not too much to say that Arahatship is Buddhism. And I will close by quoting (with the alteration of a single word) a poem by an English author, who, while not thinking at all of Buddhism, has managed to convey, in the language of the nine- teenth century, the kind of feeling that animated the Arahats of old.

" 'T is self whereby we suffer. 'T is the greed To grasp, the hunger to assimilate All that earth holds of fair and delicate, The lust to blend with beauteous lives, to feed And take our fill of loveliness, which breed This anguish of the soul intemperate.

'T is self that turns to harm and poisonous hate

The calm clear life of love that Arahats lead.

Oh ! that 't were possible this self to bum

In the pure flame of joy contemplative !

Then might we love all loveliness, nor yearn With tyrannous longings ; undisturbed might live Greeting the summer's and the spring's return, Nor wailing that their bloom is fugitive."

SIDDHARTHA could no longer find peace. He strode through the halls of his palace like a lion stung by some poisoned dart. He was unhappy.

One day, there came to him a great longing for the open fields and the sight of green meadows. He left the palace, and as he strolled aimlessly through the country, he mused:

"It is indeed a pity that man, weak as he really is, and subject to sickness, with old age a certainty and death for a master, should, in his ignorance and pride, contemn the sick, the aged and the dead. If I should look with disgust upon some fellow-being who was sick or old or dead, I would be unjust, I would not be worthy of understanding the supreme law."

And as he pondered the misery of mankind, he lost the vain illusion of strength, of youth and of life. He knew no longer joy or grief, doubt or weariness, desire or love, hatred or scorn.

Suddenly, he saw a man approaching who looked like a beggar and who was visible to him alone.

"Tell me, who are you?" the prince asked him.

"Hero," said the monk, "through fear of birth and death, I became an itinerant monk. I seek deliverance. The world is at the mercy of destruction. I think not as other men; I shun pleasures; I know nothing of passion; I look for solitude. Sometimes I live at the foot of a tree; sometimes I live in the lonely mountains or sometimes in the forest. I own nothing; I expect nothing. I wander about, living on charity, and seeking only the highest good."

He spoke. Then he ascended into the sky and disappeared. A God had taken the form of a monk in order to arouse the prince.

Siddhartha was happy. He saw where his duty lay; he decided to leave the palace and become a monk.

He returned to the city. Near the gates he passed a young woman who bowed and said to him, "She who is your bride must know supreme blessedness, O noble prince." He heard her voice, and his soul was filled with peace: the thought had come to him of supreme blessedness, of beatitude, of nirvana.

He went to the king; he bowed and said to him:

"King, grant the request I have to make. Do not oppose it, for I am determined. I would leave the palace, I would walk in the path of deliverance. We must part, father."

The king was deeply moved. With tears in his voice, he said to his son:

"Son, give up this idea. You're still too young to consider a religious calling. Our thoughts in the springtime of life are wayward and changeable. Besides, it is a grave mistake to perform austere practises in our youth. Our senses are eager for new pleasures; our firmest resolutions are forgotten when we learn the cost in effort. The body wanders in the forest of desire, only our thoughts escape. Youth lacks experience. It is for me, rather, to embrace religion. The time has come for me to leave the palace. I abdicate, O my son. Reign in my stead. Be strong and courageous; your family needs you. And first know the joys of youth, then those of later years, before you betake yourself to the woods and become a hermit."

The prince answered:

"Promise me four things, O father, and I shall not leave your house and repair to the woods."

"What are they?" asked the king.

"Promise me that my life will not end in death, that sickness will not impair my health, that age will not follow my youth, that misfortune will not destroy my prosperity."

"You are asking too much," replied the king. "Give up this idea. It is not well to act on a foolish impulse."

Solemn as Meru mountain, the prince said to his father:

"If you can not promise me these four things, do not hold me back, O father. When some one is trying to escape from a burning house, we should not hinder him. The day comes, inevitably, when we must leave this world, but what merits is there in a forced separation? A voluntary separation is far better. Death would carry me out of the world before I had reached my goal, before I had satisfied my ardor. The world is a prison: would that I could free those beings who are prisoners of desire! The world is a deep pit wherein wander the ignorant and the blind: would that I could light the lamp of knowledge, would that I could remove the film that hides the light of wisdom! The world has raised the wrong banner, it has raised the banner of pride: would that I could pull it down, would that I could tear to pieces the banner of pride! The world is troubled, the world is in a turmoil, the world is a wheel of fire: would that I could, with the true law, bring peace to all men!"

With tears in his eyes, he returned to the palace. In the great hall Gopa's companions were laughing and singing. He paid no heed to them. Night came on, and they were silent.

They fell asleep. The prince looked at them.

Gone was their studied grace, gone the sparkle of their eyes. Their hair was dishevelled, their mouths gaped, their breasts were crushed, and their arms and legs were stiffly outstretched or clumsily twisted under them. And the prince cried:

"Dead! They are dead! I am standing in a graveyard!"

And he left, and made his way toward the royal stables.

Siddhartha Leaves His Father's Palace

THE called his equerry, fleet Chandaka.

"Bring me my horse Kanthaka, at once," said he. "I would be off, to find eternal beatitude. The deep joy I feel, the indomitable strength that now sustains my will, the assurance that I have a protector even though I am alone, all these things tell me that I am about to attain my goal. The hour has come; I am on the road to deliverance."

Chandaka knew the king's orders, but he felt some superior power urging him to disobey. He went to fetch the horse.

Kanthaka was a magnificent animal; he was strong and supple. Siddhartha stroked him quietly, then said to him in a gentle voice:

"Many times, O noble beast, my father rode you into battle and defeated his powerful enemies. To-day, I go forth to seek supreme beatitude; lend me your help, O Kanthaka! Companions in arms or in pleasure are not hard to find, and we never want for friends when we set out to acquire wealth; but companions and friends desert us when it is the path of holiness we would take. Yet of this am I certain: he who helps another to do good or to do evil shares in that good or in that evil. Know then, O Kanthaka, that it is a virtuous impulse that moves me. Lend me your strength and your speed; the world's salvation and your own is at stake."

The prince had spoken to Kanthaka as he would have to a friend. He now eagerly climbed into the saddle, and he looked like the sun astride an autumn cloud.

The horse was careful to make no noise, for the night was clear. No one in the palace or in Kapilavastu was awakened. Heavy iron bars protected the gates of the city, an elephant could have raised them only with great difficulty, but, to allow the prince to pass, the gates opened silently, of their own accord.

Leaving his father, his son and his people, Siddhartha went forth from the city. He felt no regret, and in a steady voice, he cried:

"Until I shall have seen the end of life and of death, I shall not return to the city of Kapila."

Siddhartha the Hermit

KANTHAKA bravely carried him a great distance. When the sun finally peered between the eyelids of night, the most noble of men saw that he was near a wood where dwelt many pious hermits. Deer were asleep under the trees, and birds fluttered about fearlessly. Siddhartha felt rested, and he thought he need go no further. He dismounted and gently stroked his horse. There was happiness in his glance and in his voice as he said to Chandaka:

"Truly, a horse has the strength and swiftness of a God. And you, dear friend, by bearing me company, have proved to me how great is your affection and your courage. It was a noble deed and pleases me.

Those who, like yourself, can combine energy and devotion are indeed rare. You have shown that you are my friend, and you expect no reward from me! Yet it is usually a selfish interest that brings men together. I assure you, you have made me very happy. Take the horse now and return to the city. I have found the forest I was seeking."

The hero took off his jewels and handed them to Chandaka.

"Take this necklace," said he, "and go to my father. Tell him to believe in me and not give way to his grief. If I enter a hermitage, it is not because I am wanting in affection for my friends or because my enemies provoke my anger; nor is it because I seek a place among the Gods.

Mine is a worthier reason: I will destroy old age and death. Therefore, do not grieve, Chanda, and do not let my father be unhappy. I left my home to be rid of unhappiness. Unhappiness is born of desire; that man is to be pitied who is a slave to his passions. When a man dies, there are always heirs to his fortune, but heirs to his virtues are rarely found, are never found. If my father says to you, 'He left for the forest before the appointed time,' you will answer that life is so uncertain that the practise of virtue is never untimely. Say this to the king, O my friend, and do your best to make him forget me.

Tell him that I possess neither virtue nor merit; for a

man without virtue is never loved, and he who is never loved is never mourned."

With tears in his eyes, Chandaka replied:

"Oh, how they will weep, those who love you! You are young, you are beautiful, the palace of the Gods should be your home; yet you would live in the woods and sleep on the coarse grass? I knew of your cruel resolve; I should not have gone to fetch Kanthaka; but a supernatural power urged me, deceived me, and I brought him to you.

How could I have done such a thing of my own will? Sorrow will now find its way into Kapilavastu. O prince, your father loves you dearly, do not forsake him! And Mahaprajapati? What has she not done for you! She is your foster-mother; do not be ungrateful! And is there not still another woman who loves you? Do not abandon faithful Gopa! Raise your son with her help, and one day he will bring you glory!"

He wept bitterly. The hero was silent. Chanda continued:

"You are going to leave your family for ever! Oh, if you must cause them grief, spare me, at least, the anguish of imparting the sad news! What would the king say to me if he saw me return without you? What would your mother say to me? What would Gopa say?

And when I appear before your father, you ask me to deny your merit and your virtue! How can I do that, my lord? I can not lie.

And even if I should decide to lie, who would believe me? Who can be made to believe that the moon has fiery beams?"

He seized the hero's hand.

"Do not forsake us! Come back, oh, come back!"

Siddhartha still remained silent. Finally, he said in a solemn voice:

"We must part, Chanda. There comes a time when people who are bound by the closest ties must go their own ways. If, out of love for my family, I were not to leave, death would still separate us, in spite of everything. What am I now to my mother?

What is she to me? Birds that sleep in the same tree at night scatter to the four winds at the first flush of dawn; clouds that some puff of wind has brought together by another puff of wind are again dispersed.

I can no longer live in a world that is but a dream. We must part, my friend.

Tell the people of Kapilavastu that I have done nothing worthy of blame, tell them to forget their affection for me; and tell them also that they will see me again, soon, the conquerer of old age and death, unless I should fail miserably and die."

Kanthaka was licking his feet. The hero gently stroked his horse and spoke to him as though to a friend:

"Do not weep. You have shown that you are a noble animal. Be patient. The time is near when your toil will be rewarded."

Then he took a sword that Chandaka was holding. The hilt was of gold and was studded with jewels; the blade was sharp.

With one blow he cut off his hair, then tossed the sword into the air where it glistened like a new star. The Gods caught it and held it in great reverence.

But the hero was still wearing his gorgeous robe. He wanted a plain one, one suitable to a hermit. Whereupon a hunter appeared, wearing a coarse garment made of a reddish material. Siddhartha said to him:

"Your peaceful robe is like those worn by hermits; it offers a strange contrast to your savage bow. Give me your clothes and take mine in exchange. They will suit you better."

"Thanks to these clothes," said the hunter, "I can deceive the beasts in the forests. They do not fear me, and I can kill them at close range.

But if you have need of them, my lord, I shall willingly give them to you and take yours in exchange.

Siddhartha joyfully donned the coarse, reddish-colored clothes belonging to the hunter, and the hunter reverently accepted the hero's robe, then he disappeared into the sky.

Siddhartha realized that the Gods themselves had wished to present him with his hermit's robe, and he rejoiced. Chandaka was filled with wonder.

Arrayed in his reddish-colored robes, the saintly hero set out on the path to the hermitage. He was like the king of the mountains wrapped in clouds at dusk.

And Chandaka, with a heavy heart, took the road back to Kapilavastu.

Gopa and Suddhodana Grieve

GOPA had awakened in the deep of night. A strange uneasiness possessed her. She called to her beloved, Prince Siddhartha, but there was no answer.

She rose. She ran through the halls of the palace; he was nowhere to be found. She became frightened. Her maidens were asleep. A cry escaped her lips:

"Oh, wicked, wicked! You have betrayed me! You have

allowed my beloved to escape!"

The maidens awoke. They searched every room. There was no longer any doubt: the prince had left the palace. Gopa rolled on the ground; she tore her hair, and her face bore the marks of her deep despair.

"He once told me that he would go away, far away, he, the king of men! But I never thought the cruel parting would come so soon.

Oh, where are you, my well-beloved? Where are you?

I can not forget you, I, who am forlorn, so forlorn! Where are you? Where are you? You are so beautiful! Your beauty is unrivalled among men. Your eyes sparkle. You are good, and you are beloved, my well-beloved! Were you not happy? Oh, my dear, my beloved, where have you gone?"

Her companions tried in vain to console her.

"Hereafter, I will drink only to quench my thirst, I will eat only to still my hunger. I will sleep on the bare ground, for crown I will wear a hermit's braid, no more sweet-scented baths will I take, I will mortify my flesh.

The gardens are bare of flowers and of fruit; the faded garlands are heavy with dust. The palace is deserted. No longer will it ring with the happy songs of yesterday."

Mahaprajapati learned from one of her maidens of Siddhartha's flight. She went to Gopa. The two women wept in each other's arms.

King Suddhodana heard the lamentation. He asked the reason. A servant went to inquire and returned with this answer:

"My lord, the prince can not be found anywhere in the palace."

"Close the gates of the city," cried the king, "and search for my son in the streets, in the gardens, in the houses."

He was obeyed, but the prince was nowhere to be found. The king broke down.

"My son, my only child!" he sobbed, and fell into a swoon. He was soon brought to, and he ordered:

"That horsemen be dispatched in all directions, and that they bring me back my son!"

In the meanwhile, Chandaka and the horse Kanthaka were slowly returning from the hermitage. As they approached the city, they both hung their heads in dejection. Some horsemen espied them.

"It is Chandaka! It is Kanthaka!" they cried, and they galloped their horses. 'They saw that Chandaka was carrying the prince's jewels. They asked, anxiously:

"Was the prince murdered?"

"No, no," Chandaka quickly replied. "He entrusted me with his jewels that I might return them to his family. He has donned a hermit's robe, and he has entered a forest where dwell some holy men."

"Do you think," said the horsemen, "that if we went to him, we could persuade him to return with us?"

"Your words would be futile. He is obdurate. He said, 'I shall not return to Kapilavastu until I have conquered old age and death.' And what he has said, he will do."

Chandaka followed the horsemen to the palace. The king summoned him at once.

"My son! My son! Where has he gone, Chandaka?"

The equerry told him what the prince had done. The king grieved, yet he could not help admiring his son's greatness.

Gopa and Mahaprajapati entered; they had heard of Chandaka's return. They questioned him, and they learned of Siddhartha's high resolve.

"O you who were my joy," said Gopa through her tears, "you whose voice was so sweet, you who had such strength and such grace, such knowledge and such virtue!

When you spoke to me, I thought I was listening to some lovely song, and when I leaned over you, I inhaled the perfume of all the flowers.

Now I am far away from you, and I weep. What shall become of me, now, for he is gone, he who was my guide? I shall know poverty, for I have lost my treasure.

He was my eyes; I can no longer see the light; I am blind. Oh, when will he return, he who was my joy?"

Mahaprajapati saw the jewels Chandaka had brought back with him. She stood looking at them a great while. She was weeping. Then, taking the jewels, she left the palace.

Still weeping, she walked through the garden until she carne to a pool. Once again, she looked at the jewels, then threw them into the water.

Kanthaka had returned to the stables. The other horses were happy at his return and neighed in a friendly manner. But he did not hear them; he did not see them. He was very sad. He whinnied pitifully once or twice, and, suddenly, fell dead.

The Doctrine of Arata Kalama

SIDDHARTHA had entered the hermitage where holy Arata Kalama taught the doctrine of renunciation to a great number of disciples. Whenever he appeared, they all admired him; wherever he went, there shone a marvellous light. The monks listened with joy when he spoke, for his voice was sweet and powerful, and he was persuasive. One day, Arata Kalama said to him:

"You understand the law as well as I understand it; all that I know, you know. Hereafter, if you wish, we will share the work; we will both teach the disciples."

The hero asked himself: "Is the law that Arata teaches the true law? Does it lead to deliverance?"

He thought: "Arata and his disciples lead lives of great austerity. They refuse food prepared by man; they will eat only fruit, leaves and roots; they will drink only water. They are more abstemious than the birds that peck at minute seeds, than the deer that nibble at the grass, than the serpents that inhale the breeze.

When they sleep, it is under a canopy of branches; the heat of the sun scorches them; they expose their bodies to the bitter winds; they bruise their feet and their knees on the stones of the highway. To them, virtue comes only with suffering. And they think they are happy, for they believe that by practising perfect austerity, they will earn the right to ascend to the sky! Yes, they will ascend to the sky! But the human race will continue to suffer old age and death!

To lead a life of austerity and be indifferent to the constant evil of birth and death is simply to add suffering to suffering. Men tremble in the presence of death, yet they do their utmost to be reborn; they keep plunging deeper and deeper into the very pit they fear.

If it is an act of piety to mortify the flesh, then it must be impious to indulge in sensuality, but mortifications in this world are followed by gratifications in the next, and thus the reward of piety is impiety. If, to be sanctified, it is enough simply to be abstemious, then the deer would be saints, and those men also would be saints who have lost caste, for to them an evil fate has made pleasure unattainable. But, it will be said, it is the intention to suffer that develops religious virtue. The intention! We can intend to gratify our senses as well as we can intend to suffer, and if the intention to gratify our senses is worth nothing, why should the intention to suffer be of any value?"

Thus did he ponder in the hermitage of Arata Kalama. He saw the vanity of the doctrine that the master was teaching, and he said to him:

"I will not teach your doctrine, Arata. Who knows it will not find deliverance. I shall leave your hermitage, and I shall seek the rule to which we must submit before we can have done with suffering."

And the hero set out for the country of Magadha, and there, alone and absorbed in meditation, he dwelt on the slope of a mountain, near the city of Rajagriha.

5

Discovery of Buddhism

WE can now, I think, venture on an explanation of the Wheel of Life with which we opened the last lecture. You will recollect that I read you a list of the successive links in the circum-ference of that wheel, an ancient picture of which has been discovered in Ajanta. It was the discovery of the chain of causation depicted on this wheel, which, in the Vinaya account of the attainment of Buddhahood, is made the essential point of the Buddha's extraordinary insight. And the chain of causation itself is a kind of summary of the way in which the real facts of existence presented them-selves to the Buddha's mind. We had yesterday a description of the Noble Eightfold Path, and of the Ten Fetters which the Buddhist has to break. But why should he go along the path ? Why should he break the fetters? What is the prison-house in which he is chained up? What is the goal to which he hopes the path will carry him ?

The answers to these questions must occupy us to-day. The salvation the Buddhist seeks cannot be accurately described either as a salvation from hell, or as a salvation from sin. The Indian belief in transmigration made the belief in a hell (and for the matter of that, in a heaven, in the Christian sense) impossible. All the beings in all the heavens and hells would necessarily die (as we should say), fall from that state (as the Indians would say), when the causal efficacy of the Karma which put them there had been exhausted. The terrible thing was not a re-birth in hell so much as the far more staggering and terrifying conception that there was no escape from the round of trans-migration at all. A being in a state of misery, or in a state of happiness, might be perfectly sure that that state would sooner or later come to an end ; but it would come to an end only by the commencement of another state, of another birth. And that birth would be inevitably attended by all the results inherent in the limitations of individuality. And the struggle necessary to keep the individuality alive would bring with it fresh cares and troubles, old age and death, grief, lamentations, wailings, and despair.

Arahatship is no doubt an end in itself. It is a state of bliss unspeakable. But it is also an escape from the whirlpool of re-births, and it is as a salvation from that, that it is put forward as the goal to be sought for, the aim to be realised. And the wheel of life is an attempt to describe the real causes which keep men bound in the whirlpool of re-births.

This belief in the whirlpool of re-births was part of the dominant creed at the time when the Buddha worked out his system. The theologies had their theory of escape from it a theory only made work-able by the introduction of a deus ex machind. The Buddha was bound to give his answer too. It is a kind of necessary argumentum ad hominem. But though the doctrine of Arahatship can be considered on its merits, apart from the theory of transmigration, yet the Wheel of Life also is none the less a part, and an important part, of his system.

AviJJA ignorance is the first link in the chain of causation. It is the picture of Avijja which stands hard-by the first spoke in the wheel of life. The symbol in the Ajanta fresco is a blind camel led by a driver. In the Tibetan picture it is simply a blind man feeling his way with a stick. And in the reproduction of a Japanese illustration of the wheel, published last year by Professor Bastian of Berlin, the figure is a demon. In any case, what is meant is, that it is Ignorance which is the cause of Individuality. To attempt to explain what lies behind this enigmatic expression would occupy the rest of my time, nor even then perhaps would the mystery be satisfactorily cleared up. The course of reasoning is analogous to that by which a modern European philosopher seeks to find the explanation of life in the " unconscious will to live " ; and you may understand Avijja, for our present purpose, as a productive unconscious ignorance.

The second link is the SANKHARAS, or conformations (literally, Confections). In the Dialogues they are divided into three thought, word, and deed.* But in the Abhidhamma and in the later books, they are divided into fifty-two divisions of thought, word, and deed, and mean practically all those immaterial qualities and capabilities which go to make up the individual. They are represented in the Ajanta fresco, by a potter working at his wheel, surrounded by pots ; in the later Tibetan picture, by the wheel and the pots without the potter ; and in the still later Japanese picture, by the potter's wheel alone.

It is curious that, as is pointed out by Mr. Wad-dell, this is precisely the Egyptian symbol of the Creator. It represents no doubt the shaping of the crude and formless mental aggregates by the Karma, and an old Sanskrit poem sheds light upon it when it says :

" Our mind is but a lump of clay Which Fate, grim potter, holds On sorrow's wheel that rolls alway, And, as he pleases, moulds."

The third is Vl&ffANA, or Consciousness, repre-sented in the fresco and the Japanese picture by an ape ; in the Tibetan counterpart, by an ape climbing a tree. The Tibetan lamas explain this as showing the rudimentary being becoming anthropoid, but still an unreasoning automaton. I am very doubt-ful of the validity of this explanation ; but there can, I think, be no question that the stage typified is the first rise of consciousness.

The* fourth link is NAMA-RUPA, or Name and Form, represented on the fresco by two figures, the meaning of which I cannot make out. In the Tib-etan picture, it is a boat crossing a stream ; and in the Japanese, the same with a man in the boat.

The idea is no doubt that of a man crossing the ocean of life. He has now acquired a name and outward form, and has started on an earthly career as a man, endowed with self-consciousness and all the capacities of a sentient individual.

That the word " name" should imply mind is due to the pre- name was a part of his personality.

The fifth is the SAL-AYATANA, the six "pro-vinces " or " territories," 2. e., of the senses : to wit, our five senses and the mind (or mano), regarded as itself an organ of sense. These are represented in the fresco as the mask of a face, with eyes, nose, ears, and mouth, and with blank eye-sockets in the forehead to represent the inner sense or mind.

This face is, as it were, " The Empty House of the Senses," and is represented in the Tibetan picture by a house with six windows ; and in the Japanese, by the figure of a man.

The sixth link is PHASSO, or Contact, which, in the fresco, is unfortunately missing, but is repre-sented in the Tibetan picture by a man seated with an arrow entering the eye. The idea, no doubt, is, that for a sense-perception to be complete you must have the object-impression from without, as well as the sense-organ to receive the impression.

The seventh link in the chain is VEDANA, or Sensation, effaced in the fresco, but represented in both the Tibetan and Japanese pictures by lovers embracing.

Then we have TANHA, or Thirst, also effaced in the fresco, but represented in the two pictures by a man drinking. That craving should follow from sensation, and sensation from contact, is perfectly simple ; and has been well illustrated by Sir Edwin Arnold's lines in The Light of Asia :

" Trishna, that thirst which makes the living drink Deeper and deeper and deeper of the false salt waves, Whereon they float, pleasures, ambition, wealth, Praise, fame or domination, conquest, love, Rich meats and robes and fair abodes and pride Of ancient lines, and lust of days, and strife To live, and sins that flow from strife, some sweet, Some bitter. Thus Life's thirst quenches itself With draughts which double thirst."

The ninth link is UP AD ANA literally, Grasping-represented in the Tibetan picture by a man pick-ing flowers. It typifies the attachment to worldly things which the human being ignorantly grasps at, supposing they will quench this craving thirst which has arisen from sensation.

Now the tenth link is BHAVA, literally, "Becoming," the tendency to be. This idea, the symbol for which is effaced in the fresco and indistinct in the Japanese, is represented in the Tibetan picture by a pregnant woman ; and the eleventh link JATI, Birth, is represented by the birth of a child. The idea, no doubt, is that it is the grasping disposition which leads to re-birth. So Plato in his simile of re-birth (in the Phaedd) represents the soul, which should rise to heaven, as dragged down into re-existence by the steed Epithumia, that is, craving or appetite ; and he explains this by saying : " Through craving after the corporeal, which never leaves them, they are imprisoned finally in another body etc. He then goes on to give examples, and winds up with the absolutely Indian saying, that " He who is a philosopher, or lover of learning, and is entirely pure at departing, is alone permitted to attain to the divine nature." As I have quoted the whole pas-sage, together with its context, in my Hibbert Lect-curious coincidence between Eastern and Western thought.

The twelfth and last link in the chain of causation is simply the inevitable result of the eleventh the old age, decay, and death, with the accom-panying grief, which follow upon each new birth.

The whole picture of this wheel or chain of causation seems to me to be an attempt at expressing what happens in every human life. I do not think that each separate link is necessarily intended to follow the preceding one in time. It is not intended, e.g., that link No. 3 is necessarily posterior in time to link No. 2. There is a dependence of each one of these links upon the other, but the dependence is not always of the same kind, either of time or of cause and effect. This has been well pointed out by Mr. H. C. Warren of Cambridge, Mass., in a very suggestive article in the Journal of the American Oriental Society for 1893. But the interpretation of the wheel is not yet, to my mind, entirely satisfactory. The text only lies at present before us in the extremely curt phraseology of the passage I have read; and no commentary upon it is as yet accessible. And even when we have the help of further passages in the Pali, the whole subject will have to be studied by someone more intimately ac-quainted with the history of philosophic conceptions than I can claim to be. My wife has pointed out, in the Journal of the Royal Asiatic Society for 1894 (p. 388), that, in the Orphic theogony, we come across the notion of re-birth considered as a weary unending circle of birth, a wheel of From this wheel the soul longs to escape, and entreats the gods, especially Dionysos, for release from the wheel. Again, in the verses inscribed on one of the three golden funereal tablets dug up near the site of Sybaris, it is said, " And thus I escape from the cycle, the misery-laden."

Pindar, Empedokles, and Plato, as is well known, all entertained the notion of repeated re-birth in this world, which, according to the later writers, often included in its phases incarnation as an animal or even as a vegetable. It is possible that all three de-rived this notion from Pythagoras, and throughout there runs the Orphic (and also the Buddhist) idea of each re-birth being a stage in a course of moral evolution and effort after purification. Empedokles, however, sees not a wheel, but rather a toilsome road or roads of life. Professor Garbe, in his book which I quoted in the first lecture, the just published Sdnkhya Philosophic, repeats his opinion expressed in the Monist of January, 1894, that the Greeks did actually borrow, in other respects, from the Indian philosophers. And Professor von Schroeder, in his treatise Pythagoras und die Inder, seems to me to have quite clearly made out his case in favour of a borrowing by Pythagoras. It is at least certain that the students of ancient philosophy will do well to study more carefully than hitherto the Indian parallels ; and I hope I shall therefore be excused for having turned aside, in this connection, to notice a few of the most interesting.

What is at least certain is that the Buddhist, like the Vedantist, the Sankhya, and the Greek views just referred to (as well as in the Keltic parallels quoted in my Hibbert Lectures, pp. 76, 77), looked upon salvation, not as an escape from sin or hell, but from this unending, hopeless wheel of life, on which the ordinary man was being relentlessly whirled round. All the Indian philosophies unite in supposing ignorance to be the origin of the whole evil, the great enemy to be conquered. But they differ in their view as to what the destruction of this ignorance will bring about.

According to the Ve-dantist, an insight into the pregnant fact that the soul of man is identical with the great soul, the First Cause of all, will lead to a union between God and the "soul," which has only been temporarily interrupted or obscured by the conditions of individuality. So Plato, as we have seen, says that it is only the philos-opher, entirely pure at departing, who is permitted to attain to the divine nature.

Buddhism has gone a step beyond this. It holds also that that destruction of ignorance is the way of escape from the wheel of life, but the escape is not reached, and, of course, in the Buddhist system, could not be reached, in a union with God to be attained only in an after-life. The victory to be gained by the destruction of ignorance is, in Gotama's view, a victory which can be gained and enjoyed in this life, and in this life only. This is what is meant by the Buddhist ideal of Arahatship the life of a man made perfect by insight, the life of a man who has travelled along the "Noble eightfold path" and broken all the " Fetters/' and carried out in its entirety, the Buddhist system of self-culture and self-control. The Christian analogue to this state of mind (which, in English books on Buddhism, is usually called Nirvana), is the advent of the King-dom of Heaven within a man, the "peace that passeth understanding."

As I have reminded you in the last lecture the meaning of the phrase Nirvana, is literally the " going out " ; and it is used, in its primary sense, of the going out of the flame of a lamp. In its secondary ethical sense it signifies (not, of course, the going out of a " soul," nor the going out of life), but the going out of the threefold fire of lust, ill-will, and delusion or dulness or stupidity. But it involves the going out also of that " Upadana " or grasping, which would lead to the formation, in another birth, of a new individual. This point is dealt with at greater length in my manual, Buddhism, pp. no- it 5, where (already in 1877) this view of the real meaning of Nirvana, since confirmed by the publication of the texts, was first put forth.

This then is Buddha's reply to those of his contemporaries who were concerned above all things in escaping from the whirlpool of re-births. " Arahatship will save you : you can save yourselves by Arahatship."

We find a precisely similar state of things when, in the Tevijja Sutta,* the two young Brahmins come to him and ask him to shew them the way to a union with God, with Brahma. " Very well," says the reformer, "I will shew you." And he gives a long exposition of Arahatship. " That is the way/'

In both cases the exposition of Arahatship is clear enough. The obscurities begin with the reasoning which endeavours to adapt so untheological a position to a solution of difficulties really based on the current theologies. It is all very well to complain how much easier it would have been simply to deny the facts (the facts of the whirlpool of re-births, and the union with God) rather than to attempt to reconcile them with the new doctrine of Arahatship.

But that course of action could have led to only one result. Buddhism would have died in its birth. In any case Gotama adopted the opportunist position, and seems to have thought the reconciliation both clear and complete. And though it is, in my opinion, neither the one nor the other in our present state of knowledge, it is surely wiser to suspend our judgment as to the logical adequacy of the reasonings put forth till the publication of the other half of the texts shall have put us in possession of all the materials on which a judgment should really be formed.

What we have at present ascertained is that, in both cases, Arahatship is the Buddhist solution of the puzzle put. Now as to what constitutes Arahat-ship we had, in the last lecture, descriptive lists, and discussions of their details. It will be advisable, on this central and most important point of Buddhism, to quote more fully the actual words of the early Buddhist writers.

The Buddhist poems reach their highest level of beauty when they attempt to describe the glory of this state of victory over the world, and over birth and death, of an inward peace that can never be shaken, of a joy that can never be ruffled. Thus, when Kassapa, a distinguished Brahmin teacher, had left all to join the new leader, and the people were astonished at it, he is asked, in the presence of the multitude, to explain the nature qf the change that has come over him :

What hast thou seen, O thou of UruvelS, That thou, for penances so far renowned, Forsakest thus thy sacrificial fire ?

I ask thee, Kassapa, the meaning of this thing.

How comes it that thine altar lies deserted ?

What is it, in the world of men or gods, That thy heart longs for ? Tell me that, Kassapa ! "

And the convert answers : 41 That state of peace I saw, wherein the roots Of ever fresh re-birth are all destroyed, and greed And hatred and delusion all have ceased, That state from lust for future life set free, That changeth not, can ne'er be led to change.

My mind saw that ! What care I for those rites ? "

The following two poems are taken from the Sutta Nipata, from the same collection that con-tained the ballad, already quoted above, about the first meeting of Gotama and King Bimbisara.

Dhaniya Sutta.

1. Hot steams my food. My cows are milked.

So said the herdsman Dhaniya Along the banks of the Mahi With equals and with friends I dwell.

Right well is my trim cottage thatched, And on my hearth the fire burns bright.

So let the rain pour down now, if it likes, to-night !

2. Cool is my mind. No fallow land lies there So said the Exalted One- For one night only, as I wander on, I dwell upon the banks of the Mahi.

My lodging 's open to the sky. The fires Are out (for in my heart the flames Of Lust, Ill-will, and Dulness burn no more).

So let the rain -pour down now, if it likes, to-night !

3. There are no gadflies here. My kine So said the herdsman Dhaniya .

Are roaming thro' the meadows rich with grass ; Well can they bear the fickle rain god's blows.

So let the rain pour down now, if it likes, to-night !

4. My basket raft was woven well together So said the Exalted One Crossed over now, I Ve reached the farther bank And overcome the floods (the Lust of Sense The Lust of Life, Delusion, Ignorance).

So let the rain pour down now, if it likes, to-night !

5. Obedient is my wife, no wanton she, So said the herdsman Dhaniya Long has she dwelt with me, my well beloved, I hear no evil thing in her against me.

So let the rain pour down now, if it likes, to-night !

6. Obedient is my heart, wholly set free, So said the Exalted One Long has it been watched over, well subdued, No evil thing is found within my breast.

So let the rain pour down now, if it likes, to-night !

7. On my own earnings do I live at ease.

So said the herdsman Dhaniya My boys are all about me, strong in health, I hear no evil thing in them against me.

So let the rain pour down now, if it likes, to-night !

8. No man can call me servant, and I wander So said the Exalted One At will, o'er all the earth, on what I find.

I feel no need of wages, or of gain.

So let the rain pour down now, if it likes, to-night !

9. I Ve barren cows and sucking calves, So said the herdsman Dhaniya And cows in calf, and heifers sleek, And a strong bull, lord o'er the cows.

So let the rain pour down now, if it likes, to-night !

10. No barren cows have I, nor sucking calves, So said the Exalted One-No cows in calf, nor heifers sleek, Nor a strong bull, lord o'er the cows.

So let the rain pour down now, if it likes, to-night !

11. The stakes are driven in, nothing can shake them, So said the herdsman Dhaniya The ropes of Munja grass are new and strong, No calves could break them loose, and stray.

So let the rain pour down now, if it likes, to-night !

12. I Ve broken all the bonds loose, like a bull, Or like the lordly elephant, calm in his strength, Contemning the weak strands of jungle rope.

I ne'er again shall enter the dark womb.

So let the rain pour down now, if it likes, to-night !

13. Then lo ! a thunder-cloud, filling the hollows, And the high ground, that moment poured forth rain, And Dhaniya the herdsman, as he heard The god's rain rushing, yielded him, and said ;

14. 0, great the gain that has accrued to us, In that we met the Exalted One to-day !

In thee of the seeing eye we put our trust.

Be thou, mighty Sage, a teacher to us.

My wife and I will be obedient ; Under the Happy One we both will lead A holy life, and pass beyond old age and death, And put an end, for aye, to every pain !

15, The man with sons takes pride in sons, So said Mara, the Evil One The man with kine takes joy in kine.

Lusts, evil, and Karma bring delights to men ; He, who has none of these, has no delights.

1 6. He, who has sons, has sorrow in his sons, So said the Exalted One- He, who has kine, has trouble with his kine.

Lusts, evil, and Karma are the source of care ; He, who has none of these, is not careworn.

1. Rise ! sit up ! what is the use of sleeping ?

How can sleep wait upon the sick at heart ?

Upon sick men pierced with the dart of care, In whose sad heart the dart is rankling still ?

2. Rouse yourselves then, sit up ! and steadfastly Train yourselves, learn, for the sweet sake of peace !

Let not the King of Death, knowing you indolent Befool you, fallen into his deadly power !

3. That clinging bond in which both gods and men,

Craving with wants, stand caught, 0, conquer that!

Let not the moment pass ! For those who let

The moment pass them, mourn in states of woe ?

The two last lines of this verse recur at Thera Gatha, 404, and at Then Gatha, 5.

4. Carelessness is dust and dirt, and carelessness On carelessness heaped up, defiles the mind.

By earnestness and wisdom let the wise

Draw out the dart that rankles in his heart.

Utthana Sutta is ended.

Here is a passage descriptive of the bliss of the

Nirvana of Arahatship :

" Let us live happily then, free from hatred among the hating! Among men who hate let us dwell free from ill-will!

" Let us live happily then, free from ailments among the ailing ! Among men sick at heart let us dwell free from repining !

" Let us live happily then, free from care among the careworn ! Among men devoured by eagerness let us be free from excitement !

" Let us live happily then, we who have no hindrances!

We shall be like the bright gods who feed upon happiness ! "

In a later prose description of the kind of feelings that lead a man to seek after Nirvana, we find the words it is King Milinda who is speaking to Na-gasena the Buddhist

" Venerable Nagasena, your people say : ' Nirvana is

not past, nor future, nor present, nor produced, nor not produced, nor produceable,' In that case, Nagasena, does the man who, having ordered his life aright, realise Nirvana, realise something al-ready produced, or does he himself produce it first, and then realise it?"

" Neither the one, King, nor the other. And, nevertheless, King, that essence of Nirvana which he, so ordering his life aright, realises that exists."

" Do not, venerable Nagasena, clear up this puzzle by making it dark ! Make it open and plain as you elucidate it. With a will, strenuous in endeav-our, pour out upon it all that has been taught you.

It is a point on which this people is bewildered, plunged in perplexity, lost in doubt. Dissipate this guilty uncertainty ; it pierces like a dart."

" That principle of Nirvana, King, so peaceful, so blissful, so delicate, exists. And it is that which he who orders his life aright, grasping the idea of things according to the teachings of the Conquerors, realises by his wisdom even as a pupil, by his knowledge, makes himself, according to the instruc-tion of his teacher, master of an art.

" And if you ask : ' How is Nirvana to be known ? '

it is by freedom from distress and danger, by confidence, by peace, by calm, by bliss, by happiness, by delicacy, by purity, by freshness. . . .

" And if again you should ask : ' How does he who orders his life aright realise that Nirvana ? ' I should reply : ' He, King, who orders his life aright grasps the truth as to the development of all things, and when he is doing so he perceives therein birth, he perceives old age, he perceives disease, he perceives death. But he perceives not therein, whether in the beginning or the middle or the end, anything worthy of being laid hold of as lasting satisfaction . . . And discontent arises in his mind when he thus finds nothing fit to be re-lied on as lasting satisfaction, and a fever takes pos-session of his body, and without a refuge or pro-tection, hopeless, he becomes weary of repeated lives. . . . And in the mind of him who thus perceives the insecurity of transitory life, of starting afresh in innumerable births, the thought arises:

' All on fire is this endless becoming, burning and blazing ! Full of pain is it, of despair ! If only one could reach a state in which there were no becoming, there would there be calm, that would be sweet the cessation of all these conditions, the getting rid of all these defects (of lusts, of evil, and of Karma), the end of cravings, the absence of passion, peace, Nirvana ! '

" And therewith does his mind leap forward into that state in which there is no becoming, and then has he found peace, then does he exult and rejoice at the thought : * A refuge have I gained at last! ' Just, King, as a man who, venturing into a strange land, has lost his way, on becoming aware of a path, free from jungle, that will lead him home, bounds forward along it, contented in mind, exulting and rejoicing at the thought : ' I have found the way at last ! ' Just so in him who thus perceives the insecurity of transitory births there arises the thought :

' All on fire is this endless becoming, burning and blazing ! Full of pain is it and despair ! If only one could reach a state in which there were no be-coming, there would there be calm, that would be sweet the cessation of all these conditions, the getting rid of all these defects, the end of craving, the absence of passion, peace, Nirvana!' And therewith does his mind leap forward into that state in which there is no becoming, and then has he found peace, then does he exult and rejoice at the thought : * A refuge have I found at last ! * And he strives with might and main along that path, searches it out, accustoms himself thoroughly to it ; to that end does he make firm his self-possession, to that end does he hold fast in effort, to that end does he remain steadfast in love toward all beings in all the worlds ; and still to that does he direct his mind again and again, until, gone far beyond the transitory, he gains the Real, the highest fruit of Arahat-ship. And when he has gained that, King, the man who has ordered his life aright has realised, seen face to face, Nirvana ! "

Then after this discussion as to the time at which, and the manner by which, Nirvana can be obtained, the author goes on to discuss where Nirvana is stored up. The answer is that there is no such place, and the discussion then goes on :

" Venerable Nagasena, let it be granted that there is no place where Nirvana is stored up. But is there any place on which a man may stand and, by ordering his life aright, realise Nirvana ? "

" Yes, King, there is such a place'

" Which, then, Nagasena, is that place ? "

" Virtue, King, is the place. For if grounded in virtue, and careful in attention whether in the land of the Skythians or the Greeks, whether in China or in Tartary, whether in Alexandria or Nikumba, whether in Benares or in Kosala, whether in Kashmir or in Gandhara, whether on a mountain top or in the highest heavens wheresoever he may be, the man who orders his life aright will attain Nirvana."

We have several descriptions in the older books of the man who has actually attained this Nirvana of Arahatship. But there are none of them, so far as I know, that purport to contain the whole description. Perhaps we may find this in the Visuddhi Magga, or Path of Purity, now being edited and translated by Mr. Henry C. Warren of Cambridge, Mass. We have a more complete characterisation of the ideal Buddhist Recluse (which comes to much the same thing) in a work later than the Canon :

" Just, King, as a lotus flower of glorious, pure, and high descent and origin is glossy, soft, desirable, sweet-smelling, longed for, loved, and praised, untarnished by the water or the mud, graced with tiny petals and filaments and pericarps, the resort of many bees, a child of the clear, cold stream, just so is that disciple of the Noble Ones endowed with the thirty Graces. And what are the thirty ?

" i. His heart is full of affectionate, soft, and ten- der love.

" 2. Evil is killed, destroyed, cast out from within him.

" 3 and 4. Pride and self-righteousness are put an end to and cast down.

" 5. Stable and strong and established and unde- viating is his self-confidence.

" 6. He enters into the enjoyment of the heart's refreshment, the highly praised and desirable peace and bliss of the ecstasies of contemplation fully felt.

" 7. He exhales the most excellent and unequalled sweet savour of righteousness of life.

" 8. Near is he and dear to gods and men alike.

"9. Exalted by the best of beings, the Arahat Noble Ones themselves.

" 10. Gods and men delight to honour him.

"11. The enlightened, wise, and learned approve, esteem, and appreciate him.

" 12. Untarnished is he by the love either of this world or the next.

" 13. He sees the danger in the 'smallest, most insignificant offence.

" 14. Rich is he in the best of wealth the wealth that is the fruit of the Path, the wealth of those who are seeking the highest of the Attainments.

" 15. He is in receipt, in full measure, of the four requisites of a recluse (food, lodging, clothing, and medicine).

" 16. He lives without a home, addicted to that best austerity that is dependent on meditation.

" 17. He has unravelled the whole net of evil.

He has broken and burst through, doubled up and utterly destroyed, the possibility of re-birth in any of the five future states.

" 18. He has broken and burst through the five obstacles to th,e highest life in this world (lust, malice, sloth, pride, and doubt).

" 19. He is unalterable in character.

" 20. He is excellent in conduct.

"21. He transgresses none of the rules as to the four requisites of a recluse.

" 22. He has passed beyond all perplexity.

"23. His mind is set upon complete emancipation.

" 24. He has seen the truth.

" 25. The sure and steadfast place of refuge from all fear has he gained.

"26. The seven evil inclinations (to lust, and malice, and

heresy, and doubt, and pride, and desire for future life, and ignorance) are rooted out in him.

" 27. He has reached the end of the Great Evils (lust, future life, delusion, and ignorance).

" 28, 29. He abounds in peace, and the bliss of the ecstasies of contemplation.

" 30. He is endowed with all the virtues a recluse should have.

"These, King, are the thirty Graces he is adorned withal."

I might go on quoting such passages, but they would weary you, and I must find time to mention the thirty-seven constituent elements of Arahatship.

The word itself means " the-state-of-one-who-is-worthy," or "noble/' and this state of mind is divided, in the oldest books, into these thirty-seven constituent parts. They are called the Medicines Discovered by the Great Physician.

" Of all the medicines found in all the world, Many in number, various in their powers, Not one equals this medicine of the Truth.

Drink that, brethren. Drink, and drinking, live !

" For having drunk that medicine of the Truth, Ye shall have passed beyond old age, and death And evil, lusts, and Karma rooted out Thoughtful and seeing, ye shall be at rest ! "

Or, to put it in another way : Just before Gotama died, he is said f to have convened a special meeting of the Order, and to have said :

"Which then, Brethren, are the dispositions which,

when I had perceived, I made known to you ; which, when you have mastered, it behoves you to practise, meditate upon, and spread abroad, in order that pure religion may last long and be perpetuated, In the Maha Patinibbana Sutta, translated in my Buddhist in order that it may continue to be for the good and happiness of the great multitude, out of pity for the world, to the good and the gain and the weal of gods and men ? They are these :

The Four Earnest Meditations.

The Fourfold Great Struggle against Error.

The Four Roads to Saintship.

The Five Moral Powers.

The Five Organs of Spiritual Sense.

The Seven Kinds of Wisdom, and

The Noble Eightfold Path.

" Behold, now, Brethren, I exhort you, saying :

" All component things must grow old. Work out your salvation with diligence. The final passing away of the Tathagata will take place before long.

At the end of three months from this time the Tathagata will die.

" My age is now full ripe ; my life draws to its close.

I leave you, I depart, relying on myself alone.

Be earnest then, brethren, active, full of thought ;

Be steadfast in resolve ! Keep watch over your own hearts.

Who wearies not, but holds fast to this truth and law, Shall cross this sea of life, shall make an end of grief!"

Now I very deeply regret that, being obliged to put the whole of the higher Buddhism into two lectres, I am precluded from dealing at any length with any of the above thirty-seven details. I am painfully aware how uninteresting such bare lists are apt to be, when the full meaning implied by the pregnant terms enumerated is not completely brought, out and illustrated by examples drawn from similar systems in the West. But I have endeavoured, so far as in me lies, to bring out, in what I have already said, the essential points of the deeper view of life which lies behind all Buddhism ; and I can only ven-ture to trouble you now with a few general remarks on this system of ethical discipline.

And first I would observe that the whole system is based on intellectual activity. It is no doubt often related in the Buddhist books, and must often have happened, that an eloquent address on the imper-manence of all things, on the delusions of self, on the vanity of earthly things (wealth, power, and renown), will have led to the conversion of some hearer whose personal experience had prepared him for the recep- tion of the truth. But though, in that way, a hearer may, in the eloquent words of the passage I have read you from the Milinda, have leaped forward along the way and arrived by a sudden flash of in- sight at some, even advanced, stage of the Noble Path ; still it was required of him to keep up a constant intellectual activity in order to hold fast what he had attained, and reach out to further things beyond.

Secondly, it is throughout regarded that wrong belief, the nursing of delusions, the dulness which cannot open its eyes to the deep realities of life, are in themselves ethically wrong ; that to believe a lie is an obstacle to any advance along the path, and that the Arahat has to be constantly steadfast and earnest in keeping his views whole and sound.

Thirdly, that it is the greatest mistake to suppose that the suppression of desire is a part of the higher Buddhism. It is really just the contrary. Evil desires are, no doubt, to be suppressed. It is true that some of the desires which in modern Western life are held to be natural, and worthy of satisfaction, such as the desire for a wife and family, for wealth and power and titles, are, in Arahatship, regarded as obstacles to the attainment of the goal.

But to the Buddhist layman the satisfaction of these desires is freely permitted and even regulated by precept ; and it is at least an open question whether we could not match every expression as to the suppression of such desires with equivalents from the teachings of Western prophets. Even with regard to the sexual relations Gotama finds himself in agreement with many earnest Christian writers. It is at all events certain, that the ideal is not one of mere quietism, but of intellectual activity and of exalted desire, not only entertained, but reached and enjoyed. " Entering the Order did not mean' as my wife has said in the article already quoted, " mere mortification of feeling or deadening of energies. It was a diversion of both into new channels.

The Arahats are as exalted and virtually as hedonistic in their aspirations as any Christian saint. Of them too, Matthew Arnold could have said :

" Ye like angels appear Radiant with ardour divine, Beacons of hope ye appear, Languor is not in your heart, Weakness is not in your work, Weariness not on your brow."

The fourth point is the joyousness of the Arahat, springing more especially from the emancipation of heart to which he has attained, and on which so much stress is laid. Thus, in the Mahaparinibbana Sutta (a few pages after Gotama, on the eve of his decease, has insisted on his disciples being a lamp unto themselves), the Blessed One says :

"It is through not understanding and grasping four conditions, Brethren, that we have had to run so long, to wander so long, in this weary path of transmigration both you and I. And what are these four? When noble conduct is realised and known, and noble meditation and noble wisdom, and noble freedom, is realised and known, then is the craving for becoming rooted out, that which leads to renewed life is destroyed, and there is no more birth.

Righteousness, earnest thought, wisdom and freedom sublime, These are the truths realised by Gotama far-renowned.

Knowing them, he the knower, proclaimed the truth to the brethren ; The Master with eye divine, the quencher of grief must die."

The emancipation of heart is one of the " Seven Jewels " of the Blessed One, and describing it, the author of the Milinda says :

" There is one diadem that is the chief of all, and that is this diadem of Emancipation of heart !

" All the people that dwell in a house look up To their Lord when he wears his crown of gems The wide world of the gods and of men looks up To the wearer of Freedom's diadem ! "

It was the " gentle liberty " of a higher, wider law by which to regulate and concentrate their lives, that all those who had realised the doctrine of im-permanence were to strive after. The emancipation was no doubt an emancipation from delusions ; the freedom did not extend to license to revert to the errors which they had renounced, or to embrace, in intellectual anarchism, any analogous errors in their ethical development. But within those limits, which must have been clear to you from the earlier part of this lecture, there was perfect freedom from dogma, perfect liberty of thought.

But I am not concerned to defend the accuracy, or the completeness, or the adequacy of the solution put forward by Gotama of the problem of practical ethics. It is true that in my humble opinion no historian can be an adequate historian without sympathy, and indeed I confess I should not have devoted my life to the study of Buddhism, had I not felt the intrinsic worth of much that Gotama laid down. And it is at least interesting to remember that Gotama was the only man of our own race, the only Aryan, who can rank as the founder of a great religion. Not only so, but the whole intellectual and religious development of which Buddhism is the final outcome was distinctively Aryan, and Buddhism is the one essentially Aryan faith.

But we do not need to go back 2500 years to seek for truth. We have to fight out the problem of ethics for ourselves and for our own times. The point I stand here to submit to your consideration, is that the study of ethics, and especially the study of ethical theory in the West, has hitherto resulted in a deplorable failure through irreconcilable logo-machies and the barrenness of speculation cut off from actual fact. The only true method of ethical inquiry is surely the historical method. As the President of Cornell University in his " Ethical Im-port of Darwinism " has so ably put it :

"How is ethics as a science possible? If it is ever to rise above the analytic procedure of logic, it can only be by becoming one of the historical sciences. Given the earliest morality of which we have any written record, to trace from it, through progressive stages, the morality of to-day that is the problem, and the only problem, which can fall within the scope of a truly scientific ethic. The discovery of these historical sequences constitutes the peculiarity of the science, which, like every other, pre-supposes observation, analysis, and classification." Surely this is the sound gospel, and I cannot be wrong in maintaining that the study of Buddhism should be considered a necessary part of any ethical course, and should not be dismissed in a page or two, but receive its due proportion in the historical perspective of ethical evolution. I venture to appeal, therefore, in conclusion, to the friends of higher education in America, to recognise the importance of finding a place in their curriculum for the proper treatment of this most interesting and suggestive study.

ONE morning, the hero took his alms-bowl and entered the city of Rajagriha. The people who passed him on the road admired his beauty and his noble bearing. "What is this man?" they wondered. "He is like a God, like Sakra or Brahma himself." Presently, it was noised abroad that a marvellous being was wandering through the city, begging. Every one wanted to see the hero; they followed him about, and women rushed to the windows as he passed by. But he gravely pursued his way, while over the city a strange light appeared.

A man ran to inform the king that a God, no less, was begging in the streets of the city. King Vimbasara went out on the terrace of the palace; he saw the hero. His splendor dazzled him. He sent him alms, and he gave orders to have him followed, in order to discover his retreat. Thus did the king learn that the magnificent beggar lived on the slope of the mountain, near the city.

The following day, Vimbasara drove out of the city and came to the mountain. He left his chariot, and, quite alone, walked toward a tree in whose shade the hero was seated. The king paused near the tree, and, speechless with wonder, reverently gazed at the beggar.

Then, bowing humbly, he said:

"I have seen you and great is my joy! Do not remain here on the lonely mountain-side; sleep no longer on the hard ground. You are beautiful, you are resplendent with youth; come to the city. I will give you a palace, and all your desires shall be gratified."

"My lord," replied the hero, in a gentle voice, "my lord, may you live many years! Desires mean nothing to me. I lead the life of a hermit; I know peace."

"You are young," said the king, "you are beautiful, you are ardent; be rich. You shall have the loveliest maidens in my kingdom to serve you. Do not go away; stay and be my companion."

"I have given up great riches," said the hero.

"I will give you half my kingdom."

"I have given up the most beautiful of kingdoms."

"Here you may gratify all your desires."

"I know the vanity of all desire. Desires are like poison; wise men despise them. I have thrown them away as one would throw away a wisp of dry straw. Desires are as perishable as the fruit on a tree, they are as wayward as the clouds in the sky, they are as treacherous as the rain, they are as changeable as the wind! Suffering is born of desire, for no man has ever gratified all his desires. But they that seek wisdom, they that ponder the true faith, they are the ones that find peace. Who drinks salt water increases his thirst; who flees from desire finds his thirst appeased. I no longer know desire. I seek the true law."

The king said:

"Great is your wisdom, O beggar! Which is your country? Where is your father? Where is your mother? Which is your caste? Speak."

"Perhaps you have heard of the city of Kapilavastu, O king? A prosperous city it is. The king, Suddhodana, is my father. I left him in order to wander and beg."

The king replied:

"Good fortune attend you! I am happy now that I have seen you. Between your family and mine there is a friendship of long standing. Be gracious to me, and when you have gained enlightenment, deign to teach me, O master."

He bowed three times, then returned to Rajagriha.

The hero heard that there lived near Rajagriha a famous hermit named Rudraka, son of Rama. This hermit had many disciples whom he instructed in the law. The hero went to listen to his teachings, but like Arata Kalama, Rudraka knew nothing of the true law, and the hero did not tarry.

Presently he came to the banks of the Nairanjana. Five of Rudraka's disciples: Kaundinya, Asvajit, Vashpa, Mahanaman and Bhadrika, had joined him.

THE clear waters of the Nairanjana flowed through a rich and fertile land. Little villages drowsed in the shade of magnificent trees, and great meadows stretched away into the distance. The hero thought, "How pleasant it is here; what an inviting spot in which to meditate! Perhaps, here, I shall find the path to wisdom. Here I shall dwell."

He became deeply absorbed in contemplation. He was so engrossed with his thoughts that he stopped breathing, and, one day, he fell into a swoon. The Gods, who were watching him from the sky, thought he was dead, and they cried:

"Is he dead, this child of the Sakyas? Has he died and left the world to its suffering?"

Maya, the hero's mother, lived among the Gods. She heard their cries and plaints, and she feared for the life of her son. Attended by a host of Apsarases, she descended to the banks of the Nairanjana, and when she saw Siddhartha, so stiff, so inert, she wept.

She said:

"When you were born in the garden, I was assured, O my son, that you would behold the truth. And later, Asita predicted that you would set the world free. But they were all lies, these predictions. You did not win fame by any royal conquest, you did not attain supreme knowledge! You died, pitifully and alone. Who will help you, O my son? Who will bring you back to life? For ten moons I carried you in my womb, O my jewel, and now I can only grieve."

She scattered flowers over the body of her son, whereupon he stirred and spoke to her in a gentle voice:

"Have no fear, mother; your labor was not in vain; Asita told you no lie. Even if the earth crumble into dust, even if Meru sink below the waters, even if the stars fall like rain upon the earth, I shall not die. I, alone, of all men, will survive the world's ruin! Do not weep, mother! The time is approaching when I shall attain supreme knowledge."

Maya smiled at her son's words; three times she bowed, then ascended to the sky, to the music of celestial lutes.

For six years, the hero remained on the banks of the river and meditated. He never sought shelter from the wind, from the sun or from the rain; he allowed the gadflies, the mosquitoes and the serpents to sting him. He was oblivious to the boys and girls, the shepherds and woodcutters, who jeered at him as they passed by and who sometimes threw dust or mud at him. He hardly ate: a fruit and a few grains of rice or of sesame composed his fare. He became very thin; his bones showed prominently. But under his gaunt forehead, his dilated eyes shone like stars.

And yet true knowledge did not come to him. He felt he was becoming very weak, and he realized that if he wasted away, he would never reach the goal he had set for himself. So he decided to take more nourishment.

There was a village called Uruvilva near the spot where Siddhartha spent long hours in meditation. The head man of this village had ten daughters. They revered the hero, and they brought him grain and fruit by way of alms. He rarely touched these gifts, but, one day, the girls noticed that he had eaten all they had offered him. The next day, they came with a large dish full of boiled rice, and he emptied that. The following day, each one brought a different delicacy, and the hero ate them all. He began to gain flesh, and, presently, he started going to the village to beg his food. The inhabitants vied with one another in giving him alms, and, before long, he had regained his strength and his beauty.

But the five disciples who had joined him said to each other:

"His austerities did not lead him into the path of true knowledge, and now he has ceased to practice them. He takes abundant nourishment; he seeks comfort. He no longer thinks of doing holy deeds. How can he, now, attain true knowledge? We considered him a wise man, but we were mistaken: he is a madman and a fool."

And they left him and went to Benares.

Siddhartha Under the Tree of Knowledge

THE hero's clothes had become threadbare in the six years he had been wearing them, and he thought: "It would be well if I had some new clothes; otherwise I shall have to go naked, and that would be immodest."

Now, Sujata, the most devout of the ten young girls who had been bringing him food, had a slave who had just died. She had wrapped the body in a shroud made of a reddish material and had had it carried to the cemetery. The dead slave was lying in the dust. The hero saw the body as he passed; he went over to it and removed the shroud.

It was very dusty, and the hero had no water in which to wash it. Sakra, from the sky, saw his perplexity. Coming down to earth he struck the ground, and a pool appeared before the eyes of the Saint.

"Good," said he, "here is water, but I still need a wash-stone."

Sakra made a stone and set it down on the edge of the pool.

"Man of virtue," said the God, "give me the shroud; I shall wash it for you."

"No, no," replied the Saint. "I know the duties of a monk; I myself shall wash the shroud."

When it was clean, he bathed. Now, Mara, the Evil One, had been watching for him for some time. He suddenly raised the banks of the pool, making them very steep. The Saint was unable to climb out of the water. Fortunately, there was a tall tree growing near the pool, and the Saint addressed a prayer to the Goddess who lived in it.

"O Goddess, may a branch of this tree bend over me!"

A branch immediately bent over the pool. The Saint caught hold of it and pulled himself out of the water. Then he went and sat down under the tree, and he began to sew on the shroud and make a new garment for himself.

Night came on. He fell asleep, and he had five dreams.

First, he saw himself lying in a large bed that was the whole earth; under his head, there was a cushion which was the Himalaya; his right hand rested on the western sea, his left hand on the eastern sea, and his feet touched the southern sea.

Then he saw a reed coming out of his navel, and the reed grew so fast that it soon reached the sky.

Then he saw worms crawling up his legs and completely covering them.

Then he saw birds flying toward him from all points of the horizon, and when the birds were near his head, they seemed to be of gold.

Finally, he saw himself at the foot of a mountain of filth and excrement; he climbed the mountain; he reached the summit; he descended, and neither the filth nor the excrement had defiled him.

He awoke, and from these dreams he knew that the day had come when, having attained supreme knowledge, he would become a Buddha.

He rose and set out for the village of Uruvilva, to beg.

Sujata had just finished milking eight wonderful cows that she owned. The milk they gave was rich, oily and of a delicate savor. She added honey and rice flour to it, then set the mixture to boil in a new pot, on a new stove. Huge bubbles began to form and kept floating off to the right, without the liquid rising or spilling a single drop. The stove did not even smoke. Sujata was astonished, and she said to Purna, her servant:

"Puma, the Gods are favoring us to-day. Go and see if the holy man is approaching the house."

Purna, from the doorstep, saw the hero walking toward

Sujata's house. He was diffusing a brilliant light, a golden light. Puma was dazzled. She ran back to her mistress.

"Mistress, he is coming! He is coming! And your eyes will be blinded by his splendor!"

"Let him come! Oh, let him come!" cried Sujata. "It is for him that I have prepared this wonderful milk."

She poured the milk mixed with honey and flour into a golden bowl, and she awaited the hero.

He entered. The house was lighted up by his presence. Sujata, to do him honor, bowed seven times. He sat down. Sujata kneeled and bathed his feet in sweet-scented water; then she offered him the golden bowl full of milk mixed with rice flour and honey. He thought:

"The Buddhas of old, it is said, had their last meal served to them in a golden bowl, before attaining supreme knowledge. Since Sujata offers me this milk and honey in a golden bowl, the time has come for me to be a Buddha."

Then he asked the young girl:

"Sister, what must I do with this golden bowl?"

"It belongs to you," she replied.

"I have no use for such a bowl," said he.

"Then do as you please with it," said Sujata. "It would be contemptible of me to offer the food and not offer the bowl."

He left, carrying the bowl in his hands, and he walked to the banks of the river. He bathed; he ate. When the bowl was empty, he threw it into the water, and he said:

"If I am to become Buddha this very day, may the bowl go upstream; if not, may it go with the current."

The bowl floated out to the middle of the river, then rapidly started upstream. It disappeared in a whirlpool, and the hero heard the muffled ring as it landed, in the subterranean world, among those other bowls the former Buddhas had emptied and thrown away.

The hero sauntered along the banks of the river. Night slowly descended. The flowers wearily closed their petals; a sweet fragrance rose from the fields and gardens; the birds timidly rehearsed their evensongs.

It was then the hero walked toward the tree of knowledge.

The road was sprinkled with gold-dust; rare palms, covered with precious stones, lined the way. He skirted the edge of a pool whose blessed waters exhaled an intoxicating perfume. White, yellow, blue and red lotuses spread their massive petals over the surface, and the air rang with the clear songs of the swans. Near the pool, under the palms, Apsarases were dancing, while in the sky the Gods were admiring the hero.

He approached the tree. On the side of the road, he saw Svastika, the reaper.

"They are tender, these grasses you are mowing, Svastika. Give me some grass; I want to cover the seat I shall occupy when I attain supreme knowledge. They are green, these grasses you are mowing, Svastika. Give me some grass, and you will know the law some day, for I shall teach it to you, and you may teach it to others."

The reaper gave the Saint eight handfuls of grass.

There stood the tree of knowledge. The hero went to the east of it and bowed seven times. He threw the handfuls of grass on the ground, and, suddenly, a great seat appeared. The soft grass covered it like a carpet.

The hero sat down, his head and shoulders erect, his face turned to the east. Then he said in a solemn voice:

"Even if my skin should parch, even if my hand should wither, even if my bones should crumble into dust, until I have attained supreme knowledge I shall not move from this seat."

And he crossed his legs.

Mara's Defeat

THE light emanating from the hero's body reached even to those realms where Mara, the Evil One, reigned supreme. It dazzled Mara, and he seemed to hear a voice saying:

"The hero who has renounced royalty, the son of Suddhodana, is now seated under the tree of knowledge. He is concentrating his mind, he is making the supreme effort, and soon he will bring to all creatures the help which they need. The road he will have taken, others will take. Once set free, he will set others free.

Once he has found peace, he will bring peace to others. He will enter nirvana, and he will cause others to enter. He will find wisdom and happiness, and he will give them to others. Because of him, the city of the Gods will be crowded; because of him, the city of the Evil One will be deserted. And you, Mara, a commander without an army, a king without subjects, will not know where to take refuge."

Mara was filled with apprehension. He tried to sleep, but his slumber was disturbed by terrible dreams. He awoke and summoned his servants and his soldiers. When they saw him, they became alarmed, and Sarthavaha, one of his sons, said to him:

"Father, you look pale and unhappy; your heart beats fast and your limbs tremble. What have you heard? What have you seen? Speak."

"Son," replied Mara, "the days of my pride are over. I heard a voice crying in the light, and it told me that the son of the Sakyas was seated under the tree of knowledge. And I had horrible dreams. A black cloud of dust settled over my palace. My gardens were bare of leaves, of flowers and of fruit. My ponds had dried up, and my swans and peacocks had their wings clipped. And I felt alone, amid this desolation. You had all deserted me. My queen was beating her breast and tearing her hair, as though haunted by remorse. My daughters were crying out in their anguish, and you, my son, were bowing before this man who meditated under the tree of knowledge! I wanted to fight my enemy, but I could not draw my sword from the scabbard. All my subjects fled in horror. Impenetrable darkness closed in upon me, and I heard my palace crashing to the ground."

Sarthavaha said:

"Father, it is disheartening to lose a battle. If you have seen these omens, bide your time, and do not run the chance of being ingloriously defeated."

But Mara, at the sight of the legions that surrounded him, felt his courage return. He said to his son:

"To the man of energy, a battle can end only in victory. We are brave; we will surely win. What strength can this man have? He is alone. I shall advance against him with a vast army, and I shall strike him down at the foot of the tree."

"Mere numbers do not make the strength of an army," said Sarthavaha, "The sun can outshine a myriad of glowworms. If wisdom is the source of his power, a single hero can defeat countless soldiers."

But Mara paid no heed. He ordered the army to advance at once, and Sarthavaha thought:

"He who is insane with pride will never recover."

Mara's army was a fearful sight. It bristled with pikes, with arrows and with swords; many carried enormous battle-axes and heavy clubs. The soldiers were black, blue, yellow, red, and their faces were terrifying. Their eyes were cruel flames; their mouths spewed blood. Some had the ears of a goat, others the ears of a pig or of an elephant. Many had bodies shaped like a jug. One had the paws of a tiger, the hump of a camel and the head of a donkey; another had a lion's mane, a rhinoceros' horn and a monkey's tail. There were many with two, four and five heads, and others with ten, twelve and twenty arms. In place of ornaments, they wore jawbones, skulls and withered human fingers. And shaking their hairy heads, they advanced with hideous laughter and savage cries:

"I can shoot a hundred arrows at one time; I shall seize the body of the monk." "My hand can crumple up the sun, the moon and the stars; how easy it will be to crush this man and his tree." "My eyes are full of poison: they would dry up the sea; I shall look at him, and he will burn to a cinder."

Sarthavaha kept to himself. A few friends had gathered around him, and they were saying:

"Fools! You think he is mad because he meditates; you think he is craven because he is calm. It is you who are madmen, it is you who are cowards. You do not know his power; because of his great wisdom he will defeat you all. Were your numbers as infinite as the grains of sand on the banks of the Ganges, you would not disturb a single hair of his head. And you believe you can kill him! Oh, turn back! Do not try to harm him; bow before him in reverence. His reign has come. The jackals howl in the forests when the lion is away, but when the lion roars, the jackals scamper off in terror. Fools, fools! You shout with pride while the master is silent, but when the lion speaks you will take to your heels,"

The army listened with contempt to these words of wisdom spoken by Sarthavaha and his friends. It kept advancing.

Before attacking the hero, Mara sought to frighten him. He roused against him the fury of the winds. Fierce gales rushed toward him from the horizon, uprooting trees, devastating villages, shaking mountains, but the hero never moved; not a single fold of his robe was disturbed.

The Evil One summoned the rains. They fell with great violence, submerging cities and scarring the surface of the earth, but the hero never moved; not a single thread of his robe was wet.

The Evil One made blazing rocks and hurled them at the hero. They sped through the air but changed when they came near the tree, and fell, not as rocks, but flowers.

Mara then commanded his army to loose their arrows at his enemy, but the arrows, also, turned into flowers. The army rushed at the hero, but the light he diffused acted as a shield to protect him; swords were shivered, battie-axes were dented by it, and whenever a weapon fell to the ground, it, too, at once changed into a flower.

And, suddenly, filled with terror at the sight of these prodigies, the soldiers of the Evil One fled.

And Mara wrung his hands in anguish, and he cried:

"What have I done that this man should defeat me? For they are not a few, those whose desires I have granted! I have often been kind and generous! Those cowards who are fleeing could bear witness to that."

The troops that were still within hearing answered:

"Yes, you have been kind and generous. We will bear witness to that."

"And he, what proof has he given of his generosity?" continued Mara. "What sacrifices has he made? Who will bear witness to his kindness?"

Whereupon a voice came out of the earth, and it said:

"I will bear witness to his generosity."

Mara was struck dumb with astonishment. The voice continued:

"Yes, I, the Earth, I, the mother of all beings, will bear witness to his generosity. A hundred times, a thousand times, in the course of his previous existences, his hands, his eyes, his head, his whole body have been at the service of others. And in the course of this existence, which will be the last, he will destroy old age, sickness and death. As he excels you in strength, Mara, even so does he surpass you in generosity."

And the Evil One saw a woman of great beauty emerge from the earth, up to her waist. She bowed before the hero, and clasping her hands, she said: "O most holy of men, I bear witness to your generosity."

Then she disappeared.

And Mara, the Evil One, wept because he had been defeated.

6

Some Notes on the History of Buddhism

A NY presentation of Buddhism would be veiy .imperfect without at least an attempt to sketch the most instructive and suggestive history of the curious developments which, during its long career, it has, in different times and places, under-gone. This history is especially interesting from a comparative point of view. Buddhism starts with a complete philosophical and psychological theory-worked out by men of great intellectual power and considerable culture. It took its rise among an ad- vancing and conquering people full of pride in their colour and their race, in their achievements and their progress. It advocated a view in many re- spects far in advance of what had been reached and, for the matter of that, of what has even now been reached by the average philosophic and religious mind. It made its first conquests in a great conti-nent occupied by peoples of various races and hold-ing widely different views ; their leaders often, it is true, well trained in philosophic thought, but the mass of the folk entangled in multiform varieties of an indiscriminating animism. And it soon spread over the frontiers among nations, some of them more barbarous still than the then most uncultured Indians. Buddhism has been adopted by the wild hordes on the cold table-lands of Nepal,

Tartary, and Tibet, by the cultured Chinese in their varying climes, in the peninsula of Korea, whence it spread to the islands of Japan, and by the Sinhalese and Siamese under the palm groves of the south. It has penetrated on the west to the confines of Europe ; on the north it numbers its adherents amid the snow and ice of Siberia ; and in the far east it was the dominant religion for centuries in the beautiful islands of the Javanese archipelago. Wherever it has gone it has been so modified by the national characteristics and the inherited beliefs of its converts, acting upon the natural tendencies within it- self to alteration and decay, that it has developed, under these conditions, into strangely inconsistent and even antagonistic beliefs and practices. But each of these beliefs breathes more or less of the spirit of the system out of which they all alike have grown, and most interesting it is to trace the causes which have produced out of it such different results.

It would be premature to attempt, in our present state of knowledge, to trace any development in doc-trine in the sacred books themselves. Except in one particular, the system presented to our view in the dialogues, as repeated in the Anguttara and Sam-yutta Nikayas, as developed in the psychological books, and as used as the basis of the poetry, pre-sents the picture of a continuous and consistent whole. And this is not surprising considering the perfection of the system as it came from the hands of the Master, and the intellectual activity, and en-thusiastic culture, of the men by whom it was first handed down. But in the century or two after the death of Gotama, during which the books, as we have them, were put into their present shape, there was time enough for a very considerable growth of opinion concerning the person of their revered teacher.

Most of these developments were due to the later books after the canon was closed. The various de- tails referred to in Lecture III., in which the later accounts of the Jataka, and of the Sanskrit poems, have been anticipated in an unpublished Suttanta, relate only to the legend of his birth.* And even on this matter the later versions are, as one would expect, much more expanded.

But the first disruption in the Order took place on other questions, namely, on matters connected with the regulation of the Order itself. One hundred years after the death of Buddha, according to the oldest account preserved in an appendix to the Khandakas, there arose a certain party in the Order which proclaimed and practised a loosening of the rules in ten particulars. These ten particulars seem to us now to be very trumpery ; just as the disputes between the Irish and Romish sections of the Christian Church at the synod of Whitby, held in the seventh century, seem to us moderns to be concerning matters of little moment, the exact position and shape of the tonsure and the exact dating of the Easter festival. No doubt in both cases there were greater differences behind, and though these are not apparent in the most ancient Buddhist account they come out very strongly in later writers.

As I have given the whole list of the ten indulgences in my manual, Buddhism, I need not repeat them here ; and will only remind you that the last and most important of them was, that gold and silver might be received by members of the Order.

To put an end to the disputes upon these points a Council of the leading members of the Order was held at Vesāli and the heretical opinions were condemned. The long-continued struggle on the question as important for the history of Buddhism as the Arian controversy for that of Christianity agitated the whole Buddhist world to its very centre.

And the decision on the point, given at this Council of Vesali, led to a serious schism in the Buddhist Church.

Now the ten indulgences are each summed up in a single word ; and these words are, each and all of them, conspicuous by their absence from the books on the laws and regulations of the Order included in the canon, except that they appear in an historical account added, quite evidently as an appendix, to the collection of treatises, or Khandakas, described in my second lecture. This fact is of the very greatest importance in determining the date at which those Khandakas must have been composed.

The ten points in dispute were all matters of ecclesiastical law. They all related to observances of the Brotherhood. Is it probable that, in a set of rules and treatises which seek to set forth, down to the minutest detail, and even with hair-splitting diffuseness, all that has any relation to the daily life of the Brethren and the regulation of the Buddhist Order, is it probable that, in such a collection, if, when it was compiled, the struggle on these ten points had already burst into flame, there should be no reference at all, even in interpolations, to any one of these ten disputes ? That the difference of opinion on each of the ten points remains altogether unnoticed in that part of the rules and treatises where, in the natural order of things, it would be obviously referred to that the rules are not in any way altered to cover, or to suggest, any decision of the points in dispute, and that they are only mentioned in an appendix where the Council held to decide them is described, shows clearly that the rules and treatises, as we have them, must have been put together before the time when the Council of Vesali was held.

The ancient story of the Council stops at the point where the ten indulgences are rejected. But the Ceylon chronicles, which have preserved the tradition of the orthodox school (and are therefore, notwithstanding their later date, very good evidence as against that school), admit that the matter did not rest there. They say that the adherents of the ten indulgences proceeded to hold a council of their own, and I will read you the account of what they admit that the heretics did. The animus of the description only entitles it to a greater confidence.

The Dipa Vansa, the older of the two Chronicles in question, has the following words :

" The monks of the Great Council twisted the teaching round.

They broke up the original scriptures and made a new recension, A chapter put in one place they put in another, And distorted the sense and the doctrine of the Five Nikayas.

These monks who knew neither what had been spoken at length Nor what had been spoken in abstract, neither What was the obvious nor what the higher meaning Put things referring to one matter as if they referred to another, And destroyed much of the spirit by holding to the shadow of the letter.

They partly rejected the Sutta, and the Vinaya so deep,

And made another rival Sutta and Vinaya of their own.

The Parivara abstract, and the book of the Abhidhamma, The Patisambhida, the Niddesa, and a portidh of the Jataka, So much they put aside, and made others in their place. They rejected the well known rules of nouns and genders too, Of composition and of literary skill, and put others in their place."

This council of the heretics we see was called, as the orthodox chroniclers admit, " The Great Council," which seems to show that the number of its adherents was not to be despised ; and from it, in the next two centuries and a half, seventeen bodies of more or less heretical doctrine were gradually formed in the Buddhist Church. These were not sects in our sense. There was no division of organisation, or church government. There were no such things as churches, or church services ; and the divi-sions, such as they were, remained solely differences of opinion. Various schools were named, for the most part, after the names of some great teachers, or after the locality in which they took their rise.

Only a few of the names refer to matters of doctrine.

The division did not therefore correspond to the division between Greek Catholics, Roman Catholics, Episcopalians, Independents, and so forth, but rather to the division between Broad, High, and Low Church. We have, unfortunately, none of their early books surviving. It would appear, from the passage just read from the Dlpa Vansa, that all the schools continued to use the books in the Pitakas, though they made changes in some of them. For the only books which they are stated $o have rejected are those of the Abhidhamma, and three prose works included in the Appendix described to you in my second lecture, and one other, the Parivara, or student's manual, which has been added to the canon law, that is to the Rules and the Treatises.

The canon law itself was in fact retained, subject no doubt to slight alterations and differences of inter-pretation. So also it is not stated that they rejected any of the Dialogues, or even the great rearrange-ments of Buddhist doctrine in the Anguttara and Sarpyutta Nikayas.

It is scarcely credible that, had they done so, it would not have been thrown in their teeth by the orthodox chroniclers and commentators ; and it is expressly implied that they accepted, and continued to use, all the books of religious and philosophical poetry. Even as late as the time of Asoka we find that Tissa, the son of Moggall, the author of the Katha Vatthu, in his arguments against those who differed from the orthodox school, appeals through-out to the Pitaka texts, and takes it for granted that his opponents will acknowledge them as decisive.

But no doubt the leaders of the various schools did, from time to time, compile works now lost, but of which we may some day be able to gather some fragments from Sanskrit, Tibetan, and Chinese manuscripts still extant, though not translated.

As to the actual points at issue, the best authority is, of course, the Katha Vatthu itself. The author states the various theses put forward by his opponents, but does not specify who they are, nor to what school they belong. This information is afforded to us by the Commentary on the Katha Vatthu, which has been edited in full for the Pali Text Society, although it has not been translated.

This traditional interpretation and identification of the schools referred to was handed down in the seats of orthodox learning; and the Pali version of it, still preserved to us, has come from the great Buddhist seminary of the Maha Vihara in Ceylon. There is no reason why the supporters of the orthodox school should have modified or recast this tradition.

There may have been mistakes, no doubt, but, in the absence of any motive to the contrary, there is no valid reason for refusing to accept the tradition as a bona-fide statement of what they held to be true.

Now this work and its commentary are so important for a history of the development of Buddhism that, although much pressed by other work which prevented my undertaking an edition of the text, I made a complete analysis, from a manuscript in my possession, of each of the questions raised in the Katha Vatthu, and published it in 1892 in the Journal of the Royal Asiatic Society. It is impossible here to discuss the results in any detail, but two general conclusions may be stated with advantage.

In the first place, there had survived, at the time when

the Katha Vatthu was written (that is to say, in B. C. 250), only a small proportion of the seven-teen schools, whose names have been handed down by tradition. Some of them only come before us in the pages of the Katha Vatthu Commentary as the supporters of one or two theses of no very great importance.

But five of the schools are mentioned pretty fre- quently, and of these, the two principal are the Uttara-pathakas, or Northerners, and the Dakkhina- pathakas, or Southerners. This conclusion is entirely confirmed from two sources, which are mutually quite independent.

The one is the inscriptions. Among the ruins of the Buddhist topes, now being investigated by the Archeological Survey of India, are found a number of votive tablets on which are inscribed the names of the donors. For the most part these are personal names only, but quite occasionally the name of the school to which the person belonged is incidentally added. No doubt at the time when the tablets were put up there may have been two or more persons of the same name living in the 'locality, and the de-scription is added for the sake of distinction. I have collected all the instances of this in my article, and the result agrees with the conclusions derived from the Katha Vatthu and its Commentary.

The other confirmation comes from a source not so authoritative as being much later. But it is equally independent and more complete. Yuan Thsang, in the account of his travels in India, mentions, in regard to each locality, the estimated number of Buddhist recluses in each place at that time, the early part of the seventh century.

The list is a very long one, but I have thoroughly analysed it in an article in the Journal of the Royal Asiatic Society for 1892. The conclusions to be drawn from it as to the comparative prevalence of the various schools substantially coincide with the conclusions drawn from the KathaVatthu and its commentary.

The subject-matter of the differences in opinion between the orthodox and the other schools had, no doubt, in the time of Yuan Thsang assumed greater proportions. He gives no details, but it seems from the Katha Vatthu that, in B. c. 250, the differences were principally of three kinds. In the first place we find that in the North and also in the South the old heresy of the soul-theory had crept back by side issues into the doctrine from which it had been categorically and explicitly excluded by Gotama and his earlier followers. In the second place we find that the exaltation of their revered Master had led some of his followers to go far beyond the belief in objective miraculous phenomena at his birth and at his death, and had produced a belief also in the personal superiority of their Master above the ordinary laws which govern human life. They not only believed that the earth was illumined at his birth, that flowers fell from heaven, that his mother's conception was immaculate, that he was transfigured before the eyes of his disciples, that an earthquake was occasioned by his birth and death, but that he himself was " Lokuttara " (above the common, super-human, transcendental), not only in moments of supreme enlightenment, but in all the ordinary affairs of life. And thirdly, we find the germs of a belief we shall meet with farther on which proved even more disruptive in its tendency than either of the two we have mentioned that is, that the real ideal for the Buddhist to aim at was, not Arahatship, the centre point and crown of the earlier Buddhism, but Bodhisatship, the essential doctrine of what is self-complacently called by its followers the Maha Yana, or Greater Vehicle.

All these three notions do in fact hang together, support one another, and have eventually developed into a system diametrically antagonistic to Gotama's own doctrine of a salvation in this life in Arahatship by self-culture and self-control. The materials are not yet available from which an accurate history of the fall can be drawn out in consecutive order, or in sufficiency of detail ; and I do not envy the his torian who shall take up the task of tracing the gradual intrusion of animistic and transcendental views, and beliefs in the supernatural, into the purely human and psychological ethics of the earlier system. But it is already possible to show the lines along which the later speculation went, and to trace the causes of the recrudescence of the errors which Gotama's reform was intended to kill.

You will recollect that there is included in the Buddhist canon a collection of the Indian folk-lore of that time, in which Gotama the Buddha himself in a previous birth has been identified with the hero of each particular story. The greatness and good-ness and insight of the Buddha were in the eyes of his followers much too perfect to have been wrought out or developed in a single lifetime. Through ages upon ages he had gradually exercised himself in the Pdrdmitds (or sublime conditions), necessary to the attainment of Buddhahood. These are Generosity and Kindness and Renunciation and Wisdom and Resolution and Patience and Love of Truth and Energy and Good-will and Equanimity. At the end of each existence the Karma, that is, the doing or action accumulated in the previous birth, was handed on to a new individual who (though from the Christian point of view different from the others as having no continuing memory and no consciousness of identity) was, according to the Buddhist standpoint, the same individual, as being the product of the same Karma. And the Buddhist books glow with the fervour of gratitude in passages where they de-scribe the self-abnegation of the Blessed One who submitted to be born again and again, that he might! v bring about the emancipation of mankind. For all through this time, whenever he was re-born as a man, he might, according to the view even of the orthodox school, have attained to Arahatship. The Karma which he inherited would no longer, then, have been re-individualised. It would have been dissipated in the good effect which his actions, his Karma, might have had upon other individuals.

But that particular chain of existence would have been broken, the Pdrdmitds would never have been accomplished, and Gotama would not have become the Buddha. The Buddha therefore had, in his pre-vious existences, deliberately abandoned that ideal which, in his historical existence, he urged men to set before them as their goal.

It is scarcely surprising, therefore, that the mistake began to be made of regarding the Bodhisat (that is, one of the individuals in the chain of those who were perfecting the Pdrdmitds) as a higher being than the Arahat. I say the mistake, for it was a mistake in two senses. The old Buddhist tradition rarely states that the Bodhisat was consciously pur-suing the aim of becoming a Buddha. I only know of one passage older than the fifth century of our era in which this idea is put forward. And it was also a mistake from the ethical point of view.

For from the moment that Arahatship began to be looked down upon in comparison with Bodhisatship, the whole system of mental training and self-control began to be neglected and even ignored.

The results of this took a long time to work out their full effect. One standard work of perhaps the principal of the seventeen schools the Lokuttara-vadins, or Transcendentalists has survived. It is written in Sanskrit, and is being now edited, with a quite unusual degree both of care and of scholar-ship, by M. femile Senart of Paris. The date of the work has not been ascertained with any certainty, but it is probably at least as old as the second century B.C. These Transcendentalists were the school which represented most nearly the views of those who held the Great Council ; and so far as the edition has gone, it gives a very curious view of the position which they held. I have not noticed a single passage in which any of the propositions laid down in the Dialogues, is, in so many words, denied or even disputed ; but the whole point of view has become entirely different, and it must have required a considerable time for so great a change to have taken place. Practically speaking the whole burden of the Dialogues is Arahatship, or one or other of the thirty-seven constituent elements of Arahatship. In the Maha Vastu, which is the name of this manual of the Transcendentalists, Arahatship is indeed incidentally taken for granted as an ideal, if not the ideal. But the burden of the book is the consideration, from various points, of the stages which lead, not to Arahatship, but to Bodhisatship. It will be easier to speak more absolutely when M. Senart shall have finished his great work, but this is the impression which the volumes already published make upon the careful reader.

In the " Lotus of the Good Law " (the Sad-dharma Pundarika, as it is called in Sanskrit), of which we have a French translation by M. Burnouf, and a translation into English by Prof. Kern of Leiden, we find a stage far beyond that which has been reached in the Maha Vastu of the Transcen-dentalists. In the Lotus we find that Arahatship is explicitly condemned, and Bodhisàtship held up as the goal at which every good Buddhist has to aim ; and the whole exposition of this theory, so subver-sive of the original Buddhism, is actually placed in the mouth of Gotama himself. The doctrine of Bodhisatship as the ideal is here called the Greater Vehicle, as opposed to the Lesser Vehicle of Arahatship.

The Maha Yana doctors said, in effect : " We grant you

all you say about the bliss of attaining Nirvana in this life. But it produces advantage chiefly to yourselves. And according to your own theory there will be a necessity for Buddhas in the future as much as there has been for Buddhas in the past.

Greater, higher, nobler, then, than the attainment of Arahatship must be the attainment of Bodhisatship from a desire to save all living creatures in the ages that will come."

The new teaching therefore was in no conscious contradiction to the old. It accepted it all and was based upon it. Its distinguishing characteristic was the great stress which is laid on one point of the earlier doctrine to the gradual overshadowing of the rest. Its strength lay in the grandeur of its appeal to self-renunciation. It is true the newer school un-consciously thereby changed the centre point of the system, the focus of their mental vision. But it was at least no slight merit to have been led, even though they were led astray, by a sense of duty to the race. They might have been wiser, had they seen more clearly the originality of Gotama's sys-tem of ethics, and perceived that the race would really be benefited much more largely by the older doctrine of Arahatship, than by the new stress upon Bodhisatship. But readers of the Maha Yana books, tedious as these have so often been called, and rightly called, will find them acquire a new sig-nificance, and even a new beauty, when they are read in the light of this conception. The whole history of this development of belief, firstly in the putting of Arahatship into the background, and putting the Jataka stories and the road of Bodhisatship into the foreground ; and then the actual contempt of Arahatship, and the adoption, to its explicit as well as its virtual exclusion, of Bodhisatship, has yet to be written. The final step is attributed by later chroniclers, Tibetan and Chinese, to Nagarjuna. And there are works extant, though only in Tibetan and Chinese translations, which are attributed to him. These works, however, are not yet accessible to the West ; and of the Hlna Yana books (that is to say, the books of the older schools which led on to the final result) we have only the Maha Vastu, and the Sanskrit poems on the life of Buddha which were mentioned in my third lecture. But it is possible already to point out some of the results which followed from the newer doctrine. That the progress was very slow we know from the statements of Yuan Thsang. For in his time, that is, as late as the sixth century of our era, two thirds of the members of the Buddhist Order still adhered to the older doctrine. And in Nalanda, thegreat Buddhist university of that time, both the schools seem to have been represented.

As the Bodhisat theory loomed larger and larger before the minds of the Buddhists, their thoughts naturally turned with peculiar reverence to the Bodhisats of the past, the present, and the future, rather than to the Arahats whose names are recorded in the sacred books. Thus Nagarjuna himself is looked upon by the Chinese as a Bodhisat, and Yuan Thsang mentions a number of persons, leaders in the newer school, with the title of Bodhisat. So the " Lotus of the Good Law " imitates the older Dialogues by giving a kind of introductory story describing the place and the occasion, on which Gotama is said to have propounded this much later work. And the persons to whom it is addressed, the assembly which surrounded him on that occasion, consists of a number of Bodhisats, instead of the actual persons by whom we know that the historical Buddha was in his lifetime surrounded.

For not only were distinguished human beings singled out as Bodhisats, but a vast number of hypothetical beings were introduced as objects of reverence and worship on the ground that they were Bodhisats. As time went on, converts to this later Buddhism, who were well acquainted with the Hindu gods and goddesses of the day, thought to bring about a reconciliation between the two faiths by simply turning the Hindu gods and goddesses into Bodhisats, and representing them as supporters of the Buddha.

One of the chief agents in this line of development seems to have been Asanga, an influential monk of Peshawur in the Panjab, who lived and wrote the first text-book of the creed the Yogacara Bhumi Qastra about the sixth century of our era.

He managed with great dexterity to reconcile the two opposing systems by placing a number of Saivite gods in the Pantheon of his newer Buddhism, and by incorporating into it a great deal of mystic Tantric doctrine from the prevalent animism. He thus made it possible for the half-converted, rude tribes to remain Buddhists while they brought offerings, and even bloody offerings, to these more congenial shrines ; and while their practical beliefs had no relation at all to the four Truths or the Noble Eightfold Path, but busied itself almost wholly with attaining magic powers (Siddhi), by means of magic phrases (Dharani) and magic circles (Man-dala). These Maha Yana books inculcating the new doctrines were translated, along with the older ones, into Chinese. Yuan Thsang regarded himself as a Mahayanist, took many books of the Greater Vehicle back to China, and in his labours as a translator was imitated by a long line of workers in the same field. The later books were afterwards translated into Tibetan, and the new doctrine attained in Tibet to so great a development, that Tibetan Buddhism, or rather Lamaism, has come to be the exact contrary of the earlier Buddhism. It has been worked up there into a regular system which has shut out all of the earlier Buddhism, although a few of the earlier books are also to be found in Tibetan translations.

In China, on the contrary, we find no evidence of a special system. All the books, early and late, are mixed together in one heterogeneous collection.

Though no doubt the books of the Great Vehicle have by far the preponderating influence, yet books of various ages are still studied, and different schools in China have adopted different degrees of the newer doctrine.

Buddhism was introduced into Japan in the sixth century from the Korea, and having started there at so late a date, it has retained very little of the older doctrine, except the theories of impermanence, of the sorrow inherent in individuality, and of the absence of any abiding principle as set out in my fourth lecture. There are indeed now many sects of Buddhists in that country, but their divisions are entirely distinct from the divisions into Greater and Lesser Vehicle. All of them are founded on the Greater Vehicle, and they have developed in various ways along purely local lines. There are even members of the Order to be found there who are married clergy, and who preach a salvation to be reached in heaven.

But it is especially in Tibet that the doctrine of Bodhisatship has received its most curious development ; and there alone is it, that the head of the Buddhist Order has also become the temporary ruler of the state, and is considered as being him-self a living Bodhisat. In my Hibbert Lectures there will be found (pp. 192-195) a statement of the very curious and interesting similarities between this latest phase of the corruption of Buddhism, and the latest phase of Christianity in Rome.

In this connection I shall doubtless be expected to say a few words on Theosophy, if only because one of the books giving an account of that very curious and widely spread movement has been called Esoteric Buddhism, It has always been a point of wonder to me why the author should have chosen this particular title for his treatise. For if there is anything that can be said with absolute certainty about the book it is, that it is not esoteric, and not Buddhism. The original Buddhism was the very contrary of esoteric. Gotama was accus-tomed, throughout his long career, to speak quite openly to everyone of the whole of the view of life which he had to propound. No doubt there were a certain number of questions to which it was his habit to refuse to reply. These were questions the discussion of which, in his opinion, was apt to lead the mind astray, and so far from being conducive to a growth in insight, would be a hindrance to the only thing which was supremely worth aiming at, the perfect life in Arahatship. The reason for his reticence was not at all that he had formulated any doctrine upon them which he wished to conceal from some people, and reveal only to other more intimate disciples. Such questions as What shall I be during the ages of the future ? Do I after all exist, or am I not ? How am I ? This is a being : Whence did it come ? And whither will it go ? are regarded as worse than unprofitable, and the Buddha not only refused to discuss them, but held that the tendency, the desire to discuss them was a weakness, and that the answers usually given were a delusion. There are a whole set of such questions, drawn up in identical words in several of the Dialogues, a considera-tion of which is called the Walking in Delusion, the Jungle, the Wilderness, the Puppet Show, the Writhing, the Fetter of Delusion. Gotama says, just before he dies, in a passage I have already read to you: " I have preached the truth without making any distinction between exoteric and esoteric doctrine ; for in respect of the truths, Ananda, the Tathagata has no such thing as the closed fist of a teacher who keeps some things back." And it is quite impossible for anyone who reads the Pali books to avoid seeing that everything which the Master himself, and his early disciples, regarded as important is not only set out with a lavish exposition which seeks above all to make the whole matter clear to everybody, but is even explained with a length of detail which those not interested in the system find tedious in the extreme. There is not the slightest hint throughout the whole of the Pitakas of any esoteric teaching. And even as late as the Milinda we find the ideal teacher described in the following words: "He should be zealous, teach nothing partially, keep nothing secret, and hold nothing back' It is only when the Maha Yana books, written many centuries after the time of Gotama, wished to father on the Buddha opinions different from those which he actually promulgated, that we find the allegation, in Buddhist books, of an esoteric teaching. It was the only way in which the writers of those books could at the same time call themselves Buddhist followers of Gotama, and yet put forward the new ideas, contrary to those of Gotama, which they were anxious to propagate.

And not only was there nothing esoteric in the real original Buddhism. The views expressed in Esoteric Buddhism, so far as they are Indian at all, are not esoteric. The study of self-induced trance is common to all the Indian schools. All that is taught on the subject is accessible in handbooks, and the teachers who practised themselves in such things are always willing to teach them to anyone who will submit to the necessary discipline. In this sense only is it that Indian teachers, other than the Buddhist, can occasionally be described as esoteric.

And this is a sense in which the word is also applicable to our own teachers in the universities of the West. They will not admit to their classes any chance comer who has not undergone the necessary discipline to enable him to appreciate what they have to say. All the talk about " astral body " and the different kinds of " soul/' seven more or less, which is, or rather was, put forward as esoteric Buddhism, is a part of the Yoga philosophy of India, which is perfectly accessible to all the world.

And so far as I have been able to ascertain (though the

later Buddhists were much given to magic and Tantric charms), this happens to be a part of the current Indian belief on those subjects which even they have never adopted. It is of course diametric-ally opposed to all the most essential Buddhist doc-trines as set out in outline in my last two lectures.

You will see therefore, why I venture to say that the views put forward, in the work referred to, are neither esoteric, nor are they Buddhism.

At the same time it is fair to add that Theo-sophists in general do not any longer, I believe, describe their tenets under the name of Esoteric Buddhism, and we must not forget that there are Theosophists and Theosophists. There are not a few among them who are doing good service in helping to break down that ignorant self-compla- cency which regards any notions differing from the current notions held in the West as quite unworthy of notice. There are not a few of them who have really devoted themselves to a patient study of Eastern philosophies and Eastern religions, and who have rendered real service to scholarship by bringing over MSS. and providing funds for the publication of translations of Eastern books. There may be much in Theosophy which suggests a superficial curiosity into obscure questions of psycho-physics, and into half-savage practices of magic, black and white. But no one can doubt the sincerity of such Theosophists as those to whom I have just referred.

I regret that an unfortunate title, now no longer emphasised by Theosophists themselves, should have led very widely to a confusion between a great and sane system of philosophical ethics, and speculations of very doubtful validity (really in many instances, the rebound of half-trained intellects from a crass materialism) and mixed up with his-torical heresies of a most startling character.

It is very instructive to notice the fact that the name of Buddhism has been rejected by the leading expounders of Theosophy. This fact is really an unconscious tribute to the success of the efforts that have been made in the last few years to render the authorities of the real, original Buddhism accessible to the Western world. And I venture to think that the publication and translation of the Buddhist texts may possibly have no little influence among the more cultured of those Eastern peoples, who still call themselves Buddhists although they have wan-dered, in many respects, so far from the ancient faith. When Japanese students, for instance, come to our Western colleges and learn there to read their Pali and Sanskrit books under the guidance of professors trained in historical criticism, it is almost impossible that they can return to their own country without the accuracy of their knowledge being greatly improved, and their ideas of Buddhism, to some extent at least, corrected and modified. We have an admirable instance of this in the very valuable catalogue of Chinese Sanskrit books published by Mr. Bunyiu Nanjio, at the University Press of Oxford. Prepared under the guidance of the distinguished Professor of Comparative Philology at Oxford, Professor Max Muller, this book is a model of what such a catalogue ought to be, with discussions about dates, and careful indexes to all the names of the books and authors mentioned. Mr. Bunyiu Nanjio, while in London and Oxford, studied Buddhist Sanskrit, and has now returned to Japan to occupy the post of Professor at the University of Tokio.

This is one of the excellent results following on the increased intercommunication between East and West which are now becoming so frequent, and which we owe to the victories over nature achieved by Western science. It was the desire of peoples to travel and have intercourse with one another which was one of the principal means of spurring on inventions. And the inventions, in their turn, have made possible such a meeting as the Parliament of Religions at Chicago, where minds steeped exclusively in Western and New-World ideas listened, not only with interest, but also with sympathy, greatly heightened by the presence of their representatives, to the expositions of Eastern creeds.

It is true that a perusal of the numerous speeches made at that Congress (and I have read the Buddhist ones very carefully) show how astounding is the gulf on all sides between popular beliefs and the conclusions of scholarship. To take only one instance from the address on Buddha by the Right Rev.

Zitsuzen Ashitsu of Japan. He says : " The Person of Buddha is perfectly free from life and death. We call it Nehan or Nirvana. Nehan is divided into four classes:

(1) The name given to the nature of Buddha which has neither beginning nor end and is entirely clear of lust like a perfect mirror. But such an excellent nature as I have mentioned is not the peculiar property of Buddha, but every being in the world has just the same constitution.

(2) The name given to the state, little advanced from the above, where we perceive that our solicitude is fleeting, our lives are inconstant, and even that there is no such thing as Ego. In this state our mind is quite empty and clear, but there still remains one thing, the body. So it is called Uyo, or something left.

(3) The state in which our body and intellect come to entire annihilation and there is nothing traceable, therefore this state is called Muyo, or nothing left.

(4) The state when we get perfect intellectual wis-dom. We are not any more subject to birth and death. Also we become perfectly merciful ; we are not content with the

indulging state of highest Nirvana ; but we appear to the beings of every class to save them from prevailing pains by imparting the pleasure of Nirvana. Out of these four classes of Nirvana the first and last are called the Nirvana of Mahayana, the Greater Vehicle, while the remainder are that of Hina Yana, the Lesser Vehicle. We must of course take into consideration, in this quotation, the imperfection of the English. But the curious thing about it is that the views here ascribed to the Hina Yana, can not be found, so far as we know, in any Hina Yana book. And this difficulty does not seem to have occurred to the learned author, who also distinctly states that the Maha Yana books (really many centuries later) were com-piled by the disciples of the Buddha, meaning no doubt his personal followers. It will be very inter-esting to be able to trace how these notions passed through the intermediate stages between the doc-trine of the Pitakas and the doctrine here set forth.

I have not time now to discuss the resemblances and differences which are involved, but it will be apparent to you all how different is the tone of the passage I have just quoted from the passages I have had occasion to read from the Buddhist Pitakas themselves.

MONTHS passed. Then, one day, the queen knew that the time was approaching for her son to be born. She went to King Suddhodana, and she said to him:

"My lord, I would wander through the happy gardens. Birds are singing in the trees, and the air is bright with flower-dust. I would wander through the happy gardens."

"But it will weary you, O queen," replied Suddhodana. "Are you not afraid?"

"The innocent being that I carry in my womb must be born amid the innocence of budding flowers. No, I will go, O master, I will go into the flower-gardens."

The king yielded to Maya's wish. He said to his servants:

"Go into the gardens and deck them out in silver and in gold. Drape the trees with precious hangings. Let everything be magnificent, for the queen will pass."

Then he addressed Maya:

"Array yourself, to-day, in great splendor, O Maya. Ride in a gorgeous palanquin; let your most beautiful maidens carry you. Order your servants to use rare perfumes; have them wear ropes of pearls and bracelets of precious stones; have them carry lutes and drums and flutes, and sing sweet songs that would delight the Gods themselves."

Suddhodana was obeyed, and when the queen reached the palace-gates the guards greeted her with joyous cries. Bells peeled gaily, peacocks spread their gorgeous tail-feathers, and the song of swans throbbed in the air.

They came to a wood where the trees were in bloom, and Maya ordered them to set down the palanquin. She stepped out and began wandering about, aimlessly. She was happy. And behold! she found a rare tree, the branches drooping under their burden of blossoms. She went up to it; gracefully extending her hand, she drew down a branch. Suddenly, she stood very still. She smiled, and the maidens who were near her received a lovely child into their arms.

At that same moment all that was alive in the world trembled with joy. The earth quivered. Songs and the patter of dancing feet echoed in the sky. Trees of all seasons burst into flower, and ripe fruit hung from the branches. A pure, serene light appeared in the sky. The sick were rid of their suffering. The hungry were satisfied. Those to whom wine had played false became sober. Madmen recovered their reason, the weak their strength, the poor their wealth. Prisons opened their gates. The wicked were cleansed of all evil.

One of Maya's maidens hastened to King Suddhodana and joyously exclaimed:

"My lord, my lord, a son is born to you, a son who will bring great glory to your house!"

He was speechless. But his face was radiant with joy, and he knew great happiness.

Presently he summoned all the Sakyas, and he commanded them to accompany him into the garden where the child had been born. They obeyed, and, with a host of brahmans in attendance, they formed a noble retinue as they gravely followed the king.

When he came near the child, the king made a deep obeisance, and he said:

"Do you bow as I bow before the prince, to whom I give the name Siddhartha."

They all bowed, and the brahmans, inspired by the Gods, then sang:

"All creatures are happy, and they are no longer rough, those roads travelled by men, for he is born, he who gives happiness: he will bring happiness into the world. In the darkness a great light has dawned, the sun and the moon are like dying embers, for he is born, he who gives light: he will bring light into the world.

The blind see, the deaf hear, the foolish have recovered their reason, for he is born, he who restores sight, and restores hearing, and restores the mind: he will bring sight, he will bring hearing, he will bring reason into the world. Perfumed zephyrs ease the suffering of mankind, for he is born, he who heals: he will bring health into the world. Flames are no longer pitiless, the flow of rivers has been stayed, the earth has trembled gently: he will be the one to see the truth."

Asita's Prediction

THE great hermit Asita, whose austerities were pleasing to the Gods, heard of the birth of him who was to save mankind from the torment of rebirth. In his thirst for the true law, he came to the palace of King Suddhodana and gravely approached the women's quarters. His years and his learning lent him great dignity.

The king showed him the courtesies that custom prescribed and addressed him in a seemly manner:

"Happy, indeed, am I! Truly, this child of mine will enjoy distinguished favor, for the venerable Asita has come purposely to see me. Command me. What must I do? I am your disciple, your servant."

The hermit, his eyes shining with the light of joy, gravely spoke these words:

"This has happened to you, O noble, generous and hospitable king, because you love duty and because you are ever kind to those who are wise and to those who are full of years. This has happened to you because your ancestors, though rich in land and rich in gold, were above all rich in virtue. Know the reason for my coming, O king, and rejoice. In the air I heard a divine voice speaking and it said: 'A son has been born to the king of the Sakyas, a son who will have the true knowledge.' I heard these words, and I came, and my eyes shall now behold the glory of the Sakyas."

Overwhelmed with joy, the king went to fetch the child. Taking him from his nurse's breast, he showed him to the aged Asita.

The hermit noticed that the king's son bore the marks of omnipotence. His gaze hovered over the child, and presently his lashes were wet with tears. Then he sighed and turned his eyes to the sky.

The king saw that Asita was weeping, and he began to fear for his son. He questioned the old man:

"You say, O venerable roan, that my son's body differs little from that of a God. You say that his birth was a wondrous thing, that in the future his glory will be supreme, yet you look at him with eyes that are filled with tears. Is his life, then, to be a fragile thing? Was he born only to bring me sorrow? Must this new branch wither before it has burst into flower? Speak, O saintly man, speak quickly; you know the great love a father bears his son."

"Be not distressed, O king," replied the hermit. "What I have told you is true: this child will know great glory. If I weep, it is for myself. My life draws to a close and he is born, he who will destroy the evil of rebirth. He will surrender sovereign power, he will master his passions, he will understand truth, and error will disappear in the world before the light of his knowledge, even as night flees before the spears of the sun. From the sea of evil, from the stinging spray of sickness, from the surge and swell of old age, from the angry waves of death, from these will he rescue the suffering world, and together they will sail away in the great ship of knowledge.

He will know where it takes its rise, that swift, wonderful, beneficent river, the river of duty; he will reveal its course, and those who are tortured by thirst will come and drink of its waters. To those tormented by sorrow, to those enslaved by the senses, to those wandering in the forest of existences like travellers who have lost their way, he will point out the road to salvation. To those burning with the fire of passion, he will be the cloud that brings refreshing rain; armed with the true law, he will go to the prison of desires where all creatures languish, and he will break down the evil gates. For he who will have perfect understanding will set the world free.

Therefore do not grieve, O king. He alone is to be pitied who will not hear the voice of your son, and that is why I weep, I who, in spite of my austerities, in spite of my meditations, will never know his message and his law. Yes, even he is to be pitied who ascends to the loftiest gardens of the sky."

Siddhartha at the Temple

They pleased Suddhodana at first, these words of Asita's, and he pondered them. "So my son will live, and live gloriously," he thought, but then he became anxious. For it had been said that the prince would renounce royalty, that he would lead the life of a hermit, and did that not mean that at his death Suddhodana's family would cease?

But his anxiety was short-lived, for since the birth of Siddhartha the king could undertake nothing that did not prosper. Like a great river whose waters are swollen by many tributaries, each day new riches poured into his treasury; the stables were too small to hold the horses and elephants that were presented to him, and he was constantly surrounded by a host of loyal friends. The kingdom was rich in fertile lands, and sleek, fatted cattle grazed in the meadows. Women bore their children without suffering; men lived at peace with their neighbors, and happiness and tranquillity reigned in the land of Kapilavastu.

But the joy that had come to Maya proved too sweet. It soon became unbearable. The earth knew her as a mother but seven days; then she died and ascended to the sky, to be received among the Gods.

Maya had a sister, Mahaprajapati, who in beauty and virtue was almost her equal. The prince was given into

Mahaprajapati's care, and she looked after his wants as tenderly as if he were her own child. And like fire fanned by an auspicious wind, like the moon, queen of the stars in the luminous skies, like the morning sun rising over the mountains in the East, Siddhartha grew in strength and stature.

Everyone now delighted in bringing him precious gifts. They gave him toys that would amuse a child of his age: tiny animals, deer and elephants, horses, cows, birds and fish, and little chariots; and they were toys made not of wood or of clay but of gold and of precious stones. And they brought him costly materials and rare gems, pearl necklaces and jewelled bracelets.

One day, while he was playing in a garden not far from the city, Mahaprajapati thought, "It is time I taught him to wear necklaces and bracelets," and she ordered the servants to bring the jewels that had been given to him. She clasped them around his arms and his neck, but it was as if he wore none at all. The gold and the precious stones seemed dull and lifeless, so brilliant was the light he diffused. And the Goddess who lived among the flowers of that garden came to Mahaprajapati and said:

"If the earth were made of gold, a single ray of light emanating from this child, the world's future guide, would be enough to dull its splendor. The light of the stars and the light of the moon, yes, even the light of the sun, are dimmed by his refulgence. And would you have him wear jewels, baubles crudely fashioned by jewellers and goldsmiths? Woman, remove those necklaces, take off those bracelets. They are only fit to be worn by slaves; give them to the slaves. This child will have his thoughts; they are gems of a purer water."

Mahaprajapati gave heed to the words of the Goddess. She unclasped the bracelets and the necklaces, and she never wearied of admiring the prince.

The time came to take Siddhartha to the temple of the Gods. By the king's command, the streets of the city and the public squares were superbly decorated; drums were sounded and bells joyously rung. While Mahaprajapati was dressing him in his richest apparel, the child asked:

"Mother, where are you taking me?"

"To the temple of the Gods, my son," she replied. The child smiled and quietly went with her to meet his father.

It was a magnificent sight. In the procession were brahmans from the city, warriors and all the chief merchants. A host of guards followed, and the Sakyas surrounded the chariot that bore the prince and the king. In the streets the air was heavy with incense, flowers were strewn in their path, and the people waved flags and streamers as they passed.

They arrived at the temple. The king took Siddhartha by the hand and led him to the hall where stood the statues of the Gods. As the child stepped across the threshold the statues came to life, and all the Gods, Siva, Skanda, Vishnu, Kuvera, Indra, Brahma, descended from their pedestals and fell at his feet. And they sang:

"Meru, king of the mountains, does not bow before a grain of wheat; the Ocean does not bow before a pool of rainwater; the Sun does not bow before a glowworm; he who will have the true knowledge does not bow before the Gods. Like the grain of wheat, like the pool of rainwater, like the glowworm is the man or the God with stubborn pride; like Meru mountain, like the Ocean, like the Sun is he who will have supreme knowledge. Let the world pay him homage, and the world will be set free!"

Another excellent result which may, and I hope will, follow from our increased acquaintance with the actual thoughts and literature, as well as with the personalities of Oriental peoples, is a loosening of that prejudice which undoubtedly obtains, even among scholarly circles, in the West. It would be perhaps too much to complain that classical schol-ars, for instance, should have a decided repugnance to admit any actual influence on Greek thought or institutions as having been exercised by the think-ers of the East, however ungrudgingly that privi-lege is conceded to Egypt. Personally I think that they are quite in the right in maintaining that such an influence is, except in a few instances, at present entirely unproven. But surely there are many points of analogy which are most instructive, and suggest-ive at least of more than an analogical connection ; points that may throw light upon the natural course of the evolution of human conceptions and, in doing so, help to throw light on dark corners of the history of , that culture out of which our own has arisen. It is a common saying that it is impossible to know any one language well without at the same time knowing another, and I venture to think that a similar remark holds good of the history of religion or of ethics, or of institutions, or of philosophy.

Should I be considered too bold if I were to go one step farther and suggest that there are really some points in the philosophy of the East, and es-pecially of India, which are fated sooner or later to find their place in, and to exercise a not inconsid-erable influence over, the thought of Western na- tions. I know it is a common idea, and one held not only by Philistines, that the study of Buddhism, for instance, is of no use except as a matter of curiosity, since it has no connection with the origins of our own culture, which is, after all, in the commonly accepted opinion, the only progressive culture in the world. This view not only entirely ignores the value of the comparative study of all historical questions, but it ignores also, with an almost wilful ignorance, the real originality of Gotama's ethics and philosophy.

But this, I know, is not the view which is held by those I have the honour of addressing, or indeed by some of the most unprejudiced and original leaders of thought in Europe. You all know how Schopenhauer claims to have arrived, in the very deepest foundation of his system, at a practical agreement with Buddhism, and he writes, alluding to other thinkers :

"If I am to take the results of my philosophy as the standard of truth, I should be obliged to concede to Buddhism the pre-eminence over the rest. In any case it must be a satisfaction to me to find my teaching in such close agreement with a religion professed by the majority of men. This agreement must be all the more satisfactory because in my philosophising I have certainly not been under its influence."

These words are at least conclusive evidence to show that, so far as Schopenhauer is worth studying, the Buddhist philosophy is worthy of study also ; and I need not stay therefore to point out the reasons which have led me to believe that Schopen-hauer was influenced, not only by Vedantism, but also by Buddhism.

And with this great philosophical thinker I would also remind you of the words of the veteran leader of scientific thought in England, Professor Huxley, who, comparing Gotama's idealism with that of Bishop Berkeley, says, in one of his latest utter-ances :

" It is a remarkable indication of the subtlety of Indian speculation that Gotama should have seen deeper than the greatest of modern idealists."

And throughout his whole essay he insists very strongly

on the value, even to actual belief in the West, of a critical study of the Buddhist system.

Dr, Deussen, Professor of Philosophy at Kiel, has even gone so far as to publish a handbook for students entitled Elements of Metaphysics, in which Indian thought is throughout compared and used, alongside with European speculation. And I know from your presence here to-day, that you at least will cordially agree with the committee representing centres of higher education in America, that the comparative study of religious belief (which must be very largely, and even mainly, the history of Oriental belief) has come to be a matter of real importance to Western students. It would be beyond the scope of a lecturer on this subject to touch upon the possible influence of its study upon the religion of the future. But it is a matter of historic fact that the great epochs of intellectual progress have been precisely those when two different and even antagonistic systems of thought have been fermenting in the same minds. The two systems are, as it were, the father and mother, whose progeny, more like, perhaps, to one of its parents, still possesses some of the characteristics of both, and escapes from the evil results of too exclusive and narrow an interbreeding.

We may at least venture to hope that the series of lectures, of which this course is only the first in-stalment, will do much to promote that feeling of respect for opinions we ourselves can never hold, which lends so much assistance to a right under-standing of the causes at work in the evolution of thought and in the history of our race.

THE prince grew older, and the time came for him to study with the teacher who instructed the young Sakyas in the art of writing. This teacher was called Visvamitra.

Siddhartha was entrusted to his care. He was given, to write on, a tablet of gilded sandal-wood, set round with precious stones. When he had it in his hands, he asked:

"Which script, master, would you have me learn?"

And he enumerated the sixty-four varieties of script. Then again he asked:

"Master, which of the sixty-four would you have me learn?"

Visvamitra made no answer: he was struck dumb with astonishment. Finally, he replied:

"I see, my lord, that there is nothing I can teach you. Of the scripts you mentioned, some are known to me only by name, and others are unknown to me even by name. It is I who should sit at your feet and learn. No, my lord, there is nothing I can teach you."

He was smiling, and the prince returned his affectionate glance.

Upon leaving Visvamitra, the prince went into the country and started walking toward a village.

On the way, he stopped to watch some peasants working in the fields, then he entered a meadow where stood a clump of trees. They attracted him, for it was noon and very hot. The prince went and sat down in the shade of a tree; there, he began to ponder, and he was soon lost in meditation.

Five itinerant hermits passed near the meadow. They saw the prince meditating, and they wondered:

"Is he a God, he who is seated there, resting? Could he be the God of riches, or the God of love?

Could he be Indra, bearer of thunder, or the shepherd Krishna?"

But they heard a voice saying to them:

"The splendor of the Gods would pale before the splendor of this Sakya who sits under the tree and ponders majestic truths!"

Whereupon they all exclaimed:

"Verily, he who sits and meditates under the tree bears the marks of omnipotence; he will doubtless become the Buddha!"

Then they sang his praises, and the first one said: "To a world consumed by an evil fire, he has come like a lake. His law will refresh the world."

The second one said: "To a world darkened by ignorance, he has come like a torch. His law will bring light into the world."

The third one said: "Over the sea of suffering, that sea so difficult to sail, he has come like a ship. His law will bring the world safely into harbor."

The fourth one said: "To those bound in chains of evil, he has come like a redeemer. His law will set the world free."

The fifth one said: "To those tormented by old age and sickness, he has come like a savior. His law will bring deliverance from birth and death."

Three times they bowed, then continued on their way.

In the meanwhile, King Suddhodana wondered what had become of the prince, and he sent many servants out to search for him. One of them found him absorbed in meditation. The servant drew near, then suddenly stopped, overcome with admiration. For the shadows of all the trees had lengthened, except of that tree under which the prince was seated. Its shadow had not moved; it still sheltered him.

The servant ran back to the palace of the king.

"My lord," he cried, "I have seen your son; he is meditating under a tree whose shadow has not moved, whereas the shadows of all the other trees have moved and lengthened."

Suddhodana left the palace and followed the servant to where his son was seated. Weeping for joy, he said to himself:

"He is as beautiful as fire on a mountain-top. He dazzles me. He will be the light of the world, and my limbs tremble when I see him thus in meditation."

The king and his servant dared neither move nor speak. But some children passed by, drawing a little chariot after them. They were making a noise. The servant said to them, in a whisper:

"You must not make a noise."

"Why?" asked the children.

"See him who meditates under the tree? That is Prince Siddhartha. The shadow of the tree has not left him. Do not disturb him, children; do you not see that he has the brilliance of the sun?"

But the prince awoke from his meditations. He rose and approaching his father, he said to him:

"We must stop working in the fields, father; we must seek the great truths."

And he returned to Kapilavastu.

7

The Buddha Pacifies the Malcontents of Rajagriha

The number of believers was constantly increasing, and King Vimbasara gave repeated evidence to the Master of his faith and friendship. He often invited him to the palace and offered him a seat at his table, and at such times he would order the city to have a festive appearance. The streets were carpeted with flowers, and the houses decorated with banners. The sweetest perfumes filled the air, and the inhabitants dressed in their brightest clothes. The king himself would come forward to greet the Blessed One and would shade him from the sun with his golden parasol.

Many young nobles put all their faith in the law taught by the Blessed One. They wanted to become saints; they abandoned family and fortune, and the Bamboo Grove was soon filled with devout disciples.

But there were many in Rajagriha who were disturbed to see the great number of converts the Buddha was making, and they went about the city, voicing their anger.

"Why has he settled in our midst, this son of the Sakyas?" they would ask. "Were there not enough monks already, preaching to us about virtue? And they did not lure our young men away like this master. Why, even our children are leaving us. Because of this son of the Sakyas, how many women are widows! Because of this son of the Sakyas, how many families are childless! Evil will befall the kingdom, now that this monk has settled in our midst!"

The Master soon had a great many enemies among the inhabitants of the city. Whenever they met his disciples, they would taunt them or make sarcastic remarks.

"The great monk came to the city of Rajagriha and conquered the Bamboo Grove; will he now conquer the entire kingdom of Magadha?" said one as he went by.

"The great monk came to the city of Rajagriha and took Sanjaya's disciples away from him; who will he lure away to-day?" said another.

"A plague would be less harmful than this great monk," said a third; "it would kill fewer children."

"And it would leave fewer widows," a woman sighed.

The disciples made no reply. But they felt the anger of the populace growing, and they told the

Master of the evil words they had heard.

"Do not let it disturb you, O disciples," replied the Buddha. "They will soon stop. To those who follow you with jeers and insults, speak quiet, gentle words. Say to them, 'It is because they know the truth, the real truth, that the heroes convince, that the perfect ones convert. Who dares offend the Buddha, the Saint who converts by the power of truth?' Then they will be silent, and in a few days, when you wander through the city, you will meet only with respect and praise."

It happened as the Buddha had said. The evil voices were silenced, and every one in Rajagriha did honor to the Master's disciples.

Suddhodana Sends Messengers to His Son

KING Suddhodana heard that his son had attained supreme knowledge and that he was living at Rajagriha, in the Bamboo Grove. He had a great desire to see him again, and he sent a messenger to him, with these words: "Your father, King Suddhodana, longs to see you, O Master."

When the messenger arrived at the Bamboo Grove, he found the Master addressing his disciples.

"There is a forest clinging to the slope of a mountain, and at the foot of the mountain, a wide, deep pool. Wild beasts live on the banks of this pool. A man appears who would harm these beasts, who would make them suffer, who would let them die. He closes up the good path that leads away from the pool, the path that is safe to travel, and he opens up a treacherous path that ends in a dreadful swamp. The beasts are now in danger; one by one, they will perish. But let a man appear who, on the contrary, seeks the welfare of these wild beasts, who seeks their comfort, their prosperity. He will destroy the treacherous path that ends in a swamp, and he will open up a safe path that leads to the peaceful mountain top.

Then the beasts will no longer be in danger; they will thrive and multiply. Now understand what I have told you, O disciples. Like these beasts on the banks of the wide, deep pool, man lives near the pleasures of the world. He who would do him harm, who would make him suffer, who would let him die, is Mara, the Evil One. The swamp wherein all beings perish is pleasure, desire, ignorance. He who seeks the welfare, the comfort, the prosperity of all is the Perfect One, the Saint, the blessed Buddha. It was I, O disciples, who opened up the safe path; it was I who destroyed the treacherous path. You will not go to the swamp; you will climb the mountain and reach the bright summit. All that a master can do who pities his disciples and who seeks their welfare, I have done for you, O my disciples."

The messenger listened in a transport of delight. Then he fell at the Master's feet and said:

"Receive me among your disciples, O Blessed One."

The Master extended his hands and said: "Come, O monk."

The messenger stood up, and, suddenly, his clothes, of their own accord, took the shape and color of a monk's robe. He forgot everything, and the message that Suddhodana had entrusted to him was never delivered.

The king became weary of waiting for his return. Each day, the desire to see his son became more intense, and he sent another messenger to the Bamboo Grove. But for this man's return he also waited in vain. Nine times he sent messengers to the Blessed One, and nine times the messengers, upon hearing the sacred word, decided to remain and become monks.

Suddhodana finally summoned Udayin.

"Udayin," said he, "as you know, of the nine messengers who set out for the Bamboo Grove, not one has returned, not one has sent me word how my message was received. I do not know if they spoke to my son, if they even saw him. It grieves degreesme, Udayin. I am an old man. Death lies in wait for me. I may live till to-morrow, but it would be rash to count on the days that follow after. And before I die, Udayin, I want to see my son. You were once his best friend; go to him now. I can think of no one who would be more welcome. Tell him of my grief; tell him of my wish, and may he not be indifferent!"

"I shall go, my lord," replied Udayin.

He went. Long before he arrived at the Bamboo Grove,

he had made up his mind to become a monk, but King Suddhodana's words had affected him deeply, and he thought, "I shall tell the Master of his father's grief. He will be moved to pity and will go to him."

The Master was happy to see Udayin become one of his disciples.

Winter was almost over. It was a favorable time to travel, and Udayin said to the Buddha, one day:

"The trees are budding; they will soon be in leaf. See the bright rays of the sun shining through the branches. Master, this is a good time to travel. It is no longer cold, nor it is yet too warm; and the earth wears a lovely mantle of green. We shall have no trouble finding food on the way. Master, this is a good time to travel."

The Master smiled at Udayin and asked:

"Why do you urge me to travel, Udayin?"

"Your father, King , would be happy to see you, Master."

The Buddha considered a moment, then he said: "I shall go to Kapilavastu; I shall go and see my father."

WHEN Vimbasara heard that the Master was leaving the Bamboo Grove, to be gone for some time, he went to see him with his son, Prince Ajatasatru.

The Master looked at the young prince; then turning to the king, he said:

"May Ajatasatru be worthy of your love, O king."

Again he looked at the prince, and he said to him:

"Now listen well, Ajatasatru, and ponder my words. Cunning does not always succeed; wickedness does not always prevail. A story will prove this, the story of something that happened long ago, something I saw with my own eyes. I was then living in a forest; I was a tree-God. This tree grew between two pools, one small and unattractive, the other wide and beautiful. The little pool was full of fish; in the larger one, lotuses grew in great profusion. During a certain summer of oppressive heat, the little pool almost completely dried up; while the large pool, sheltered from the sun as

it was by the lotuses, always had plenty of water and remained pleasantly cool. A crane, passing between these two pools, saw the fish and stopped. Standing on one leg, he began to think: 'These fish would be a lawful prize. But they are quick; they are likely to escape if I attack them too hastily. I must use cunning Poor fish! They are so uncomfortable in this dried-up pool! And over there is that other pool, full of deep, cool water, where they could swim about to their heart's content!' A fish saw the crane deep in thought and looking as solemn as a hermit, and he asked, 'What are you doing there, venerable bird? You seem immersed in thought.' 'I am meditating, O fish,' said the crane, 'yes, indeed, I am meditating. I am wondering how you and your friends can escape your sad fate.' 'Our sad fate! What do you mean?' 'You suffer in that shallow water, O unhappy fish! And each day, as the heat becomes more intense, the water will fall still further, and then what will become of you? For presently the pool will be completely dry, and you will all perish! Poor, poor fish! I weep for you.' All the fish had heard what the crane said. They were filled with dismay. 'What will become of us,' they cried, 'when the heat will have dried up the pool?'

They turned to the crane. 'Bird, O venerable bird, can you not save us?' The crane again pretended to be lost in thought; finally, he replied, 'I believe I see a way out of your misery.' The fish listened eagerly. The crane said, 'There is a marvellous pool quite near here. It is considerably larger than the one in which you live, and the lotuses that cover the surface have protected the water from the summer's thirst. Take my word for it, go live in that pool. I can pick you up in my bill, one at a time, and carry you there. In that way, you will all be saved.'

The fish were happy. They were about to accept the crane's suggestion when a crayfish spoke up. 'I have never heard anything quite so strange,' he exclaimed. The fish asked him, 'What is there to astonish you about that?' 'Never,' said the crayfish, 'never, since the beginning of the world, did I know a crane to take an interest in fish, unless it was perhaps to eat them.' The crane assumed an offended air and said, 'What, you wicked crayfish, you suspect me of trying to deceive these poor fish who are in imminent danger of death! O fish, I only want to save you; it is your welfare I seek. Put my good faith to a test if you wish. Choose one of your number, and I shall carry him in my bill to the lotus pool. He will see it; he can even swim around a few times; then I shall pick him up and bring him back here. He will tell you what to think of me.' 'That seems quite fair,' said the fish. To make this trip to the pool, they chose one of the older fish who, although half blind, was considered quite a sage. The crane carried him to the pool, dropped him in, and let him swim about as much as he pleased. The old fish was delighted, and when he returned to his friends, he had only words of praise for the crane. The fish were now convinced that they would owe their lives to him. 'Take us,' they cried, 'take us and carry us to the lotus pool.' 'Just as you wish,' said the crane, and with his bill he again picked up the old, half-blind fish. But this time he did not carry him to the pool. Instead, he dropped him on the ground and stabbed him with his bill; then he ate him and left the bones at the foot of a tree, the tree of which I was the God. This done, the crane returned to the small pool and said, 'Who will come with me now?'

The fish were eager to see their new home, and the crane had only to make a choice that would satisfy his appetite. Presently, he had eaten them all, one after another. Only the crayfish remained. The crayfish had already shown that he distrusted the bird, and he was now saying to himself, 'I doubt very much that the fish are in the lotus pool. I am afraid the crane has taken advantage of their faith in him. Still, it would be well for me to leave this miserable pool and go to the other one which is so much larger and more comfortable. The crane must carry me, but I must run no risk. And if he has deceived the others, I must avenge them.' The bird approached the crayfish. 'It is your turn, now,' said the crane. 'How will you carry me?' asked the crayfish. 'In my bill, like the others,' replied the crane. 'No, no,' said the crayfish; 'my shell is slippery; I might fall out of your bill. Rather, let me hold on to your neck with my claws; I shall be careful not to hurt you.' The crane agreed. He stopped at the foot of the tree. 'What are you doing?' asked the crayfish. 'We are only half-way. Are you tired? Yet the distance is not great between the two pools!' The crane was at a loss for an answer. Besides, the crayfish was beginning to tighten the hold on his neck. 'And what have we here!' exclaimed the crayfish. 'This pile of fish-bones at the foot of the tree is evidence of your treachery. But you will not deceive me as you deceived the others. I shall kill you, if I must die in the attempt.' The crayfish tightened his claws. The crane was in great pain; with tears in his eyes, he cried, 'Dear crayfish, do not hurt me. I shall not eat you. I shall carry you to the pool.

' 'Then go,' said the crayfish. The crane walked to the edge of the pool and extended his neck over the water. The crayfish had only to drop into the pool. Instead, he tightened his grip, and so powerful were his claws that the crane's neck was severed. And the tree-God could not help exclaiming, 'Well done, crayfish!' " The Master added:

"Cunning does not always succeed. Wickedness does not always prevail. Sooner or later the treacherous crane meets a crayfish. Always remember that, Prince Ajatasatru!"

Vimbasara thanked the Master for the valuable lesson he had taught his son. Then he said:

"Blessed One, I have a request to make."

"Speak," said the Buddha.

"When you are gone, O Blessed One, I shall be unable to do you honor, I shall be unable to make you the customary offerings, and it will grieve me. Give me a lock of your hair, give me the parings of your finger-nails; I shall place them in a temple in the midst of my palace. Thus, I shall retain something that is a part of you, and, each day, I shall decorate the temple with fresh garlands, and I shall burn rare incense."

The Blessed One gave the king these things for which he had asked, and he said:

"Take my hair and take these parings; keep them in a temple, but, in your mind, keep what I have taught you."

And as Vimbasara joyfully returned to his palace, the Master left for Kapilavastu.

IT was a great distance from Rajagriha to Kapilavastu, and the Master was walking slowly. Udayin decided to go ahead and inform Suddhodana that his son was on his way to see him, for the king would then be patient and would cease to grieve.

Udayin flew through the air, and, in a trice, had arrived at Suddhodana's palace. He found the king in deep despair.

"My lord," said he, "dry your tears. Your son will be in Kapilavastu before long."

"Oh, it is you, Udayin!" exclaimed the king. "I thought that you, too, had forgotten to deliver my message, and I had given up hope of ever seeing my beloved son. But you have come at last, and joyful is the news you bring. I shall weep no more; I shall now patiently await the blessed moment when these eyes shall look again upon my son."

He ordered that Udayin be served a splendid repast.

"I will not eat here, my lord," said Udayin. "Before I touch any food, I must know if my master has been properly served. I shall return to him the way I came."

The king protested.

"It is my wish, Udayin, that you receive your food from me, each day; and it is also my wish that my son receive his food from me, each day of this journey which he has undertaken to please me. Eat, and I shall then give you food to take to the Blessed One."

When Udayin had eaten, he was given a bowl of delicious food to take to the king's son. He tossed the bowl into the air; then he rose from the ground and flew away. The bowl fell at the Buddha's feet, and the Buddha thanked his friend. Each day thereafter, Udayin flew to the palace of King Suddhodana to fetch the Master's food, and the Master was pleased with the zeal his disciple showed in serving him.

He finally arrived at Kapilavastu. To receive him, the Sakyas had assembled in a park bright with flowers. Many of those present were extremely proud, and they thought, "There are some here who are older than Siddhartha! Why should they pay him homage? Let the children, let the young men and young maidens, bow before him; his elders will hold their heads high!"

The Blessed One entered the park. All eyes were

dazzled by the brilliant light he diffused. King Suddhodana was deeply moved; he made a few steps in his direction. "My son . . ." he cried. His voice faltered; tears of joy coursed down his cheeks, and he slowly bowed his head.

And when the Sakyas saw the father paying homage to the son, they all humbly prostrated themselves.

A magnificent seat had been prepared for the Master. He sat down. Then the sky opened, and a shower of roses descended on the park. Earth and atmosphere were impregnated with the perfume. The king and all the Sakyas gazed in wonderment. And the Master spoke.

"I have already, in some former existence, seen my family grouped around me and heard them sing my praises as with one voice. At that time King Sanjaya was reigning in the city of Jayatura. His wife's name was Phusati, and they had a son, Visvantara. When he came of age, Visvantara married Madri, a princess of rare beauty. She bore him two children: a son, Jalin, and a daughter, Krishnajina. Visvantara owned a white elephant that had the marvellous power to make the rain fall at will. Now, the distant kingdom of Kalinga was visited by a terrible drought. The grass withered; the trees bore no fruit; men and beasts died of hunger and of thirst. The king of Kalinga heard of Visvantara's elephant and of the strange power it possessed.

He sent eight brahmans to Jayatura to get it and return with it to their unfortunate country. The brahmans arrived during a festival. Riding on the elephant, the prince was on his way to the temple, to distribute alms. He saw these envoys of the foreign king. 'What brings you here?' he asked them. 'My lord,' replied the brahmans, 'our kingdom, the kingdom of Kalinga, has been visited by drought and famine. Your elephant can save us, by bringing us the rain; will you part with him?' 'It is little you ask,' said Visvantara.

'You could have asked me for my eyes or my flesh! Yes, take the elephant, and may a refreshing rain fall upon your fields and upon your gardens!'

He gave the elephant to the brahmans, and they joyfully returned to Kalinga. But the inhabitants of Jayatura were greatly distressed; they feared a drought in their own country. They complained to King Sanjaya. 'My lord,' said they, 'your son's action was reprehensible. His elephant protected us from famine. What will become of us now, if the sky withholds its rain? Show him no mercy, O king; let Visvantara pay for this folly with his life.' The king wept. He tried to put them off with promises, and at first they would not listen, but they finally relented and asked that the prince be exiled to some remote and rocky desert. The king was obliged to give his consent.

'When my son hears of his exile,' thought Sanjaya, 'he will take it to heart.' But this was not the case. Visvantara simply said, 'I shall leave tomorrow, father, and I shall take none of my treasures with me.' Then he went to look for Madri, his princess. 'Madri,' said he, 'I must leave the city; my father has exiled me to a cruel desert, where it will be hard to find a livelihood. Do not come with me, O beloved; too great are the hardships you will have to endure. You will have to leave the children behind, and they will die of loneliness. Stay here with them; remain on your golden throne; it was I my father exiled, not you.' 'My lord,' replied the princess, 'if you leave me behind I shall kill myself, and the crime will lie at your door.' Visvantara was silent. He gazed at Madri; he embraced her.

'Come,' said he. Madri thanked him, and she added, 'I shall take the children with me; I can not leave them here, to die of loneliness.' The following day, Visvantara had his chariot made ready; he got in with Madri, Jalin and Krishnajina, and as they drove out of the city, King Sanjaya and Queen Phusati wept and sobbed pitifully. The prince, his wife and the children were already far from the city when they saw a brahman approaching. 'Traveller,' said the brahman, 'is this the road to Jayatura?' 'Yes,' replied Visvantara, 'but why are you going to Jayatura?'

'I come from a distant country,' said the brahman. 'I heard that there lived in Jayatura a generous prince named Visvantara. He once owned a marvellous elephant that he gave to the king of Kalinga. He is very charitable, they say. I want to see this kindly man; I want to ask him for a donation. I know that no one has ever appealed to him in vain.' Visvantara said to the brahman, 'I am the man you seek; I am Visvantara, son of King Sanjaya. Because I gave my elephant to the king of Kalinga, my father sent me into exile. What can I give you, O brahman?' When he heard these words, the brahman complained bitterly. He said in a pitiful voice: 'So they deceived me! I left my home, full of hope, and, disappointed, I must now return!' Visvantara interrupted him. 'Console yourself, brahman. Not in vain have you appealed to Prince Visvantara.' He unharnessed the horses and gave them to him. The brahman thanked his benefactor and left. Visvantara then continued on his way. He was now drawing the chariot himself. Presently, he saw another brahman approaching. He was a little, frail old man, with white hair and yellow teeth. 'Traveller,' he said to the prince, 'is this the road to Jayatura?' 'Yes,' replied the prince, 'but why are you going to Jayatura?' 'The king of that city has a son, Prince Visvantara,' said the brahman. 'Visvantara, according to the stories I have heard, is extremely charitable; he saved the kingdom of Kalinga from famine, and whatever is asked of him is never refused. I shall go to Visvantara, and I know he will not deny my request.' 'If you go to Jayatura,' said the prince, 'you will not see Visvantara; his father has exiled him to the desert.' 'Woe is me!' cried the brahman.

'Who now will help me in my feeble old age? All hope has fled, and I shall return to my home as poor as when I left!' He wept. 'Do not weep,' said Visvantara; 'I am the man you seek. You have not met me in vain. Madri, Jalin, Krishnajina, get down from the chariot! It is no longer mine: I have given it to this old man.' The brahman was overjoyed. The four exiles continued on their way. They were now on foot, and when the children were tired, Visvantara would carry Jalin, and Madri Krishnajina. A few days later, they saw a third brahman approaching. He was going to Jayatura to see Prince Visvantara and ask him for alms. The prince stripped himself of his clothes, in order that the brahman should not leave him empty-handed. Then he walked on. And a fourth brahman approached. His skin was dark, his glance fierce and imperious. 'Tell me,' he said in a harsh voice, 'is this the road to Jayatura?' 'Yes,' replied the prince, 'and what takes you to Jayatura?' The brahman wanted to see Visvantara, who was sure to give him a magnificent present. When he learned that he was in the presence of the unhappy, exiled prince, he did not weep; in an angry voice, he said, it was a hard road 1 travelled, and it must not have been in vain.

You have undoubtedly brought along some valuable jewelry which you can give me.' Madri was wearing a necklace of gold. Visvantara asked her for it; she smiled and handed it to him, and the brahman took the necklace and went away. Visvantara, Madri, Jalin and Krishnajina kept on walking. They crossed raging torrents; they ascended ravines covered with underbrush; they travelled over rocky plains seared by a merciless sun. Madri's feet were cut by the stones; Visvantara's heels were worn to the bone, and wherever they passed, they left a trail of blood. One day, Visvantara, who was walking ahead, heard some one sobbing. He turned around and saw Madri sitting on the ground, lamenting her fate.

He was seized with anguish, and he said, 'I begged and pleaded with you, my beloved, not to follow me into exile, but you would not listen. Come, stand up; however great our weariness, the children must not suffer for it; we must not mind our wounds.' Madri saw that his feet were bleeding, and she cried, 'Oh, how much greater is your suffering than mine! I shall control my grief.' She tried to stand up, but her limbs gave way, and once again she burst into tears. 'All my strength has left me,' she sobbed; 'even the love I bear my husband and my children is not enough to sustain my courage. I shall die of hunger and of thirst in this dreadful land; my children will die, and perhaps my well-beloved.' From the sky, Indra had been watching Visvantara and his family. He was touched by Madri's grief, and he decided to come down to earth. He assumed the form of a pleasant old man, and, astride a swift horse, he advanced to meet the prince. He accosted Visvantara and addressed him in an engaging manner. 'From your appearance it is evident, my lord, that you have suffered great hardship. There is a city not far from here. I shall show you the way. You and your family must come to my home and stay as long as you please.' The old man was smiling. He urged the four exiles to get on his horse, and as Visvantara seemed to hesitate, he said, 'The horse is powerful, and you are not heavy. As for me, I shall walk; it will not tire me, for we have not far to go.' Visvantara was astonished to learn that a city had been built in this cruel desert; besides, he had never heard of the city. But the old man's voice was so pleasant that he decided to follow him, and Madri was so weary that he accepted the invitation to ride with her and the children.

They had gone about three hundred paces when a magnificent city appeared before them. It was immense. A wide river flowed through it, and there were many beautiful gardens and orchards full of ripe fruit. The old man led his guests to the gates of a shining palace. 'Here is my home,' said he; 'here, if you wish, you may dwell the rest of your days. Please enter.' In the great hall, Visvantara and Madri sat on thrones of gold; at their feet, the children played on heavy rugs, and the old man presented them with many beautiful robes. Exquisite food was then served to them, and they appeased their hunger. But Visvantara was lost in thought. Suddenly, he rose from his seat, and he said to the old man, 'My lord, I am disobeying my father's commands. He banished me from Jayatura, where he is king, and he ordered me to spend the rest of my life in the desert. I must not enjoy these comforts, for they were forbidden. My lord, permit me to leave your house.' The old man tried to dissuade him, but it was futile; and followed by Madri and the children, Visvantara left the city. Outside the gates, he turned around to take a last look, but the city had disappeared; where it had once stood, there was now only burning sand. And Visvantara was happy that he had not remained longer. He finally came to a mountain, overrun by an immense forest, and there he found a hut that a hermit had once occupied. Out of leaves, he made a couch for himself and his family, and there, at last, undisturbed by remorse, he found rest and peace. Every day, Madri went into the forest to gather wild fruit; it was the only food they had, and they drank the water of a clear, bubbling spring they had discovered near the hut. For seven months they saw no one; then, one day, a brahman passed by. Madri was away, gathering fruit, and Visvantara was watching the children while they played in front of the hut.

The brahman stopped and observed them carefully. 'Friend,' he said to the father, 'will you give me your children?' Visvantara was so taken aback that he was unable to reply. He glanced anxiously at the brahman and finally questioned him. 'Yes, will you give me your children? I have a wife, much younger than myself. She is rather a haughty woman. She is tired of doing household work, and she asked me to find two children who could be her slaves. Why not give me yours? You seem to be very poor; it must be hard for you to feed them. In my home they will have plenty to eat, and I shall try to have my wife treat them as kindly as possible.' Visvantara thought, 'What a painful sacrifice I am being asked to make. What shall I do? In spite of what the brahman says, my children will be very unhappy in his home; his wife is cruel, she will beat them and will give them only scraps of food. But since he has asked me for them, have I the right to refuse?' He thought a while longer, then he finally said, 'Take the children with you, brahman; let them be your wife's slaves.' And Jalin and Krishnajina, their faces wet with tears, went away with the brahman. Madri, in the meanwhile, had been gathering pomegranates, but each time she picked one off the tree, it slipped out of her hand. This frightened her, and she hurried back to the hut. She missed the children, and turning to her husband she asked, 'Where are the children?' Visvantara was sobbing. 'Where are the children?' Still no reply. She repeated the question a third time. 'Where are the children?' And she added, 'Answer, answer quickly. Your silence is killing me.' Visvantara spoke; in a pitiful voice, he said, 'A brahman came; he wanted the children for slaves!' 'And you gave them to him!' cried Madri. 'Could I refuse?' Madri swooned; she was unconscious a long time. When she recovered, her lamentations were pitiful. She cried, 'Oh, my children, you who would rouse me from my slumber at night; you who would be given the choicest fruit I had gathered, a wicked man has taken you away! I can see him forcing you to run, you who have just learned to walk. In his home, you will go hungry; you will be brutally beaten. You will be working in the house of a stranger. You will furtively watch the roads, but neither father nor mother will you ever see again. And your lips will be parched; your feet will be hurt by the sharp stones; the sun will burn your cheeks. Oh, my children, we were always able to spare you the hardships we had to endure. We carried you across the fearful desert; you did not suffer then, but now, what will you suffer?' She was still weeping when another brahman came through the forest. He was an old man and walked with great difficulty. He stared at the princess with watery eyes, then he addressed Prince Visvantara. 'My lord, as you see, I am old and feeble. I have no one at home to help me when I get up in the morning or when I go to bed at night; I have neither son nor daughter to look after me. Now, this woman is young; she seems quite strong. Let me take her for a servant. She will help me to get up; she will put me to bed; she will watch over me while I sleep. Give me this woman, my lord; you will be doing a good deed, a saintly deed, that will be praised throughout the world.' Visvantara had listened attentively; he was pensive. He looked at Madri. 'Beloved, you heard what the brahman said; what would you answer?' She replied, 'Since you have given away our children: Jalin, the best-beloved, and darling Krishnajina, you can give me to this brahman; I shall not complain.' Visvantara took Madri's hand and placed it in the brahman's hand. He felt no remorse; he was not even weeping.

The brahman received the woman; he thanked the prince and said, 'May you know great glory, Visvantara; may you become the Buddha some day!' He started away, but turned, suddenly, and came back to the hut. And he said, 'I shall look for a servant in some other land; I shall leave this woman here, to remain with the Gods of the mountain, and the Goddesses of the forest and of the spring; and, hereafter, you must give her to no one.' While the old brahman was speaking, his appearance gradually changed; he became very beautiful; his face was gloriously radiant. Visvantara and Madri recognized Indra. They fell at his feet and worshipped him; and the God said to them, 'Each one of you may ask one favor of me, and it shall be granted.' Visvantara said, 'Oh, that I might become the Buddha some day and bring deliverance to those who are born and who die in the mountains!' Indra replied, 'Glory be to you who, one day, shall be the Buddha!' Madri spoke next. 'My lord, grant me this favor: may the brahman, to whom my children were given, decide to sell them instead of keeping them in his home, may he find a buyer only in Jayatura, and may that buyer be Sanjaya himself.' Indra replied, 'So be it!' As he ascended to the sky, Madri murmured, 'Oh, that King Sanjaya might forgive his son!' And she heard the God say, 'So be it!' In the meantime, Jalin and Krishnajina had arrived at their new home. The brahman's wife was very pleased with these two young slaves, and she lost no time putting them to work. She delighted in giving orders, and the children had to obey her slightest whim. At first, they did their best to carry out her wishes, but she was such an exacting mistress that they soon lost all desire to please, and many were the reprimands and the blows they received. The more harshly, they were treated, the more discouraged they became, and the woman finally said to the brahman, 'I can do nothing with these children. Sell them and bring me other slaves, slaves who know how to work and obey.' The brahman took the children and went from city to city, trying to sell them, but no one would buy: the price was too high. He finally arrived in Jayatura. One of the king's counsellors passed them in the street; he stared at the children, at their emaciated bodies and sun-burned faces, and, suddenly, he recognized them by their eyes. He stopped the brahman and asked, 'Where did you get these children?' 'I got them in a mountain forest, my lord,' replied the brahman. 'They were given to me for slaves; they were unruly, and I am now trying to sell them.' The king's counsellor became anxious; turning to the children, he asked, 'Does this servitude mean that your father is dead?' 'No,' replied Jalin, 'both our parents are alive, but father gave us to this brahman.' The counsellor ran to the palace of the king. 'My lord,' he cried, 'Visvantara has given your grandchildren, Jalin and Krishnajina, to a brahman. They are his slaves. He is dissatisfied with their service, and is taking them from city to city, in order to sell them!' King Sanjaya ordered the brahman and the children brought before him at once. They were soon found, and when the king saw the misery that had come to these children of his race, he wept bitter tears. Jalin addressed him in a pleading voice. 'Buy us, my lord, for We are unhappy in the Brahman's home, and we want to live with you, who love us. But do not take us by force; our father gave us to the brahman, and from this sacrifice he expects to receive great blessings, for himself and for all creatures.' 'What price do you want for these children?' the king asked the brahman. 'You may have them for a thousand head of cattle,' replied the brahman. 'Very well.' The king turned to his counsellor and said, 'You who will now rank next to me in my kingdom, give this brahman a thousand head of cattle, and pay him also a thousand measures of gold.' Then the king, accompanied by Jalin and Krishnajina, went to Queen Phusati.

At the sight of her grandchildren, she laughed and wept for joy; she dressed them in costly clothes, and she gave them rings and necklaces to wear. Then she asked them about their father and mother. 'They live in a rude hut, in a forest, on the slope of a mountain,' said Jalin. 'They have given away all their possessions. They live on fruit and water, and their only companions are the wild beasts of the forest.' 'Oh, my lord' cried Phusati, 'will you not recall your son from exile?' King Sanjaya sent a messenger to Prince Visvantara; he pardoned him, and ordered him to return to Jayatura. When the prince drew near the city, he saw his father, his mother and his children advancing to greet him. They were accompanied by a great crowd of people who had heard of Visvantara's sufferings and of his virtue, and who now forgave him and admired him. And the king said to the prince, 'Dear son, I have done you a grave injustice; know my remorse. Be kind to me: forget my blunder; and be kind to the inhabitants of the city: forget that they ever wronged you. Never again will your acts of charity give us offense.' Visvantara smiled and embraced his father, while Madri fondled Jalin and Krishnajina, and Phusati wept for joy. And when the prince passed through the gates of the city, he was acclaimed as with one voice. Now, Visvantara was I, O Sakyas! You acclaimed me as they once acclaimed him. Walk in the path that leads to deliverance."

The Blessed One was silent. The Sakyas had listened attentively; they now bowed before him and withdrew. However, not one of them had thought of offering him his meal on the morrow.

THE following day, the Master went through the city, begging his food from house to house. He was soon recognized, and the people of Kapilavastu exclaimed:

"What a strange sight! Prince Siddhartha, who once drove through these streets, dressed in magnificent robes, now wanders from door to door, begging his food, in the humble garb of a monk."

And they rushed to the windows; they ascended to the terraces, and great was their admiration for the beggar.

One of Gopa's maidens heard the excitement as she was leaving the palace. She asked the reason and was told. She immediately ran back to her mistress.

"Your husband, Prince Siddhartha," said she, "is wandering through the city, like a mendicant monk!"

Gopa gave a start. She thought, "He who once, for all

his gorgeous jewels, was radiant with light, now wears coarse clothes, now has for sole adornment the divine brilliance of his person." And she murmured, "How beautiful he must be!"

She ascended to the terrace of the palace. Surrounded by a crowd of people, the Master was approaching. A majestic splendor emanated from his person. Gopa trembled with joy, and in a voice full of fervor she sang:

"Soft and shining is his hair, brilliant as the sun his forehead, radiant and smiling his sweeping glance! He stalks like a lion through the golden light!"

She went to the king.

"My lord," said she, "your son is begging in the streets of Kapilavastu. An admiring throng follows him about, for he is more beautiful than ever before."

Suddhodana was greatly disturbed. He left the palace, and approaching his son, he said to him:

"What are you doing? Why do you beg your food? Surely you must know that I expect you at the palace, you and your disciples."

"I must beg," replied the Blessed One; "I must obey the law."

"We are a race of warriors," said the king; "no Sakya was ever a beggar."

"You belong to the Sakya race; I, in the course of my previous existences, have sought supreme knowledge; I have learned the beauty of charity; I have known the joy of self-sacrifice. When I was the child Dharmapala, the queen, my mother, was playing with me one day, and she forgot to greet my father, King Brahmadatta, as he passed by. In order to punish her, he ordered one of the guards to cut off my hands, for he thought it would hurt her more to see me suffer than to suffer herself. My mother pleaded with him and offered her hands instead, but he was inexorable, and he was obeyed. I was smiling, and to see me smile, soon brought a smile to my mother's face. My father then ordered the guard to cut off my feet. This was done, and still I kept smiling. In a violent rage, he cried, 'Cut off his head!' My mother became terrified; she cowered before him. 'Cut off my head,' she begged, 'but spare your son, O king!' The king was about to yield when I spoke up in a childish voice. 'Mother, it is for your salvation that I give my head. When I am dead, let my body be placed on a pike and exposed to view; let it be food for the birds of the air.' And, as the executioner seized me by the hair, I added, 'Oh, that I might become the Buddha and set free all who are born and who die in the worlds!' And now, King Suddhodana, now at last 1 have attained wisdom; I am the Buddha; I know the path that leads to deliverance. Do not disturb me at my task. Be wide awake; be quick of apprehension; follow the sacred path of virtue. He sleeps in peace who leads a life of holiness, he sleeps on earth and in the other worlds."

King Suddhodana wept with admiration. The Buddha continued:

"Learn to distinguish true virtue from false virtue; learn to know the true path from the false path. He sleeps in peace who lead a life of holiness, he sleeps on earth and in the other worlds!"

The king fell at his feet; he believed in him, completely. The Blessed One smiled, then entered the palace and sat down at his father's table.

Gopa's Great Virtue

PRESENTLY the women of the palace came to pay homage to the Master. Gopa, alone, was missing. The king evinced his surprise.

"I asked her to come with us," said Mahaprajapati. "'I shall not go with you,' she answered. 'I may be wanting in virtue; I may not deserve to see my husband. If 1 have done nothing wrong, he will come to me of his own accord, and I shall then show him the respect that is his due.'"

The Master left his seat and went to Gopa's apartments. She had discarded her costly raiment and her soft veils; she had flung aside her bracelets and her necklaces; she was wearing a reddish-colored robe, made of some coarse material. At the sight of her thus attired, he smiled with happiness. She fell at his feet and worshipped him.

"You see," said she, "I wanted to dress as you are dressed; I wanted to know about your life in order to live as you live. You eat but once a day, and I eat but once a day. You gave up sleeping in a bed; look around: no bed will you see, for here is the bench on which I sleep. And from now on.

I shall have done with sweet perfumes, and no longer shall I put flowers in my hair."

"I was aware of your great virtue, Gopa," replied the Master. "It has not failed you, and I praise you for it. How many women are there in this world who would have had the courage to do as you did?"

And seating himself, he spoke these words:

"Women are not to be trusted. For one who is wise and good, more than a thousand can be found who are foolish and wicked. Woman is more mysterious than the path of a fish through the water; she is as fierce as a robber, and like the robber, she is deceitful; she will rarely tell the truth, for to her a lie is like the truth and the truth like a lie. Often have I told my disciples to avoid women. It displeases me even to have them speak to them. Yet you, Gopa, are not false; I believe in your virtue.

Virtue is a flower not easily found; a woman must have clear eyes in order to see it; she must have pure hands in order to gather it Mara hides his pointed arrows under flowers oh, how many women love treacherous flower, flowers that inflict wounds which never heal! Unhappy women! The body is but foam and they know it not. They cling to this world, then the day comes when King Death claims them for his own. The body is less substantial than a mirage:

who knows that will break Mara's flowered arrows, who knows that will never meet King Death. Death carries away the woman who heedlessly gathers flowers, even as the torrent, swollen by the storm, carries away the drowsy village. Gather flowers, O woman, take joy in their colors, drink in their perfume; Death lies in wait for you, and before you are satisfied, you will be his. Consider the bee: it goes from flower to flower, and, harming no one, simply takes the nectar from which honey is made."

Nanda Renounces Royalty

WHEN Siddhartha had retired from the world, King Suddhodana had chosen Nanda, another one of his sons, to succeed him to the throne. Nanda was happy to think that one day he would be king, and he was also happy at the thought of his coming marriage to Princess Sundarika, to beautiful Sundarika whom he loved dearly.

The Master feared for his brother; he was afraid he would stray into the path of evil. One day, he he went to him and said:

"I have come to you, Nanda, because I know you are very happy, and I want to hear from your own lips the reason for this happiness. So speak, Nanda; bare your heart to me."

"Brother," replied Nanda, "I doubt if you would understand, for you once spurned sovereign power I and you deserted loving Gopa!"

"You expect to be king some day, and that is why you are happy, Nanda!"

"Yes. And I am also happy because I love Sundarika, and because Sundarika will soon be my bride."

"Poor man!" cried the Master. "How can you be happy, you who live in darkness? Would you see the light? Then first rid yourself of happiness: fear is born of happiness, fear and suffering. He neither fears nor suffers who no longer knows happiness. Rid yourself of love: fear is born of love, fear and suffering. He neither fears nor suffers who no longer knows love. If you seek happiness in the world, your efforts will come to nothing, your pleasure will turn to pain; death is always present, ready to swoop down on the unfortunate and still their laughter and their song. The world is but flame and smoke, and everything in the world suffers from birth, from old age and from death. Since you first began pitifully to wander from existence to existence, you have shed more tears than there is water in the rivers or in the seas. You have grieved and you have wept at being thwarted in your desires, and you have wept and you have grieved when that happened which you dreaded. A mother's death, a father's death, a brother's death, a sister's death, the death of a son, the death of a daughter, oh, how many times, down through the ages, have these not caused you heartache? And how many times have you not lost your fortune? And each time you had cause for grief, you wept and you wept and you wept, and you have shed more tears than there is water in the rivers or in the seas!"

Nanda, at first, paid little heed to what the Buddha

was saying, but as he began to listen the words moved him deeply. The Master continued:

"Look upon the world as a bubble of foam; let it be but a dream, and sovereign death will pass you by."

He was silent.

"Master, Master," cried Nanda, "I will be your disciple! Take me with you."

The Master took Nanda by the hand and left the palace. But Nanda was pensive; he was afraid he had been hasty. Perhaps he would bitterly regret what he had done. For whatever might be said of it, it was pleasant and noble to exercise sovereign power. And Sundarika? "How beautiful she is," he thought; "shall I ever see her again?" And he uttered a deep sigh.

But he still followed the Master. He was afraid, to speak to him. He feared his rebuke as he feared his scorn.

Suddenly, as they turned the corner of a street, he saw a young girl approaching. She was smiling. He recognized Sundarika, and he lowered his eyes.

"Where are you going?" she asked him.

He did not answer. She turned to the Master. "Are you taking him with you?"

"Yes," replied the Master.

"But he will come back soon?"

Nanda wanted to cry, "Yes, I shall come back soon, Sundarika!" But he was afraid, and without a word, his eyes still downcast, he went off with the Master.

Then Sundarika knew that Nanda was lost to her, and she wept.

The Buddha Leaves Kapilavastu

ONE day, gentle Gopa stood looking at her son Rahula.

"How beautiful you are, my child!" she exclaimed. "How your eyes sparkle! Your father owes you a pious heritage; you must go and claim it.

Mother and child ascended to the terrace of the palace. The Blessed One was passing in the street below. Gopa said to Rahula:

"Rahula, do you see that monk?"

"Yes, mother," replied the child. "His body is covered with gold."

"He is as beautiful as the Gods of the sky! It is the light of holiness that makes his skin shine like gold. Love him, my son, love him dearly, for he is your father. He once possessed great treasures; he had gold and silver and glittering jewels; now, he goes from house to house, begging his food. But he has acquired a marvellous treasure: he has attained supreme knowledge. Go to him, my son; tell him who You are, and demand your heritage."

Rahula obeyed his mother. He was presently standing before the Buddha. He felt strangely happy.

"Monk," said he, "it is nice to stand here, in your shadow."

The Master looked at him. It was a kindly glance, and Rahula, taking heart, began walking beside him. Remembering his mother's words, he said:

"I am your son, my Lord. I know that you possess the greatest of treasures. Father, give me my heritage."

The Master smiled. He made no reply. He continued to beg. But Rahula remained at his side; he followed him about and kept repeating:

"Father, give me my heritage."

At last the Master spoke:

"Child, you know nothing about this treasure that you have heard men praise. When you claim your heritage, you think you are claiming material things of a perishable nature. The only treasures known to you are those dear to human vanity, treasures that greedy death wrests from the false rich. But why should you be kept in ignorance? You are right to claim your heritage, Rahula. You shall have your share of the jewels that are mine. You shall see the seven jewels; you shall know the seven virtues, and you shall learn the true value of faith and purity, modesty and reserve, obedience, abnegation and wisdom. Come, I shall give you in charge of holy Sariputra; he will teach you."

Rahula went with his father, and Gopa rejoiced. King Suddhodana, alone, was sad: his family was deserting him! He could not help speaking his mind to the Master.

"Do not grieve," replied the Master, "for great is the treasure they will share who hearken to my words and follow me! Bear your grief in silence; be like the elephant wounded in battle by the arrows of the enemy: no one hears him complain. Kings ride into battle on elephants that are under perfect control; in the world, the great man is the man who has learned to control himself, the man who bears his grief in silence. He who is truly humble, he who curbs his passions as one curbs wild horses, is envied by the Gods. He does no evil. Neither in the mountain-caves nor in the caverns of the sea can you escape the consequences of an evil deed; they follow you about; they sear you; they drive you mad, for they give you no peace! But if you do good, when you leave the earth your good deeds greet you, like friends upon your return from a voyage. We live in perfect happiness, we who are without hatred in a world full of hatred. We live in perfect happiness, we who are without sickness in a world full of sickness. We live in perfect happiness, we who are without weariness in a world full of weariness. We live in perfect happiness, we who possess nothing. Joy is our food, and we are like radiant Gods. The monk who lives in solitude preserves a soul that is full of peace; he contemplates the truth with a clear, steady gaze, and enjoys a felicity unknown to ordinary mortals."

Having consoled King Suddhodana with these words, the Blessed One left Kapilavastu and returned to Rajagriha.

Anathapindika's Offering

THE Master was in Rajagriha when a rich merchant named Anathapindika arrived from Cravasti. Anathapindika was a religious man, and when he heard that a Buddha was living in the Bamboo Grove, he was eager to see him.

He set out one morning, and as he entered the Grove, a divine voice led him to where the Master was seated. He was greeted with words of kindness; he presented the community with a magnificent gift, and the Master promised to visit him in Cravasti.

When he returned home, Anathapindika began to wonder where he could receive the Blessed One. His gardens did not seem worthy of such a guest. The most beautiful park in the city belonged to Prince Jeta, and Anathapindika decided to buy it.

"I will sell the park," Jeta said to him, "if you cover the ground with gold coins."

Anathapindika accepted the terms. He had chariot-loads of gold coins carried to the park, and presently only a small strip of ground remained uncovered. Then Jeta joyfully exclaimed:

"The park is yours, merchant; I will gladly give you the strip that is still uncovered."

Anathapindika had the park made ready for the Master; then he sent his most faithful servant to the Bamboo Grove, to inform him that he was now prepared to receive him in Cravasti.

"O Venerable One," said the messenger, "my master falls at your feet. He hopes you have been spared anxiety and sickness, and that you are not loath to keep the promise you made to him. You are awaited in Cravasti, O Venerable One."

The Blessed One had not forgotten the promise he had made to the merchant Anathapindika; he wished to abide by it, and he said to the messenger, "I will go."

He allowed a few days to pass; then he took his cloak and his alms-bowl, and followed by a great number of disciples, he set out for Cravasti. The messenger went ahead, to tell the merchant he was coming.

Anathapindika decided to go and meet the Master. His wife, his son and his daughter accompanied him, and they were attended by the wealthiest inhabitants of the city. And when they saw the Buddha, they were dazzled by his splendor; he seemed to be walking on a path of molten gold.

They escorted him to Jeta's park, and Anathapindika said to him:

"My Lord, what shall I do with this park?" "Give it to the community, now and for all time," replied the Master.

Anathapindika ordered a servant to bring him a golden bowl full of water. He poured the water over the Master's hands, and he said:

"I give this park to the community, ruled by tne Buddha, now and for all time."

"Good!" said the Master. "I accept the gift. This park will be a happy refuge; here we shall live in peace, and find shelter from the heat and from the cold. No vicious animals enter here: not even the humming of a mosquito disturbs the silence; and here there is protection from the rain, the biting wind and the ardent sun. And this park will inspire dreams, for here we shall meditate hour after hour. It is only right that such gifts be made to the community. The intelligent man, the man who does not neglect his own interests, should give the monks a proper home; he should give them food and drink; he should give them clothes. The monks, in return, will teach him the law, and he who knows the law is delivered from evil and attains nirvana."

The Buddha and his disciples established themselves in Jeta's park,

Anathapindika was happy; but, one day, a solemn thought occurred to him.

"I am being loudly praised," he said to himself, "and yet what is so admirable about my actions? I present gifts to the Buddha and to the monks, and for this I am entitled to a future reward; but my virtue benefits me alone! I must get others to share in the privilege. I shall go through the streets of the city, and from those whom I meet, I shall get donations for the Buddha and for the monks. Many will thus participate in the good I shall be doing."

He went to Prasenajit, king of Cravasti, who was a wise and upright man. He told him what he had decided to do, and the king approved. A herald was sent through the city with this royal proclamation:

"Listen well, inhabitants of Cravasti! Seven days from this day, the merchant Anathapindika, riding an elephant, will go through the streets of the city. He will ask all of you for alms, which he will then offer to the Buddha and to his disciples. Let each one of you give him whatever he can afford."

On the day announced, Anathapindika mounted his finest elephant and rode through the streets, asking every one for donations for the Master and for the community. They crowded around him: this one gave gold, that one silver; one woman took off her necklace, another her bracelet, a third an anklet; and even the humblest gifts were accepted.

Now, there lived in Cravasti a young girl who was extremely poor. It had taken her three months to save enough money to buy a piece of coarse material, out of which she had just made a dress for herself. She saw Anathapindika with a great crowd around him.

"The merchant Anathapindika appears to be begging," she said to a bystander.

"Yes, he is begging," was the reply.

"But he is said to be the richest man in Cravasti. Why should he be begging?"

"Did you not hear the royal proclamation being cried through the streets, seven days ago?"

"No."

"Anathapindika is not collecting alms for himself. He wants every one to participate in the good he is doing, and he is asking for donations for the Buddha and his disciples. All those who give will be entitled to a future reward."

The young girl said to herself, "I have never done anything deserving of praise. It would be wonderful to make an offering to the Buddha. But I am poor. What have I to give?" She walked away, wistfully. She looked at her new dress. "I have only this dress to offer him. But I can not go through the streets naked."

She went home and took off the dress. Then she sat at the window and watched for Anathapindika, and when he passed in front of her house, she threw the dress to him. He took it and showed it to his servants.

"The woman who threw this dress to me," said he, "probably had nothing else to offer. She must be naked, if she had to remain at home and give alms in this strange manner. Go; try to find her and see who she is."

The servants had some difficulty finding the young girl. At last they saw her, and they learned that their master had been correct in his surmise: the dress thrown out of the window was the poor child's entire fortune. Anathapindika was deeply moved; he ordered his servants to bring many costly, beautiful clothes, and he gave them to this pious maiden who had offered him her simple dress.

She died the following day and was reborn a Goddess in Indra's sky. But she never forgot how she had come to deserve such a reward, and, one night, she came down to earth and went to the Buddha, and he instructed her in the holy law.

The New Disciples

THE Master remained in Cravasti for some time; then he left, to return to Rajagriha where King Vimbasara awaited him. He had stopped to rest in a village that was about halfway, when he saw seven men approaching. He recognized them. Six were relatives, and they were among the wealthiest and most powerful of the Sakyas. Their names were Anuruddha, Bhadrika, Bhrigu, Kimbala, Devadatta and Ananda. The seventh was a barber named Upali.

Anuruddha, one day had said to himself that it was a disgrace that none of the Sakyas had seen fit to follow the Buddha. He decided to set a good example, and as there was no reason for hiding his intention, he mentioned it first to Bhadrika, who was his best friend. Bhadrika approved of his decision, and after giving it some thought, resolved to do likewise. These two then won over Ananda, Bhrigu, Kimbala and Devadatta, by convincing them that there was no higher calling than that of a monk.

The six princes then set out to join the Buddha.

They had hardly left Kapilavastu when Ananda, glancing at Bhadrika, exclaimed:

"How now, Bhadrika! You would lead a life of holiness, and you keep all your jewels?"

Bhadrika blushed; but then he saw that Ananda was also wearing his jewelry, and he laughingly replied:

"Look at yourself, Ananda."

It was now Ananda's turn to blush.

Whereupon they all looked at one another, and they found they were still wearing their jewels. It made them feel ashamed; they lowered their eyes, and were walking along the road in silence when they met the barber Upali.

"Barber," said Ananda, "take my jewels; I give them to you."

"And take mine," said Bhadrika.

The others also handed their jewels to Upali. He was at a loss for an answer. Why should these princes, who had never seen him before, give him such presents? Should he accept them? Should he refuse?

Anuruddha understood the barber's hesitation. He said to him:

"Do not be afraid to accept these jewels. We are on our way to join the great hermit who was born to the Sakyas, we are on our way to join Siddhartha, who has become the Buddha. He will instruct us in the knowledge, and we shall submit to his rule."

"Princes," asked the barber, "are you going to become monks?"

"Yes," they answered.

He then took the jewels and started for the city. But, suddenly, he thought, "I am acting like a fool. Who will ever believe that princes thrust these riches upon me? I shall be taken for a thief, or perhaps for an assassin. The least that can happen to me is that I shall incur the deep displeasure of the Sakyas. I shall not keep the jewels." He hung them on a tree that stood beside the road. And he thought, "Those princes are setting a noble example. They had the courage to leave their palaces; do I, who am nothing, lack the courage to leave my shop? No. I shall follow them. I, too, shall see the Buddha, and may he receive me into the community!"

He followed the princes at a distance. He was shy about joining them. Bhadrika happened to turn around. He saw Upali; he called him.

"Barber, why did you throw away our jewels?" he asked.

"I, too, want to become a monk," replied the barber.

"Then walk with us," said Bhadrika. But Upali still hung back. Anuruddha said to him:

"Walk beside us, barber. Monks make no distinctions,

except for age and for virtue. When we stand before the Buddha, you must even be the first to address him, and the first to ask him to receive you into the community. For by yielding to you, the princes will show that they have put aside their Sakya pride."

They continued on their way. Suddenly, a hawk swooped down on Devadatta's head and carried off a diamond he had been wearing in his hair. This exposed his vanity, and it made the princes smile. Devadatta, now, had not a single jewel left, but his companions, in their hearts, still questioned the sincerity of his faith.

THE Master was happy to number these relatives among his disciples, and he took them with him to the Bamboo Grove. There, poor Nanda was suffering. He kept thinking of Sundarika; she often appeared to him in his dreams, and he regretted having left her. The Buddha knew of his unhappiness, and he decided to cure him.

One day, he took him by the hand and led him to a tree where a hideous monkey was sitting.

"Look at that monkey," said he, "is she not beautiful?"

"I have rarely seen one as ugly," replied Nanda.

"Really?" said the Master. "And yet she resembles Sundarika, your former betrothed."

"What are you talking about!" exclaimed Nanda. "Do you mean to say that this monkey looks like Sundarika, who is grace, who is beauty itself?"

"In what way is Sundarika different? Are they not both females, do they not both awaken the desire of the male? I believe you would be willing to leave the path of holiness and run to Sundarika's arms, just as somewhere in this wood there is a monkey that can be roused to a frenzy of love by the violent ardor of this female. They will both become old and decrepit, and then you, as well as the monkey, will wonder what could have caused your folly. They will both die, and perhaps you and the monkey will then understand the vanity of passion. Sundarika is no different from this monkey."

But Nanda was not listening. He was sighing. He was dreaming that he saw slender, graceful Sundarika wandering in a garden bright with flowers.

"Take the hem of my cloak!" the Blessed One said, imperiously.

Nanda obeyed. He felt the earth suddenly give way under him, and a fierce wind sweep him to the sky. When he regained his feet, he found himself in a marvellous park. He was walking on a path of gold, and the flowers were living jewels, fashioned out of rubies and fragrant sapphires.

"You are in Indra's sky," said the Blessed One. "Open your sightless eyes."

Nanda saw a house of shining silver surrounded by an emerald field. An Apsaras, far lovelier than Sundarika, was standing at the door. She was smiling. Maddened by desire, Nanda rushed to her, but she stopped him with a sudden gesture.

"Be pure on earth," she said to him; "keep your vows, Nanda. After your death, you will be reborn here; then you may come to my arms."

The Apsaras disappeared. Nanda and the Master returned to earth.

Nanda forgot Sundarika. He was haunted by the lovely vision he had seen in the celestial gardens, and, out of love for the Apsaras, he now resolved to lead a pure life.

But the monks still looked at him with disapproval.

They would not speak to him; often, when they met him in the Bamboo Grove, they would smile at him scornfully. This made him unhappy. He thought, "They seem to bear me ill will; I wonder why?" One day, he stopped Ananda who was passing, and he asked him:

"Why do the monks avoid me? Why do you not speak to me any more, Ananda? Formerly, in Kapilavastu, we were friends as well as relatives. What have I done to offend you?"

"Poor man!" replied Ananda. "We, who meditate on the saintly truths, have been forbidden by the Master to speak to you, who meditate on the charms of an Apsaras!"

And he left.

Nanda was very disturbed. He ran to the Master; he fell at his feet and wept. The Master said to him:

"Your thoughts are evil, Nanda. You are a slave to your feelings. First it was Sundarika, now it is an Apsaras, who turns your head. And you would be reborn! Reborn among the Gods? What folly, what vanity! Strive to attain wisdom, Nanda; give heed to my teachings, and kill your devouring passions."

Nanda pondered the Buddha's words. He became a most obedient disciple, and gradually he purified his mind. Sundarika no longer appeared to him in his dreams, and now, when he thought of the Apsaras, he laughed at having wanted to become a God for her sake. One day, when he saw a hideous monkey watching him from a tree-top, he cried in a triumphant voice:

"Hail, you that Sundarika can not equal in grace; hail, you that are lovelier far than the loveliest Apsaras!"

He took great pride in having conquered his passions. "I am a true saint," he said to himself, "and in virtue I will not yield even to my brother."

He made a robe for himself of the same size as the Master's. Some monks saw him in the distance, and they said:

"Here comes the Master. Let us rise and greet him."

But as Nanda drew near, they saw their mistake.

They were embarrassed, and as they sat down again, they said:

"He has not been in the community as long as we have; why should we rise in his presence?"

Nanda had been pleased to see the monks rise at his approach; he was abashed to see them sit down again. But he was afraid to complain; he felt they would blame him. Yet it was no lesson to him; he continued to walk through the Bamboo Grove, wearing a robe that was like the Buddha's. In the distance, he was taken for the Master, and the monks would rise from their seats; but at his approach, they would laugh and sit down again.

Finally, a monk went to the Buddha and told him. He was very displeased. He assembled the monks, and in front of them all, he asked Nanda:

"Nanda, did you really wear a robe of the same size as mine?"

"Yes, Blessed One," replied Nanda; "I wore a robe of the same size as yours."

"What!" said the Master, "a disciple dares to make a robe for himself of the same size as the Buddha's! What do you mean by such audacity? An action of this kind does not tend to arouse the faith of the unbeliever, nor does it help to strengthen the faith of the believer. You must shorten your robe, Nanda, and, in the future, any monk who makes a robe for himself of the same size as the Buddha's, or larger than the Buddha's, will be committing a grave offense, an offense for which he will be severely punished."

Nanda saw the error of his ways, and he realized that to be a true saint, he would have to conquer his pride.

The Death of Suddhodana

NEAR the city of Vaisali, there was an immense wood that had been presented to the Master, and there he was living when the news came to him that his father, King Suddhodana, had fallen sick. The king was an old man; the illness was serious; it was feared that he was dying. The Master decided to visit him, and flying through the air he came to Kapilavastu.

The king lay mournfully on his couch. He was gasping for breath. Death was very near. Yet he smiled when he saw his son. And the Master spoke these words:

"Long is the road you have travelled, O king, and always did you strive to do good. You knew nothing of evil desires; your heart was innocent of hatred, and anger never blinded your mind. Happy is he who is given to doing good! Happy is he who looks into a limpid pool and sees his unsullied countenance, but far happier is he who examines his mind and knows the purity thereof! Your mind is pure, O king, and your death as calm as the close of a lovely day."

"Blessed One," said the king, "I understand now the inconstancy of the worlds. I am free of all desire; I am free of the chains of life."

Once again, he paid homage to the Buddha. Then he turned to the servants, assembled in the hall.

"Friends," said he, "I must have wronged you many

times, yet never once did you show me that you bore malice. You were kind and good. But before I die, I must have your forgiveness. The wrongs I did you were unintentional; forgive me, Friends."

The servants were weeping. They murmured: "No, you have never wronged us, lord!" Suddhodana continued:

"And you, Mahaprajapati, you who were my pious consort, you whom I see in tears, calm your grief. My death is a happy death. Think of the glory of this child you brought up; gaze at him in all his splendor, and rejoice."

He died. The sun was setting.

The Master said:"Behold my father's body. He is no longer what he was. No one has ever conquered death. He who is born must die. Show your zeal for good works; walk in the path that leads to wisdom. Make a lamp of wisdom, and darkness will vanish of its own accord. Do not follow evil laws; do not plant poisonous roots; do not add to the evil in the world.

Like the charioteer who, having left the highroad for a rough path, weeps at the sight of a broken axle, even so does the fool, who has strayed from the law, weep when he falls into the jaws of death. The wise man is the torch that gives light to the ignorant; he guides mankind, for he has eyes, and the others are sightless."

The body was carried to a great funeral pile. The Master set fire to it, and while his father's body was being consumed by the flames, while the people of Kapilavastu wept and lamented, he repeated these sacred truths:

"Suffering is birth, suffering is old age, suffering is sickness, suffering is death. O thirst to be led from birth to birth! Thirst for power, thirst for pleasure, thirst for being, thirsts that are the source of all suffering! O evil thirsts, the saint knows you not, the saint who extinguishes his desires, the saint who knows the noble eight-fold path."

Mahaprajapati is Admitted to the Community

Mahaprajapati was musing. She knew the vanity of this world. She wanted to flee the palace, to flee Kapilavastu, and lead a life of holiness.

"How happy is the Master! How happy are the disciples!" she thought. "Why can I not do as they do? Why can I not live as they live? But they oppose women. We are not admitted to the community, and I must remain in this mournful city, to me deserted; I must remain in this mournful palace, empty in my sight!"

She grieved. She laid aside her costly robes; she gave her jewels to her handmaidens, and she was humble before all creatures.

One day, she said to herself:

"The Master is kind; he will take pity on me. I shall go to him, and perhaps he will be willing to receive me into the community."

The Master was in a wood, near Kapilavastu. Mahaprajapati went to him, and in a timid voice, she said:

"Master, only you and your disciples can be really happy. Yet I, too, like you and those who accompany you, wish to walk in the path of salvation. May the favor be granted me to enter the community, O Blessed One."

The Master remained silent. She continued:

"How can I be happy in a world I despise? I know its meretricious joys. I long to walk in the path of salvation. May the favor be granted me to enter the community, O Blessed One. And I know many women who are willing to follow me. May the favor be granted us to enter the community, O Blessed One."

The Master still remained silent. She continued:

"My palace is cheerless and dreary. The city is wrapped in darkness. The embroidered veils weigh heavily upon my brow; the diadems, the bracelets and the necklaces hurt me. I must walk in the path of salvation. Many earnest women, many women of great piety, are ready to follow me. May the favor be granted women to enter the community, O Blessed One."

For the third time, the Master remained silent. Mahaprajapati, her eyes full of tears, returned to her gloomy palace.

But she would not accept defeat. She resolved to seek the Master once again and plead with him.

He was then in the great wood, near Vaisali. Mahaprajapati cut off her hair, and putting on a reddish-colored robe made of a coarse material, she set out for Vaisali.

She made the trip on foot; she never once complained of weariness. Covered with dust, she finally arrived at the hall where the Buddha was meditating. But she did not dare to enter; she stood outside the door, with tears in her eyes. Ananda happened to pass by. He saw her and asked:

"O queen, why have you come here, dressed in this manner? Why are you standing before the Master's door?"

"I dare not enter his presence. Three times, already, he has denied my plea, and that which he has thrice refused, I have come to ask him again: that the favor be granted me, that the favor be granted women, to enter the community."

"I shall intercede for you, O queen," said Ananda.

He entered the hall. He saw the Master, and he said to him:.

"Blessed One, Mahaprajapati, our revered queen, is standing before your door. She dares not appear before you; she is afraid you will again turn a deaf ear to her plea. Yet it is not the plea of a foolish woman, Blessed One. Would it mean so much to you to grant it? The queen was a mother to you, once; she was always kind to you; surely she deserves to be heard. Why should you not receive women into the community? There are women of great piety, women with the saintly courage to keep in the path of holiness."

"Ananda," said the Master, "do not ask me to permit women to enter the community."

Ananda left. The queen was waiting for him.

"What did the Master say," she asked, anxiously.

"He denies your plea. But do not lose hope."

The following day, .Ananda again went to the Blessed One.

"Mahaprajapati has not left the wood," said he. "She is thinking of the happy days of her youth. Maya was then alive; Maya, the most beautiful of all women; Maya, to whom a son would be born. Maya's sister was a noble woman: she knew nothing of envy: she loved this child, even before it came into the world. And when it was born, to bring joy to all creatures, Queen Maya died. Mahaprajapati was kind to the motherless boy: he seemed so frail. She protected him from harm; she gave him devoted nurses; she shielded him from the influence of evil servants; she lavished her care and her tenderness upon him. He grew older, and still she would not leave him. She anticipated his least wishes; she worshipped him. And he attained the happiest fortune; he is the giant tree that shelters the wise; and now, when she would seek a humble place in his shadow, she is refused the peace and rest to which she aspires. O Master, be not unjust; receive Mahaprajapati into the community."

The Master pondered; then he gravely spoke these words:

"Listen, Ananda. Go to Mahaprajapati and tell her that I am willing to receive her into the community, but that she must conform to certain very strict rules. These are the observances I shall require of the women in the community: a nun, even if she has been a nun for a hundred years, must rise in the presence of a monk and show him every mark of deep respect, even though he has been a monk for only a day; the nuns must go to the monks for a public confession of their transgressions and for instruction in the sacred word; nuns guilty of a grave offense must submit to a fitting punishment, for fifteen days, in front of the whole community of monks and nuns; before nuns are admitted to the community, their constancy and their virtue must be tried for a period of two years; the nuns will not be allowed to exhort the monks, but the monks will be allowed to exhort the nuns. These are the observances which, in addition to the observances already known to the monks, will be required of all the nuns."

Mahaprajapati joyfully promised to observe these rules. She entered the community, and within a few months, many women had followed her example.

But, one day, the Master said to Ananda:

"If women had not been admitted to the community, Ananda, chastity would have been preserved a long time, and the true faith would have lived, vigorous and serene, for a thousand years.. But now that women are admitted to the community, Ananda, chastity will be in danger, and the true faith, in all its vigor, will live only five hundred years."

The Buddha Exposes the Imposters

FROM Vaisali, the Master went to Cravasti, to Jeta's park. One day, King Prasenajit came to see him. "My Lord," said the king, "six hermits have recently arrived in Cravasti. They do not believe in your law. They maintain that your knowledge is not equal to theirs, and they have tried to astonish me by performing numerous prodigies. I believe their statements to be untrue, but it would be well, my Lord, if you were to confound their audacity. The world's salvation depends upon your glory. So appear before these cheats and impostors and silence them."

"King," replied the Buddha, "order a great hall to be built near the city. Have it finished in seven days. I shall proceed there. Arrange to have the evil hermits present, and you will then see who performs the greatest prodigies, they or I."

Prasenajit ordered the hall to be built.

While awaiting the day of the trial, the lying hermits sought to delude the Master's faithful followers, and those who refused to listen to their evil words incurred their bitter enmity. Now, the Master had no truer friend in Cravasti than Prince Kala, a brother of Prasenajit. Kala had shown his utter contempt for the hermits, and they decided to take their revenge.

Kala was a very handsome man. One day, as he was walking through the royal gardens, he met one of Prasenajit's wives, and she playfully threw him a garland of flowers. The hermits heard of the incident, and they told the king that his brother had tried to seduce one of his wives. The king flew into a great rage, and without giving Kala a chance to justify himself, he had his hands and feet cut off.

Poor Kala suffered pitifully. His friends stood around his couch, weeping. One of the evil hermits happened to pass by.

"Come, show your power," they said to him. "You know that Kala is innocent. Make him well again!"

"He believes in the son of the Sakyas," replied the hermit. "It behooves the Sakyas' son to make him well again."

Then Kala began to sing:

"How can the Master of the worlds fail to see my misery? Let us worship the Lord who no longer knows desire; let us adore the Blessed One who takes pity on all creatures."

Ananda suddenly appeared before him.

"Kala," said he, "the Master has taught me the words that will heal your wounds."

He recited a few verses, and the prince immediately recovered the use of his limbs.

"Henceforth," he exclaimed, "I shall serve the Master! However humble the tasks which he may assign to me, I shall perform them with joy, to please him."

And he followed Ananda to Jeta's park. The Master received him graciously and admitted him to the community.

The day arrived on which the Master was to compete with the hermits. Early in the morning, King Prasenajit went to the hall he had had built for this occasion. The six hermits were already there. They exchanged glances and smiled.

"King," said one of them, "we are the first to arrive at

the place of meeting."

"Do you suppose the one we are expecting will really come?" said another.

"Hermits," said the king, "do not scoff at him. You know how he sent one of his disciples to cure my brother whom I had unjustly punished. He will come. He may even be here, in our midst, without our knowing it."

As the king finished speaking, a luminous cloud filled the hall. It became lighter and lighter; it melted into the daylight, and the Buddha appeared, arrayed in golden splendor. Behind him stood Ananda and Kala. Ananda held a red flower in his hand, Kala a yellow flower, and never, in all the gardens of Cravasti, had any one seen two such flowers as these.

Prasenajit showed his profound admiration. The evil hermits ceased their laughter.

The Blessed One spoke:

"The glowworm shines for all to see, as long as the sun stays hidden, but when the blazing star appears, the poor worm quenches his feeble light.

The impostors spoke loudly as long as the Buddha was silent, but now that the Buddha speaks, they weep with fear and are silent."

The hermits were alarmed. They saw the king viewing them with a scornful eye, and they hung their heads in shame.

Suddenly, the roof of the hall disappeared, and on the dome of the sky, stretching from the east to the west, the Master traced a course over which he proceeded to travel. At the sight of this prodigy, his most insolent rival fled in terror. The hermit imagined he was being pursued by a howling pack. of hounds, and he never stopped running until he came to the edge of a pool. There, he tied a stone to his neck and threw himself into the water. A fisherman found his body the following day.

In the meanwhile, the Master had created a being in his own image, and, with him, he was now walking in the celestial path. And his great voice was heard, saying:

"O my disciples, I am about to ascend to the abode of the Gods and the Goddesses. Maya, my mother, has summoned me; I must instruct her in the law. I shall remain with her three months. But, each day, I shall descend to earth, and Sariputra, alone, will know where to find me; he will rule the community according to my instructions. And while I am absent from the sky, I shall leave with my mother, to instruct her, this being whom I have created in mine own image."

Suprabha

AT the end of three months, the Master descended to earth and took the road to Cravasti. As he was approaching Jeta's park, he met a young girl. She was the servant of a wealthy inhabitant of the city who happened to be working in the fields that day. She was taking him a bowl of rice for his meal. At the sight of the Buddha, she felt strangely happy.

"It is the Master, the Blessed One," she thought. "My eyes behold him; my hands could almost touch him, he is so near. Oh, what a holy joy it would be to give him alms! But I have nothing of my own."

She sighed. Her glance fell on the bowl of rice.

"This rice . . . My master's meal . . . No master can reduce to slavery one who is already a slave. Mine could strike me, but what of that! He could put me in chains, but

I would bear them lightly. I shall give the rice to the Blessed One."

She presented the bowl to the Buddha. He accepted it and continued on his way to Jeta's park. The young girl, her eyes shining with happiness, went to look for her master.

"Where is my rice?" he asked, as soon as he saw her.

"I gave it to the Buddha as an alms. Punish me if you will, I shall not weep; I am too happy for what I have done."

He did not punish her. He bowed' his head and said:

"No, I shall not punish you. I am asleep and your eyes are open. Go; you are no longer a slave."

The young girl made a deep obeisance.

"With your permission then," said she, "I shall go to Jeta's park, and I shall ask the Blessed One to instruct me in the law."

"Go," said the man.

She went to Jeta's park; she sat at the Buddha's feet, and she became one of the most saintly women in the community.

Among those who sought instruction from the Blessed One at the same time as this young slave was Suprabha, the daughter of a prominent citizen of Cravasti. Suprabha was very beautiful. To see her was to fall in love with her, and she was courted by all the distinguished young men of the city. This caused her father no little concern. "To which one shall I give her in marriage?" he would repeatedly ask himself; "those whom I refuse will become my bitter enemies."

And for hours at a time, he would remain deep in thought.

One day, Suprabha said to him:

"You seem to be troubled, dear father. What is the reason?"

"Daughter," he replied, "you alone are the cause of my anxiety. There are so many in Cravasti who wish to marry you!"

"You are afraid to make a choice from among my suitors," said Suprabha. "Poor men! If they but knew my thoughts! Do not be anxious, father! Tell them to assemble, and, according to the ancient custom, I shall go among them, and I myself shall choose a husband from their number."

"I shall do as you wish, daughter."

Suprabha's father went to King Prasenajit and received permission to have a herald proclaim throughout the city:

"That seven days from this day, there will be held an assembly of all the young men who wish to marry Suprabha. The young girl herself will select a husband from among their number."

On the seventh day, a host of suitors gathered in the magnificent garden belonging to Suprabha's father. She appeared, riding in a chariot. She was holding a yellow banner on which was painted the picture of the Blessed One. She was singing his praises. They all looked at her in amazement, and they wondered, "What will she say to us?" She finally addressed the young men.

"I can not love any of you," said she, "but do not think that I spurn you. Love is not my aim in life; I want to take refuge with the Buddha. I shall go to the park where he dwells, and he will instruct me in the law."

Mournfully, the young men withdrew, and Suprabha

went to Jeta's park. She heard the Blessed One speak; she was admitted to the community, and she became a most devoted nun.

One day, as she was leaving the sacred gardens, she was recognized by one of her former suitors who happened to be passing with several friends.

"We must carry off this woman," said he. "I loved her once; I still love her. She shall be mine."

His friends agreed to help him. Before Suprabha was aware of it, she was surrounded, and they suddenly rushed upon her. But as they were about to seize her, she directed her thought toward the Buddha, and, immediately, she rose in the air. A crowd gathered; Suprabha soared above them for a while, then, flying with the grace and majesty of a swan, she returned to her sacred dwelling.

And their cries followed her:

"O saintly one, you make manifest the power of the faithful; O saint, you render manifest the power of the Buddha. It would be unjust to condemn you to the earthly pleasures of love, O saintly one, O saint."

Virupa

KING Prasenajit had a daughter named Virupa. She had reached a marriageable age. Unfortunately, she was extremely ugly; no prince or warrior would have her for a wife, and even the merchants looked at her askance.

But presently a wealthy stranger came to live in Cravasti. His name was Ganga. The king thought, "Ganga has never seen my daughter. Perhaps he will not refuse to marry her." And he summoned him to the palace.

Ganga was highly flattered by Prasenajit's offer. He was of humble birth, and although, as a merchant, he had amassed a great fortune, he had never dreamed of marrying a princess. He therefore accepted the proposal.

"Then come to the palace this very evening," said the king, "and take my daughter home with you."

He obeyed. The night was dark, and the wedding took place without Ganga having seen his betrothed. Then Virupa accompanied her husband to his home.

Ganga saw his wife the next day. Her ugliness frightened him. He wanted to turn her out of the house, but he did not dare; he feared the king's vengeance. He kept her at home, but she was virtually a prisoner; she was not allowed to go out, for any reason whatsoever.

She was very unhappy. In vain she gave her husband constant proof of her affection; he only showed his aversion and his contempt for her. He never looked at her. He hardly spoke to her. And Virupa felt lonely and forlorn.

One day, Ganga was invited to a feast given by some of his friends. "Whoever comes without wife," he was warned, "will be fined five hundred pieces of gold."

Ganga decided to attend; it would relieve the monotony of his existence. But he did not want to show Virupa to his friends; he was afraid of being ridiculed. "I shall pay the five hundred pieces of gold," he thought, "and they will not make fun of me."

That day, Virupa was sadder than usual. She knew where her husband had gone, and she wept. She said to herself:

"What good is a life as dreary as mine? I never have any pleasure. My master loathes me. And I can not blame him; I am ugly; every one has told me so. I have brought joy to no one. Oh, I loathe myself. Death would be better than this life I lead; death would be sweet. I shall kill myself."

She took a rope and hung herself.

At that same moment, in Jeta's park, the Master was wondering, "Who is suffering to-day in Cravasti? Whom can I save from misery? To what unfortunate being can I lend a helping hand?"

By his power of divination, he learned of Virupa's distress. He flew to Ganga's house; he entered. Virupa was still alive. The Master loosened the rope she had fastened about her neck. She breathed deeply and looked around. She recognized the Master. She fell at his feet and made him a pious offering. Then he said:

"Look at yourself in a mirror, Virupa."

She obeyed. She uttered a cry of joy and astonishment. She was as beautiful as a daughter of the Gods. Again she wanted to worship the Buddha, but he had disappeared.

In the meanwhile, Ganga had not been spared the banter of his friends.

"Why did you come without your wife?" they asked him. "Are you afraid to let us see her? She must be very beautiful. You jealous husband!"

Ganga was at a loss for an answer. The feast bored him. One of his friends handed him a cup of intoxicating wine.

"Drink, Ganga," said he. "We laugh, and you are almost in tears. Come, laugh with us. Drink; this wine will teach you to laugh."

Ganga took the cup. He drank. He became livelier. He drank again. Presently, he was drunk. And he kept on drinking until, finally, he fell into a heavy sleep.

"Let us hurry over to his house, while he is asleep," said his friends. "We shall see his wife, and we shall find out why he keeps her out of sight."

They entered Ganga's home. Virupa had the mirror in her hand; she was looking at herself. Her eyes were bright with happiness. All the guests admired her, and they went away, quietly, saying, "We now understand Ganga's jealousy."

Ganga was still sleeping. They awoke him and said:

"Great is your felicity, friend. What did you do that was so pleasing to the Gods, to deserve a wife of such rare beauty?"

"This is too much!" cried Ganga. "What have I ever done to you that you should insult me so cruelly?"

And he abruptly left them. He was raging with anger and mortification. He flung open the door of his house; he strode through the halls, muttering imprecations; but, suddenly, the curses died upon his lips. He turned pale with astonishment. Before him was standing a woman of incomparable beauty. She was smiling. He slowly came to his senses; then he, too, smiled, and he asked:

"O you who appear before me like some radiant Goddess new-risen from her bed of flowers, O well-beloved, who made you so beautiful?"

Virupa told him the story. From that day, she and her husband knew true happiness, and they both sought every opportunity to evince their faith in the Buddha and show him their gratitude.

Sinca's Deceit

IN the meanwhile, the evil hermits, whose imposture the Buddha had exposed, were being treated with contempt by the populace, and each day their desire for vengeance grew more intense. They had established themselves near Jeta's park, and night and day they spied upon the Buddha and his disciples. But all in vain; they saw nothing that gave them the slightest excuse for slandering the community.

At last, one of the hermits said to his companions:

"We have long been observing the conduct of these monks. Their virtue can not be denied. Still, we must turn the minds of the people against them, and I think I have found a way. I know a young girl of great charm. Her name is Sinca. She is very clever at practising deceit. She will not refuse to help us, and soon the glory of this Sakya will vanish."

The hermits sent word to Sinca. She came. "Why did you send for me?" she asked.

"Do you know the monk from Kapilavastu, the one who is worshipped as the Buddha?"

"No, but I know of his great fame. I have been told of the many prodigies he has performed."

"This man is our bitterest enemy, Sinca. He treats us shamefully and would destroy our power. Now, you believe in us; come, take our part. She who will have conquered the conqueror may well be proud; she will be famous among women, and the world will ring with her praises."

Sinca was carried away by the hermit's words. She assured him that the Buddha would soon be disgraced and his name hated throughout the earth.

Each day, now, she went to Jeta's park, at a time when those who had been listening to the Master preach were beginning to leave. She was dressed in flaming red, and she carried flowers in her arms. And if, by chance, some one asked her, "Where are you going?" she would reply,

"What business is it of yours?" When she came to the park, she waited until she was quite alone; then, instead of entering the Buddha's domain, she set out for the dwelling of the evil hermits. There, she spent the night, but at dawn she returned to the gates of the park, and when she was sure to be seen by the early risers on their way to their devotions, she would leave and return home. And to those who asked, "Where do you come from, so early in the morning?" she would reply, "What business is it of yours?"

At the end of one month, she gave a different answer. In the evening she would say, "I am going to Jeta's park, where the Blessed One is waiting for me," and in the morning, "I have just come from Jeta's park, where I spent the night with the Blessed One." And there were some poor, credulous people who believed her and who suspected the Master of unchastity.

The sixth month, she took a piece of cloth and wrapped it around her body. "She is pregnant," they thought, and the fools maintained that the Master's virtue was only a pretense.

When the ninth month arrived, she tied a wooden ball to the thick girdle about her waist, and when she walked, she assumed a languorous gait. Finally, one night, she entered the hall where the Master was expounding the law. Boldly, she faced him, and her strident voice interrupted his speech.

"Sweet is your voice and honeyed your words as you instruct the people in the law. While I, who am pregnant because of you, I, who am soon to become a mother, have not even a place for my confinement! You would deny me the very oil and butter I need.

If it would make you blush, now, to look after me, you could at least entrust me to one of your disciples, or to King

Prasenajit, or to the merchant Anathapindika. But no! I am nothing to you any more, and little you care about the child that will be born! You would know all the joys of love, but the responsibilities you would ignore!"

"Is that a lie or are you telling the truth, Sinca?" asked the Master, calmly. "Only you and I know."

"You know very well I am not lying," cried Sinca.

The Master retained his composure. But Indra, who had been watching from the sky, decided it was time to expose Sinca's impudence. He had four Gods take the form of mice. They crawled under her robe and gnawed at the string that was holding the wooden ball. The ball fell to the ground.

"There, your child is born," exclaimed the Master with a laugh.

The disciples turned upon. Sinca in their rage. They reviled her; they spat in her face; they beat her. She fled. She was weeping with pain and shame and anger. Suddenly, red flames sprang up around her and enveloped her in a mantle of fire, and she, who had dared to slander the Buddha, came to a cruel and terrible end.

The Buddha Tames a Wild Buffalo

THE Master left Jeta's park. He stopped in the cities and in the villages to preach the law, and full many there were to adopt the true faith.

One day, an old man and his wife invited the Master to take his meal with them.

"My Lord," said the old man, "we have long been eager to hear your word. We are happy, now that we know the sacred truths, and among your friends you will find none more devout than we."

"I am not surprised," replied the Buddha, "for you and I were near relations in our former existences."

"Master," said the woman, "my husband and I have lived together since our early youth; we have now attained a ripe old age. Life has been kind to us. Never has the slightest quarrel come between us. We still love each other as in the days gone by, and the evening of our lives is as sweet as was the dawn. May it be granted us, my Lord, to love each other in our next existence as we have loved one another in this life."

"It will be granted," said the Master; "the Gods have protected you!"

He continued on his way. He saw an old woman drawing water from a well by the side of the road. He approached her.

"I am thirsty," said he. "Will you give me a drink?"

The old woman stared at him. She was deeply moved. She began to weep. She wanted to embrace the Master, but she was afraid. The tears coursed down her cheeks.

"Embrace me," said the Master.

The old woman ran to his arms, and she murmured:

"Now I can die happy. I have seen the Blessed One, and it was given me to embrace him."

He went on. He came to a vast forest where a herd of buffaloes lived with their keepers. One of these buffaloes was a very powerful animal. He had an ugly temper. He barely tolerated the presence of his keepers, and at the approach of a stranger he would become aggressive. When the stranger came near, he would attack him with his horns, and he would often wound him seriously. Sometimes he killed him.

The keepers saw the Blessed One walking along, quietly, and they shouted:

"Take care, traveller. Do not come near us. There is a vicious buffalo here."

But he paid no attention to the warning. He made straight for the spot where the buffalo was grazing.

All at once, the buffalo raised his head and sniffed noisily; then, lowering his horns, he rushed at the Master. The keepers trembled. "Our voices were not loud enough," they cried; "he did not hear us." But, suddenly, the animal stopped short; he knelt before the Master and began licking his feet. There was a look of pleading in his eyes.

The Master gently stroked the buffalo. He spoke to him in a quiet voice:

"Say to yourself that all earthly things are transitory, that peace is found only in nirvana. Do not weep. Believe in me, believe in my goodness, in my compassion, and your condition will change. You will not be reborn among the animals, and, in time, you will attain the sky and dwell among the Gods."

From that day, the buffalo was extremely docile. And the keepers, who had expressed their admiration for the Master and who had given him what alms they could afford, were instructed in the law, and they became known for their piety, even among the most pious.

Dissension Among the Monks

THE Master arrived at the city of Kausambi, and there, at first, he was very happy. The inhabitants eagerly listened to his words, and many of them became monks. King Udayana was among the believers, and he allowed his son

Rashtrapala to enter the community.

Yet it was in Kausambi that the Master met with one of his great sorrows. A monk, one day, was reprimanded for committing some minor offense. He would not own himself in the wrong; so he was punished. He refused to submit to the punishment, and, as he was a pleasant man, of great wit and learning, there were many to take his part. In vain the others besought him to return to the straight path.

"Do not assume that conceited air," they said to him; "do not consider yourself incapable of making mistakes. Heed our wise advice. Address the other monks as they should be addressed who profess a faith that is also yours; they will address you as he should be addressed who professes a faith that is also theirs. The community will grow, the community will flourish, only if the monks will take counsel from one another."

"It is not for you to tell me what is right or wrong," he replied. "Stop reproving me."

"Do not say that. Your words offend against the law. You are defying discipline; you are sowing discord in the community. Come, mend your ways. Live at peace with the community. Avoid these quarrels, and be faithful to the law."

It was useless. They then decided to expel the rebel, but, once again, he refused to obey. He would remain in the community: since he was innocent, there was no need to submit to an unjust punishment.

The Master finally intervened. He tried to pacify the monks; he pleaded with them to forget their grievances and to unite, as before, in the performance of their sacred duties, but no one paid any attention. And, one day, a monk even had the audacity to say to him:

"Keep still, O Master; do not bother us with your speeches. You have arrived at a knowledge of the law; meditate upon it. You will find your meditations quite delightful. As for us, we shall know where to go; our quarrels will not keep us from finding the way. Meditate, and be quiet."

The Master was not angry. He tried to speak, but it was impossible. He saw then that he could never convince the monks of Kausambi; they seemed to be possessed with some sudden folly. The Master decided to forsake them, but first he said to them:

"Happy is he who has a faithful friend; happy is he who has a discerning friend. What obstacles could two wise and virtuous friends not overcome? But he who has no faithful friend resembles a king without a country: he must roam in solitude, like the elephant in the wild forest. Yet it is better to travel alone than in the company of a fool. The wise man should follow a lonely path; he should avoid evil and should preserve his serenity, like the elephant in the wild forest."

He left. No one tried to stop him. He went to a village where he knew he would find his disciple Bhrigu. Bhrigu was overjoyed to see him, and the Master was not a little comforted. Then, Anuruddha, Nanda and Kimbala joined him. They gave him every proof of their respect and friendship, and they lived at peace with one another. And the Master thought, "So there are some, among my disciples, who love me and who do not quarrel."

One day, as he sat down in the shade of a tree and began thinking of the troublous times in Kausambi, a herd of elephants stopped to rest not far from him. The biggest elephant went down to the river and drew water which he brought back to the others. They drank; then, instead of thanking him for doing them this service, they abused him, they beat him with their trunks, and, finally, they drove him away. And the Master saw that his own experience was not unlike that of the elephant: they were both victims of gross ingratitude. The elephant noticed the sadness in his face; he drew near and looked at him tenderly; then left, to go in search of food and drink for him.

The Master finally returned to Cravasti and rested in Jeta's park.

But it still grieved him to think of the cruel monks of Kausambi. One morning, however, he saw them enter the park. They were in great distress: alms had been denied them, for every one was indignant at their treatment of the Master. They had come to beg his forgiveness. The guilty monk confessed himself to have been in the wrong, and his punishment was light. His adversaries, as well as his friends, admitted the error of their ways, and all promised strictly to obey the rules. And the Master was happy: there was no longer any dissension in the community.

Kuvalaya the Dancer

ONE day, he returned to the country of Rajagriha.

In a field, not far from the city, he came upon a brahman named Bharadvaja. It was the harvest season, and the brahman and his servants were joyously celebrating. They were laughing and singing as the Master went by. He held out his alms-bowl, and those who recognized him, greeted him and made him many friendly offerings. This displeased Bharadvaja. He went up to the Master, and he said to him in a loud voice:

"Monk, tarry not in our midst; you set an evil example. We work, we that are here, and with watchful eyes, we observe the changes of seasons. When it is time to plow, my servants plow; when it is time to sow, they sow; and I plow and sow with them. Then the day comes when we harvest the fruit of our labor. We provide our own food, and when it is stored away, we have good reason to rest and play. While you, you roam the streets and walk the roads, and the only trouble you deign to take is to hold out a bowl to those you meet. It would be better far for you to work; it would be better far to plow and sow."

The Master smiled and answered:

"Friend, like you I plow and sow, and when my work is done, I eat."

"You plow? You sow?" said Bharadvaja. "How can I believe that? Where are your cattle? Where is your grain? Where is your plow?"

The Master said:

"Purity of understanding, that is the glorious seed I sow. Works of holiness are the rain that falls upon the fertile earth where the seed sprouts and ripens. And mine is a mighty plow: it has wisdom for its plowshare, the law for its handles, and an active faith is the powerful bullock yoked to its pole. Desire is uprooted like weeds in the fields I plow, and I gather in the richest of harvests, nirvana."

He continued on his way. But the brahman Bharadvaja followed him; he would now hear the sacred word.

They entered the city. On the public square, a large crowd was watching a troop of dancers. The daughter of the leader -was attracting particular attention. Such grace and beauty had seldom been seen, and, whenever she appeared, those who were not master of their passions burned with the desire to possess her. Her name was Kuvalaya.

She had just finished dancing. Ardent eyes were still fastened upon her. She was aware of her power, and full of pride and audacity, she shouted 'to the crowd:

"Admire me, my lords! In all Rajagriha is there one who can surpass Kuvalaya in beauty, are there any who can even equal her?"

"Yes, woman," replied the brahman Bharadvaja. "What is your beauty when compared with the beauty of the Master?"

"I would see this Master whose beauty you praise," said Kuvalaya; "lead me to him."

"Here he is," said the Blessed One.

And he came forward.

The dancer stared at him.

"You are beautiful," she said at last. "I shall dance for you."

Kuvalaya danced. The dance began slowly. She had wrapped all her veils about her, even covering her face, and the beauty once so boldly flaunted was now only a dim promise. She was like the moon, hiding behind soft clouds from the gaze of night. A cloud flew away; a faint ray escaped through the rift. The dance became more rapid; one by one the veils fell away, and the queen of the stars appeared in all her glory. Faster and faster she whirled; suddenly, a blinding light flashed in her eyes, and she stopped. She was naked. The crowd gasped and surged forward.

"Unhappy woman!" said the Buddha.

He looked at her intently. Whereupon Kuvalaya's cheeks became sunken, her forehead wrinkled and her eyes grew dull. Only a few ugly teeth were left in her mouth; only a few thin strands of grey hair still hung from her head, and she was stooped as with age. The Blessed One had punished her as he had once punished Mara's daughters when they had tried to tempt him; he had changed the beautiful dancer into a shrivelled old woman.

She sighed:

"Master, I know the great wrong I have done. An ephemeral beauty had made me vain. You taught me a bitter lesson, but I feel that some day I shall be happy to have received it. Let me learn the sacred truths; then may I be released for ever from this body that, even when it was the delight of men, was nothing but a loathsome corpse."

The Master granted Kuvalaya's request, and she became one of the most devout of the Buddha's faithful followers.

IN the city of Atavi there ruled a king who was very fond of hunting. One day, he saw an enormous deer and started in pursuit. The deer was fleet of foot, and in the heat of the chase, the king lost sight of the other hunters. Finally, the prey escaped, and weary and discouraged, the king sat down under a tree. He fell asleep.

It happened that a wicked God named Alavaka lived in the tree. He liked to feed on human flesh, and he killed and devoured all who came near him. He saw the king; he rejoiced, and the poor hunter was about to be dealt a severe blow when a noise fortunately awoke him. He realized that his life was threatened; he made an attempt to rise, but the God took him by the throat and held him down. Then the king tried to plead with him.

"Spare me, my lord!" said he. "By your terrifying appearance, I know you to be one of the Gods that eat human flesh. Oh, deign to be kind to me. You will have no cause to regret your mercy. I shall reward you with magnificent gifts."

"What care I for gifts!" replied Alavaka. "It is your flesh

I want; it will appease my hunger."

"My lord," replied the king, "if you let me return to Atavi, I shall send you a man every day to satisfy your hunger."

"When you get back to your home, you will forget this promise."

"No," said the king, "I never forget a promise. Besides, if I should once fail to make this daily offering, you have only to come to my palace and tell me of your grievance, and, immediately, without resisting, I shall follow you, and you may devour me."

The God allowed himself to be persuaded, and the king returned to the city of Atavi. But he kept thinking of his cruel promise; there was no way he could evade it, and henceforth he would have to he a hard and ruthless master.

He sent for his minister and told him what had happened. The minister considered for a moment, then said to the king:

"My lord, in the prison of Atavi there are criminals who have been condemned to death. We can send them to the God. When he sees that you are keeping faith with him, perhaps he will relieve you of your promise."

The king approved of the suggestion. Guards were sent to the prison, and to those whose days were numbered they said:

"Not far from the city there is a tree inhabited by a God who is very fond of rice. Whoever leaves a plate of rice for him at the foot of the tree will be granted a full pardon."

Whereupon, each day, one of these men, carrying a plate of rice, joyously set out for the tree, never to return.

Presently, there were no men condemned to death left

in prison. The minister ordered the judges to be extremely severe and to acquit no one accused of murder except on irrefutable proof of his innocence, but it was in vain; some new way had to be found for appeasing the hunger of the God. Then they began to sacrifice the thieves.

In spite of all their efforts to apprehend the guilty, the prison was again empty, and the king and his minister were compelled to look for victims among the worthy inhabitants of the city. Old people were carried off and forcibly led to the tree, and if the guards were not fleet-footed, the God would sometimes devour them and the victims as well.

A vague uneasiness possessed the city of Atavi. The old people were seen to disappear; no one knew what became of them. And, each day, the king's remorse grew more poignant. But he lacked the courage to sacrifice his life to the welfare of his people. He thought:

"Will no one come to my assistance? There lives in Cravasti, and sometimes in Rajagriha, I have been told, a man of great power, a Buddha, whose prodigies are loudly praised. They say he is fond of travelling. Why, then, does he not come into my kingdom?"

By his power of divination, the Buddha knew of the king's desire. He flew through the air and came to Alavaka's tree. There, he sat down.

The God saw him. He started walking toward him, but, suddenly, he became powerless. His knees trembled. Fury seized him.

"Who are you?" he asked, fiercely.

"A being far more powerful than yourself," replied the Buddha.

Alavaka was in a terrible rage. He would have liked to torture this man who was sitting on the ground in front of him, this man whom he could not reach; he would have liked to torture him to death. The Buddha never lost his composure.

Alavaka finally managed to control himself. He thought that cunning would perhaps succeed where strength had failed, and in a pleasant voice he said:

"I see you are a wise man, my Lord; it is always a pleasure for me to interrogate men of wisdom. I ask them four questions. If they can answer, they are free to go wherever they please; if they can not answer, they remain my prisoners, and I devour them when I feel so disposed."

"Ask me the four questions," said the Buddha.

"I must warn you," said Alavaka, "that no one has ever answered them. You will find scattered around the bones of those I interrogated in the past."

"Ask me the four questions," repeated the Buddha.

"Well then," said Alavaka, "how can man avoid the river of passions? How can he cross the sea of existences and find safe harbor? How can he escape the tempests of evil? How can he be left untouched by the storm of desires?"

In a quiet voice, the Buddha replied:

"Man avoids the river of passions if he believes in the Buddha, in the law and in the community; he crosses the sea of existences and finds safe harbor if he understands works of holiness; he will escape the tempests of evil if he performs works of holiness; he will be left untouched by the storm of desires if he knows the sacred path that leads to deliverance."

When Alavaka heard the Master's answers, he fell at his feet and worshipped him, and he promised to change his savage ways. Then, together, they went to Atavi, to the palace of the king.

"King," said the God, "I release you from your pledge."

The king was happier than he had ever been before. When he knew who had saved him, he cried:

"I believe in you, my Lord, who have saved me and saved my people; I believe in you, and I shall dedicate my life to proclaiming your glory, the glory of the law and the glory of the community."

Devadatta Expelled from the Community

THE monk Devadatta was possessed of an arrogant nature. He was impatient of any restraint. He aspired to supplant the Buddha, but the monks, he knew, would not join him in an open revolt. For that he needed the support of some king or prince.

"King Vimbasara is an old man," he said to himself, one day; "Prince Ajatasatru, who is young and brave, is eager to succeed him to the throne. I could advise the prince to his advantage, and, in return, he could help me to become the head of the community."

He went to see Ajatasatru. He addressed him in flattering terms; he praised his strength, his courage, his beauty.

"Oh, if you were king," said he, "what glory would come to Rajagriha! You would conquer the neighboring states; all the sovereigns of the world would pay you homage: you would be the omnipotent master, and you would be worshipped like a God."

With such words as these, Devadatta won Ajatasatru's confidence. He received many precious gifts, and he became still more arrogant.

Maudgalyayana noticed Devadatta's frequent visits to the prince. He decided to warn the Blessed One.

"My Lord," he began, "Devadatta is very friendly with Prince Ajatasatru."

The Blessed One interrupted him.

"Let Devadatta do as he pleases; we shall soon know the truth. I am aware that Ajatasatru pays him homage; it does not advance him a single step in the path of virtue. Let Devadatta glory in his arrogance! It will be his ruin. As the banana-tree and the bamboo-tree bear fruit only to die, so will the honors Devadatta is receiving simply hasten his downfall."

Devadatta soon reached the height of vanity. He could not abide the Buddha's grandeur, and, one day, he made bold to say to him:

"Master, you are now well along in years; it is a great hardship for you to rule the monks; you should retire. Meditate in peace upon the sublime law you have discovered, and the community let me take charge of."

The Master smiled quizzically.

"Be not concerned about me, Devadatta; you are too kind. I shall know when it is time to retire. For the present, I shall stay in charge of the community.

Besides, when the time does come, I shall not give it even to Sariputra or Maudgalyayana, those two great minds that are like blazing torches, and you want it, Devadatta, you who have such a mediocre intelligence, you who shed even less light than a night-lamp!"

Devadatta bowed respectfully before the Master, but he could not hide the fire of anger in his eyes.

The Master then sent for learned Sariputra.

"Sariputra," said he, "go through the city of Rajagriha and cry in a loud voice: 'Beware of Devadatta! He has strayed from the path of righteousness. The Buddha is not responsible for his words or for his actions; the law no longer inspires him, the community no longer interests him. Henceforth, Devadatta speaks only for himself.'"

It grieved Sariputra to have such a painful mission to perform; however, he understood the Master's reasons, and he went through the city crying Devadatta's shame. The inhabitants stopped to listen, and some thought, "The monks envy Devadatta his friendship for Prince Ajatasatru." But the others said, "Devadatta must have committed a serious offense, for the Blessed One thus publicly to denounce him."

Ajatasatru's Treachery

DEVADATTA was musing: "Siddhartha thought to humiliate me by making light of my intelligence. I shall show him he is mistaken. My glory will overshadow his: the night-lamp will become the sun. But King Vimbasara is his faithful friend; he protects him. As long as the king is living, I can do nothing. Prince Ajatasatru, on the other hand, honors me and holds me in high esteem; he reposes implicit confidence in me. If he were to reign, I would get everything I desire."

He went to Ajatasatru's palace.

"Oh, prince," said he, "we are living in an unfortunate age! They that are best fitted to govern are likely to die without ever having reigned. Human life is so brief a thing! Your father's longevity causes me no little concern for you."

He kept on talking, and he was presently giving the prince most evil advice. The prince was weak; he listened. Before long, he had decided to kill his father."

Night and day, now, Ajatasatru wandered through

the palace, watching for an opportunity to slip into his father's apartments and make away with him. But he could not escape the vigilance of the guards. His restlessness puzzled them, and they said to King Vimbasara:

"O king, your son Ajatasatru has been behaving strangely of late. Could he be planning an evil deed?"

"Be silent," replied the king. "My son is a man of noble character. It would not occur to him to do anything base."

"You ought to send for him, O king, and question him."

"Be silent, guards. Do not accuse my son lightly."

The guards continued to keep a close watch, and at the end of a few days, they again spoke to the king. To convince them that they were mistaken, the king summoned Ajatasatru. The prince appeared before his father. He was trembling.

"My lord," said he, "why did you send for me?"

"Son," said Vimbasara, "my guards say that you have been behaving strangely of late. They tell me you wander through the palace, acting mysteriously, and that you shun the gaze of those you meet. Son, are they not lying?"

"They are not lying, father," said Ajatasatru

Remorse suddenly overwhelmed him. He fell at the king's feet, and out of the depths of his shame, he cried:

"Father, I wanted to kill you."

Vimbasara shuddered. In a voice full of anguish, he asked:

"Why did you want to kill me?"

"In order to reign."

"Then reign," cried the king. "Royalty is not worth a

son's enmity."

Ajatasatru was proclaimed king the next day.

The first thing he did was to have great honors paid to his father. But Devadatta still feared the old king's authority; he decided to use his influence against him.

"As long as your father is allowed his freedom," he said to Ajatasatru, "you are in danger of losing your power. He still retains many followers; you must take measures to intimidate them."

Devadatta again was able to impose his will on Ajatasatru, and poor Vimbasara was thrown into prison. Ajatasatru presently decided to starve him to death, and he allowed no one to take him any food.

But Queen Vaidehi was sometimes permitted to visit Vimbasara in his prison, and she would take rice to him which he ate ravenously. Ajatasatru, however, soon put a stop to this; he ordered the guards to search her each time she went to see the prisoner. She then tried to hide the food in her hair, and when this, too, was discovered, she had to use great ingenuity to save the king from dying of hunger. But she was repeatedly found out, and Ajatasatru, finally, denied her access to the prison.

In the meanwhile, he was persecuting the Buddha's faithful followers. They were forbidden to look after the temple where Vimbasara, formerly, had placed a lock of the Master's hair and the parings of his finger-nails. No longer were flowers or perfume left there as pious offerings, and the temple was not even cleaned or swept.

In Ajatasatru's palace there dwelt a woman named Srimati. She was very devout. It grieved her to be unable to perform works of holiness, and she wondered how, in these sad times, she could prove to the Master that she had kept her faith. Passing in front of the temple, she complained bitterly to see it so deserted, and when she noticed how unclean it was, she wept.

"The Master shall know that there is still one woman in this house who would honor him," thought Srimati, and at the risk of her life, she swept out the temple and decorated it with a bright garland.

Ajatasatru saw the garland. He was greatly incensed and wanted to know who had dared to disobey him. Srimati did not try to hide; of her own accord, she appeared before the king.

"Why did you defy my orders?" asked Ajatasatru.

"If I defied your orders," she replied, "I respected those of your father, King Vimbasara."

Ajatasatru did not wait to hear further. Pale with fury, he rushed at Srimati and stabbed her with his dagger. She fell, mortally wounded; but her eyes were shining with joy, and in a happy voice, she sang:

"My eyes have seen the protector of the worlds; my eyes have seen the light of the worlds, and for him, in the night, I have lighted the lamps. For him who dissipates the darkness, I have dissipated the darkness. His brilliance is greater than the brilliance of the sun; his rays are purer than the rays of the sun, and my rapt gaze is dazzled by the splendor. For him who dissipates the darkness, I have dissipated the darkness."

And, dead, she seemed to glow with the light of sanctity.

First. If material constitution, that is, inheritance, which makes for identity, modified by the tendency to variation, is the cause of character, then, as the laws of matter do not vary, we have no way of accounting for the tendency to variation itself. It is an unknown *x*, an ultimate fact with nothing behind it.

Whereas, if the psychical characteristics—the soul, to take the shortest word—are the dominant factor, the tendency to variation follows as a matter of course.

Second. If material constitution is the cause of character, the range of variation ought to be equally great in different forms of animal life; for p. 54 instance, in men, sheep, and herring. Whereas, if the variation is determined by the character, we ought to find the greatest variation where the characters are most complex,—which we do.

Third. Family resemblance often asserts itself most clearly in the second generation. And it will be noticed that the very close resemblance of a child to a grandparent is generally associated with two facts,—one, that the ancestor in question has been dead less than ten years; the other, that the very marked resemblance occurs but once, no matter how numerous the grandchildren may be. Heredity by physical transmission offers no explanation of either fact. Whereas, from three to ten years is the ordinary interval for p. 55 reincarnation, and the single resemblance is the natural result of the rebirth of a single soul.

The apparent bearing of Mendel's law here is too obvious to be overlooked. But it is perhaps too early to be sure just what is behind Mendel's law. Now, if character reincarnates, what becomes of it between whiles, between the time of one man's death and the next man's birth?

Let me remind you of Darwin again. "Those characteristics are most sure to be transmitted which have been longest transmitted." But as I have tried to show you, character is built up of reflexes which are essentially and necessarily the oldest things about the individual organism. Therefore, according to Darwin, the character is p. 56

exactly what we should expect to find transmitted.

But this does not answer the question of what becomes of it in the interval between death and birth. A living man's character we know, but a dead body has no character. If that character persists, it must be somewhere in the mean time. There is a gap here to be filled up.

Is there?

Let me ask you to recall that subject of breakfast. Remember that no consciousness but immediate sensory consciousness is conditioned by space and time. Remember that immediate sensory consciousness depends on the action of the matter of the external universe on the matter of the body, and stops at death. And then consider p. 57 the question of what has become of the reincarnating entity in the interval. From the point of view of that entity the interval as we know it does not exist, and it is our error to suppose that it does,—an error arising as usual from our disastrous habit of thinking in terms based on matter.

Is, then, rebirth in one's own family the only alternative?

By no means. The soul follows its strongest ties. These are generally the family ties, but not always; and the soul always finds its own level where its own character is most at home. If it is too sensual and self-absorbed, that is, too centripetal, to find a human birth at all, it will find its birth as an animal; and if it is not only too self-centred but too actively hostile to p. 58 everything outside itself to find a birth even as an animal, it will be born lower still.

On the other hand, if its main trait is centrifugal and altruistic, it will be born where those qualities have fullest play in a higher state of existence.

This higher state is mainly altruistic. The animal

kingdom is mainly selfish. Human life is partly one and partly the other.

Now, a word in conclusion about the material environment and incidents of a given life. I have said that consciousness is continuous. That means you cannot, so to speak, pick up a single idea alone any more than you can pick up a single knot in the middle of a fish-net. You may pick up any knot you like, but you will get also what p. 59 is tied to it. And if, at any point of the summed-up consciousness of a man's life, there is tied the record of an injury done to another man, that record will infallibly remain tied; and when, in a later life, in disentangling the threads of his own existence in terms of time and space, he comes again to that particular point, that injury will return against him with the accuracy of a spring which expends when released the exact energy required to compress it, and the blow he receives will be just as hard as the blow he gave. Action and reaction are equal and opposite.

From a higher point of view the case may be put in this way. Consciousness is continuous. Therefore, there is but one ultimate consciousness. p. 60 All beings are therefore one; and when one man strikes another, he strikes all men, including himself. Just when and where and how in terms of space and time he feels his own blow depends on circumstances, but sooner or later he will. A good deed comes back to the doer in just the same way.

I just said that consciousness is one, and all beings are therefore one. The difference in beings, therefore, is how much they realize of this universal consciousness. The process of evolution is the process of increase of the amount realized. The only thing that prevents a man from realizing the whole of it is the accumulated habit of countless generations of thinking in terms of self, that is, of the material self. It was not the fault of our p. 61 struggling predecessors on this planet that they thought in these terms. Natural selection took care of that. They had to, or die.

This universal consciousness is what all existence started from and is returning to. How easily it can be reached by organized beings depends on their place in the scale of evolution. The fish is farther from it than the dog, and the dog farther than we, and we farther than higher beings. The important thing to us is that, having evolved to the stage of human beings on our road to it, we can now see where we are going, and can greatly increase our speed if we like.

There are two ways in which this may be done. Character, as I have so often said, is habitual consciousness; p. 62 and I have compared the consciousness, that is, the man, to the dial of a watch that registers either the movement of external nature or the impulse of the will. The two ways of growth correspond to this. In Buddhism they are called respectively the Objective or Exterior and the Subjective or Interior Methods or Systems. 1

One is through the external acts of daily life, by so ordering them that the lower reflexes are gradually eliminated and the higher ones left and developed. In other words, by doing good actions.

The other is internal, through the p. 63 alteration of the character and consciousness by the direct action of the will.

The first involves the simple practice of ordinary morality. It is safe and sure, and for people occupied with the ordinary affairs of life, usually the best. The character is gradually altered, just as it was built up, by contact with the external world. The ordinary process of evolutionary growth is accelerated, but there is no break in it.

The second way equally involves the practice of

morality in daily life. In addition, it involves the direct action of the will on the character. It is generally difficult, and except for people of thoroughly good character, or under the guidance of people of thoroughly good character, liable to be dangerous. p. 64 The reason is obvious. In most people the character, especially in the lower reflexes, is stronger than the will, even when the will does not habitually aid and abet them. In a direct conflict between will and character, the character is apt to get the upper hand. I have spoken of the external material universe as a sort of pendulum or balance wheel to the organism. In the present case the simile is exact. It goes at a certain rate, and keeps the delicate machinery of the human consciousness from deviating very far from that rate. It limits, to a certain extent, the amount of good or harm a man can do to other men and consequently to himself. But if the balance wheel is disconnected even temporarily, as in meditation, the first tendency of the p. 65 clock is to obey the pressure of the mainspring, and run down violently and perhaps disastrously. If we try to check this pressure with the key, we hold it in very unstable equilibrium. And if we try with the key to make the hands go at any even rate, it is almost impossible.

Now, the spring is the character, and the key is the will, and if the character is bad, the result is disastrous, because in most people, as I have repeated so often, natural selection has made the lower reflexes strongest, and it is consequently those that come into play first.

Such exercise of the will acting directly on the character has two effects: It expands the consciousness, and solidifies the character by strengthening p. 66 the reflexes. But if the consciousness is expanded and the reflexes are strengthened in the direction of matter, the clock-hands are going round the wrong way, and the second state of the man is worse than the first.

The ultimate object of life is to acquire freedom from the limitations of the material world by substituting volitional for sensory consciousness. They are limitations to be outgrown. There is a story of the last century that Emerson was stopped in the street by an excited member of the now forgotten sect of Millerites, who exclaimed, "Mr. Emerson, do you know that the world is going to be destroyed in ten days?" "Well," said Emerson, "I don't see but we p. 67 shall get along just as well without it."

Such beings, if we may trust the p. 68 highest authorities, have the aspect of human beings. They have arms and legs and eyes and ears, noses and mouths, and none of these organs appear to be atrophied from disuse. Their pleasures may be more refined than ours and more intense, their bodies of finer matter than ours; but they are still separate individuals, and in so far forth their existence is governed by the laws of separation, which are the laws of matter. The distinctions of subject and object, of ego and non-ego, of external and internal, of active and passive, still hold good, and such beings live under the same laws of action and reaction and interaction that govern us. The highest form of happiness we can conceive for them is p. 69 expressed in expanded terms of our own lives, in an inexhaustible opportunity for the satisfaction of an inexhaustible desire, whether for work or play or worship.

INDEX

BIBLIOGRAPHIES

Jataka Tales, by Ellen C. Babbitt; illustrations by Ellsworth Young; New York, The Century Co. [1912]

The Path of Light, by L.D. Barnett, New York: E.P. Dutton and Company; [1909]

Buddhism and Immortality, by William Sturgis Bigelow; Boston and New York: Houghton Mifflin Company [1908]

The Fo-Sho-Hing-Tsan-King: A Life of Buddha by Asvaghosha Bodhisattva, translated from Sanskrit into Chinese by Dharmaraksha A.D. 420, and From Chinese into English, by Samuel Beal; (Sacred Books of the East Vol. 19) Oxford, The Clarendon Press; [1883]

The She-rab Dong-bu (The Tree of Wisdom) by Nagarjuna; edited and translated by W. L. Cambell; Calcutta, [1919]

The Jtaka, Volume IV. tr by W.H.D. Rouse; ed. by E. B. Cowell, Cambridge University Press [1901]

Pio, Edwina. *Buddhist Psychology: A Modern Perspective.* New Delhi: Abhinav Publ., 1988.

Powers, John. *The Yogacara School of Buddhism: A Bibliography.* Metuchen, NJ: Scarecrow Press, 1991.

Prebish, Charles S. *Historical Dictionary of Buddhism.* Metuchen, NJ: Scarecrow Press, 1993.

Red Pine. *The Collected Songs of Cold Mountain.* Port